FOWLER'S GUIDE TO:
SURREY

First Edition 1994
Published by Fowler's Guides
Orchard House, Park Lane,
Reigate, Surrey, RH2 8JX.

© Competex Ltd 1994
Registered at Stationers' Hall 1994

ISBN 0-9524868-0-6

Printed in Great Britain by
Claremont Press, Horsham.

Introduction

Surrey stretches only 40 miles from East to West and barely 25 miles from the Thames to the Sussex border. Almost all of the County is within easy reach of London, with excellent road and rail facilities. London's two main airports are on its boundary.

Full of variety, the County has everything to offer, ranging from the delightful village green, the cosy pub or stunning view, to the hustle and bustle of town life. In the countryside an active farming community shares with the visitor a multitude of well run farm attractions. Surrey's two main rivers, the Wey and the Mole, meander through the countryside and are crossed by some of the prettiest bridges. Eating places abound, from the most elegant to the simplest, offering a wide variety of European and ethnic food.

But Surrey is not just village life and gourmet eating. The large towns offer the best in shops and leisure facilities, whilst the beautiful countryside boasts some of the finest golf courses in the South East of England. There are watersports facilities on many of the artificial lakes, and two of the UK's biggest theme parks, Chessington World of Adventures and Thorpe Park, are located within 16 miles of each other. The four main race courses of Epsom, Kempton, Lingfield and Sandown are well spread through the County, and a day at the races is easy to arrange wherever you happen to be.

Culturally, visitor and resident are extremely well served. There are six major theatres, some often showing pre-West End productions, and many smaller theatre groups involving local communities. Historic houses, vernacular architecture and a host of fascinating churches serve as a remarkable record of Surrey's past, shaped as it was by its residents, some of whom were England's greatest heroes. In years gone by, Surrey's proximity to London made it an attractive place of inspiration and relaxation for a multitude of literary and artistic figures. At that time, the river Thames provided a natural boundary between the great metropolis and Surrey's leafy lanes. Now, that function has largely been taken over by London's orbital M25.

This short introduction would not be complete without a mention of Surrey's great gardens and one of England's most famous gardeners, Gertrude Jekyll. Her influence on horticultural matters continues to be felt in Surrey to this day. Indeed, few towns or villages are without their own garden centre or specialist nursery.

This guide tells you, in the simplest of formats, what is available and where to find it. The aim is to stimulate awareness of what is around us, and a curiosity to discover more; to encourage the resident to explore beyond his or her own familiar territory, and to persuade the visitor to spend time sampling Surrey's many delights.

About this Guide

Listed in this guide are some 2,600 establishments in just over 200 towns and villages, below each of which we mention those other destinations within easy reach.

You will find approximately:

685 pubs	70 book shops
445 restaurants	65 golf courses
260 take-aways	65 guest houses
170 hotels & inns	45 art & craft shops
165 antique dealers	40 wine bars
80 tea rooms	35 art galleries

130 garden centres and nurseries

You will also find over 350 other establishments: museums, historic houses, theatres, cinemas, leisure centres, swimming pools, parks & gardens, farm attractions, and a whole host of fun activities, from windsurfing and go-karting to paintball and dry ski slopes. Although technically no longer in Surrey, Hampton Court and Chessington have been included as we consider them sufficiently important.

In each category we have included every establishment that we know about. We do not inspect them and therefore no opinions are offered. Our editorial comments are intended to be of a factual nature designed to whet the reader's appetite and to give an overall impression. Some establishments have taken the opportunity to give additional information about themselves which we believe to be accurate and which we publish in good faith. We apologise for any errors or omissions you may find and would seek to rectify these in future reprints.

We wish our readers as much fun using this guide as we have had in compiling it, and would like to thank all those friendly and patient Surrey residents who have assisted in its preparation. This is a true explorers guide, for you will find that there is a great deal more to discover in this beautiful county than meets the eye from the M3 or M25. We recommend the use of a good road atlas, particularly to find some of the remoter areas and that excellent cup of tea or pint of beer!

C.R.S. Fowler
M.T.B. Fowler
R.A.C. Fowler

Index of Advertisers

Acknowledgements

Cover photographs are by courtesy of Chobham Golf Club, Farnham Castle, Loseley Park, and the Royal Horticultural Society, Wisley.

Copies of this guide may be obtained directly from the publisher, price £5.00, including postage and packing.

Symbols

★ Establishments known to be recommended in other guides.

◆ Pubs and Inns known to have a separate dining room.

Abinger Common
(including Abinger Hammer & Sutton Abinger)

Abinger is a scattered village in wooded hill country, and still has its old village stocks, a whipping post and many old houses. Abinger Hammer was a medieval centre of the iron industry, and the name recalls the forge hammers of the 17th century. There is still a working smithy, but the old hammer ponds are now planted with watercress. The village clock, with a figure of a blacksmith who strikes the hour with his hammer, was built as a memorial to the first Lord Farrer of Abinger Hall in 1903. Sutton Abinger is a small village set on the slopes of Abinger Common, overlooking the Tillingbourne valley.

CROSSWAYS FARM. One of the finest examples in Surrey of a small Jacobean house, where George Meredith(1828-1909) the novelist is reputed to have based Diana of the Crossways in 1885. The house is open by appointment.

FRIDAY STREET. A cluster of cottages set beside a hammer pond, which was used to power the bellows and forge hammers of iron works in the surrounding forests during the 17th century.

GODDARDS. An Edwardian country house built in 1898 in a beautiful setting on the slopes of Leith Hill as a hostel for young women. The house was designed by Sir Edwin Lutyens(1869-1944), and the garden by Gertrude Jekyll(1843-1932). The house is now administered by the Lutyens Trust and is open to the public.

ST JAMES'S CHURCH. A Norman church with a 13th century chancel, badly damaged by a flying bomb in the Second World War and then by fire in 1964. The war memorial in the churchyard was carved by Lutyens in 1921.

STEPHAN LANGTON INN. Named after Stephen Langton(c1150-1228), King John's Archbishop of Canterbury and signatory to the Magna Carta, who was born in Friday Street.

Antique Dealers
Abinger Bazaar, *Guildford Road, Abinger Hammer, RH5 6SA* ☎ *01306 730756.*
Stirling Antiques, *Aberdeen House, Guildford Road, Abinger Hammer, RH5 6RY*
☎ *01306 730706.*

Farm Shop
Kingfisher, *Guildford Road, Abinger Hammer, RH5 6QX* ☎ *01306 730703.*
MEMBER OF 'A TASTE OF SURREY' - WATERCRESS GROWERS.

Fish Farm
Tillingbourne Trout Farm, *Guildford Road, Abinger Hammer, RH5 6SA* ☎ *01306 730449.*
MEMBER OF 'A TASTE OF SURREY' - FRESH & SMOKED TROUT.

Guest House
Leylands Farm, *Leylands Lane, Abinger Common, RH5 6JU* ☎ *01306 730115.*

Historic Building
Goddards, *Abinger Lane, Abinger Common, RH5 6JH* ☎ *01306 730487.*
TELEPHONE FOR VISITING TIMES AND INFORMATION ON AVAILABILITY FOR MEETINGS AND RECEPTIONS.

Pubs
◆Abinger Arms, *Guildford Road, Abinger Hammer, RH5 6RZ* ☎ *01306 730145.*
★◆Stephan Langton Inn, *Friday Street, Abinger Common, RH5 6JR* ☎ *01306 730775.*
FIFTY COVER RESTAURANT. FULL À LA CARTE MENU AND BAR SNACKS AVAILABLE. PRIVATE FUNCTION ROOM FOR WEDDINGS AND PARTIES.
★Volunteer, *Water Lane, Sutton Abinger, RH5 6PR* ☎ *01306 730798.*

Restaurants
★Abinger Hatch, *Abinger Lane, Abinger Common, RH5 6HZ* ☎ *01306 730737.*
Frog Island, *Hatch Marsh, Guildford Road, Abinger Hammer, RH5 6SA* ☎ *01306 731463.*

Tea Room
Clockhouse Tea Rooms, *Dorking Road, Abinger Hammer, RH5 6RX* ☎ *01306 730811.*

See also Forest Green, Gomshall, Holmbury St Mary, Holmwood, Peaslake, Ranmore Common, Shere, Westcott, Wotton.

Addlestone

A small hamlet until the 19th century when farming began to develop and the arrival of the railway in 1848 led to increased building. Addlestone expanded greatly between the two World Wars.

THE CROUCH OAK. To the north of the village by the Victory Park recreation ground stands an ancient tree, thought to be over a thousand years old, which once marked the boundary of Windsor Forest.

Antique Dealer
  Aladdins Cave Antiques, *15 Station Road, Addlestone, KT15 2AL* ☎ *01932 844178.*
Boat Hire
  Chris Cruises, *27 Green Lane, Addlestone, KT15 2TZ* ☎ *01932 855120.*
Book Shop
  Crouch Oak Bookshop, *80 Station Road, Addlestone, KT15 2AD* ☎ *01932 855374.*
Cafe Bars
  Victoria Cafe, *169 Station Road, Addlestone, KT15 2BA* ☎ *01932 843476.*
Farm Shop
  Crockford Bridge Farm, *New Haw Road, Addlestone, KT15 2BU* ☎ *01932 820751.*
Garden Centres & Nurseries
  Crockford Bridge Farm, *New Haw Road, Addlestone, KT15 2BU* ☎ *01932 820751.*
  Crockford Park Nurseries, *40 Crockford Park Road, Addlestone, KT15 2LX* ☎ *01932 847647.*
  Woburn Hill Nursery, *Woburn Hill, Addlestone, KT15 2QF* ☎ *01932 821066.*
Golf Course
  Abbey Moor Golf Club, *Green Lane, Addlestone, KT15 2XU* ☎ *01932 570741.*
Inn
◆Crouch Oak, *138 Station Road, Addlestone, KT15 2BE* ☎ *01932 842562.*
Library
  SCC Lending Library, *Church Road, Addlestone, KT15 1RW* ☎ *01932 843648.*
Model Shop
  Addlestone Models, *63 Station Road, Addlestone, KT15 2AR* ☎ *01932 845440.*
Pick Your Own
  Crockford Bridge Farm, *New Haw Road, Addlestone, KT15 2BU* ☎ *01932 853886.*
Pubs
  Cricketers, *32 Rowtown, Addlestone, KT15 1EY* ☎ *01932 842808.*
  Dukes Head, *2 Station Road, Addlestone, KT15 2AJ* ☎ *01932 858373.*
  Holly Tree, *25 High Street, Addlestone, KT15 1TT* ☎ *01932 843097.*
  Magnet, *21 Station Road, Addlestone, KT15 2AL* ☎ *01932 847908.*
  Pelican, *Hamm Moor Lane, Addlestone, KT15 2SB* ☎ *01932 843032.*
  Queens Arms, *107 Church Road, Addlestone, KT15 1SF* ☎ *01932 847845.*
  Waggon & Horses, *43 Simplemarsh Road, Addlestone, KT15 1QH* ☎ *01932 847767.*
◆Woburn Arms, *Addlestone Moor, Addlestone, KT15 2QH* ☎ *01932 563314.*
  OPEN ALL DAY. RESTAURANT. FUNCTION ROOM. BUSINESS, PRIVATE PARTIES ETC. ALL MAJOR CREDIT CARDS.
Putting Green
  Victory Park Recreation Ground.
Restaurants
  New Fortune Inn, *174 Station Road, Addlestone, KT15 2BD* ☎ *01932 851287.*
  Perfect Pizza, *68 Station Road, Addlestone, KT15 2AF* ☎ *01932 841511.*
  Taj Mahal Tandoori, *186 Station Road, Addlestone, KT15 2BD* ☎ *01932 857955.*
  Vesuvio, *178 Station Road, Addlestone, KT15 2BD* ☎ *01932 846752.*
  Wan Fu, *17 Station Road, Addlestone, KT15 2AL* ☎ *01932 849167.*

Sports & Leisure Centre
Abbeylands Sports Centre, *School Lane, Addlestone, KT15 1TD* ☎ *01932 858966.*
Swimming Pool - Outdoor
Abbeylands Sports Centre ☎ *01932 858966.*
Take-Aways
Chinese, *38 High Street, Addlestone, KT15 1TR* ☎ *01932 845388.*
Fish Basket, *133 Station Road, Addlestone, KT15 2AT* ☎ *01932 844396.*
Golden House, *19 High Street, Addlestone, KT15 1TL* ☎ *01932 840873.*
JB's Takeout, *131 Station Road, Addlestone, KT15 2AT* ☎ *01932 842200.*
Kwok Lai, *45 Green Lane, Addlestone, KT15 2TX* ☎ *01932 831111.*
Muffins, *54 Station Road, Addlestone, KT15 2AF* ☎ *01932 842639.*
Piggy's, *13 Station Road, Addlestone, KT15 2AL* ☎ *01932 821874.*
Sun On, *116 Church Road, Addlestone, KT15 1SG* ☎ *01932 846213.*
The Chippy, *49 Green Lane, Addlestone, KT15 2TX* ☎ *01932 847423.*

See also Byfleet, Chertsey, Chobham, Lyne, New Haw, Ottershaw, Shepperton, Sheerwater, Thorpe, Virginia Water, Weybridge, Woodham.

Albury

(including Albury Heath)

The village was originally situated within the grounds of the Albury Park estate, until in 1918 the estate was purchased by Henry Drummond, a wealthy banker, who arranged for the entire village to be removed to its present location outside the estate. Martin Tupper(1810-1889) the poet and inventor lived in Albury.

ALBURY PARK. A large Queen Anne country mansion now owned by the Country Houses Association. The interior was altered in 1802 by Sir John Soane(1753-1837), and the exterior was rebuilt in Gothic style in 1847 by A W Pugin(1812-1852), when more than 40 ornate brick chimneys were added. The 14 acres of park and gardens, which are open to the public, were laid out in the 1670s by the diarist and landscape gardener John Evelyn(1620-1706) for his friend Henry Howard, later 6th Duke of Norfolk. Owners of the mansion have included successive Dukes of Norfolk and Earls of Aylesford.

CATHOLIC APOSTOLIC CHURCH & CHAPTER HOUSE. Built in 1840 by Henry Drummond for the Irvingite Sect, the church now remains closed awaiting the second coming.

CHURCH OF ST PETER & ST PAUL. Built by Henry Drummond in 1842 to replace the Saxon Church when the village was moved outside the estate boundary.

SAXON CHURCH. In use as the parish church until 1841 and then left to decay. Recently rescued by The Churches Conservation Trust which rebuilt the chancel. The south transept was designed by Pugin as a decorative mortuary chapel for the Drummond family. The church is now redundant and stands in private grounds, but access is permitted. There is one service a year at mid summer.

SHERBOURNE FARM. A traditional working farm set in the Tillingbourne valley close to the North Downs Way, home to a wide variety of domesticated animals thriving in a natural environment. Displays of old farm tools and, according to the time of year, lambing, shearing, calving, planting and harvesting.

Farm Attraction
Sherbourne Farm, *Shere Road, Albury, GU5 9BW* ☎ *01483 202586.*
Historic Building
The Mansion, *Albury Park, Albury, GU5 9BB* ☎ *01483 202964.*
Inn
★◆Drummond Arms Inn, *The Street, Albury, GU5 9AG* ☎ *01483 202039.*

Pub
★◆William IV, *Dark Lane, Little London, Albury Heath, GU5 9DG* ☎ *01483 202685.*

See also Blackheath, Bramley, Burpham, Chilworth, Clandon, Gomshall, Merrow, Newlands Corner, Peaslake, Shalford, Shamley Green, Shere, Wonersh.

Alfold
(including Alfold Crossways)

Alford dates back to the 13th century and was involved in the medieval glass industry centred in Chiddingfold.

St Nicholas's Church. An interesting church with evidence of every architectural style from the 12th to the 15th century, but spared of Victorian renovations. The belfry is supported by a massive 14th century oak structure. In the churchyard is the grave of Jean Carre, one of the last of the French glass makers who worked in nearby Sidney Wood and died in 1572.

Antique Dealers
  Alfold Antiques, *Country Gardens Garden Centre* ☎ *01403 753442.*
  Pine Workshop, *Byways Cottage, Dunsfold Road, Alfold Crossways, GU6 8JB*
  ☎ *01403 752850.*
Farm Attraction
  Countryways Experience, *Springbok Estate, Alfold, GU6 8EX* ☎ *01403 753589.*
Garden Centre & Nursery
  Country Gardens, *Medland, Horsham Road, Alfold, GU6 8JE* ☎ *0403 752359.*
Golf Course
  Wildwood Golf Club, *Horsham Road, Alfold, GU6 8JE* ☎ *01403 753255.*
Pubs
  Alfold Barn, *Alfold Crossways, GU6 1DA* ☎ *01403 752288.*
  Crown, *Loxwood Road, Alfold, GU6 8ET* ☎ *01403 752216.*

Three Compasses, *Dunsfold Road, Alfold, GU6 8HY* ☎ *01483 275729.*

Tea Room

Countryways Experience ☎ *01403 753589.*

See also Dunsfold. 1 mile from the Sussex boundary.

Ash

(including Ash Vale & Ash Wharf)

During medieval times a sprawling and thinly populated parish, Ash still retains a large swathe of heathland used mainly by the army as rifle ranges. The Basingstoke Canal which winds through the parish once transported agricultural produce, building materials and coal for this area as it became heavily developed. Parts of old Ash can still be seen between the Greyhound pub and St Peter's church.

HARTSHORN COTTAGE. Once the Hartshorn Inn and supposedly one of Dick Turpin's ports of call, this cottage certainly dates from the late 17th century, and possibly even from as far back as 1350.

ST PETER'S CHURCH. The original church was built around 1200, but little remains from this period after the heavy restoration work carried out in the 1860s.

Hotels & Inns

Ash Vale Hotel, *Vale Road, Ash Vale, GU12 5LW* ☎ *01252 24917.*

Ashbourne Court Hotel, *Ashbourne Close, Ash, GU12 6AG* ☎ *01252 26769.*

Lion Brewery, *104 Guildford Road, Ash, GU12 6BT* ☎ *01252 331392.*

B&B ACCOMMODATION. EXCELLENT BAR MEALS ALL DAY AND EVENING. LIVE ENTERTAINMENT. FUNCTION ROOM.

Mountain Biking

Willow Park Mountain Bikes, *Youngs Drive, off Shawfield Road, Ash, GU12 6RE* ☎ *01483 723757.*

Museum

Royal Army Medical Corps Historical Museum, *Keogh Barracks, Ash Vale, GU12 5RQ* ☎ *01252 340212.*

Pubs

Anglers Rest, *Frimley Road, Ash Vale, GU12 5PH* ☎ *01252 540022.*

Bricklayers Arms, *42 Ash Street, Ash, GU12 6LR* ☎ *01252 22228.*

Cannon, *147 Ash Street, Ash, GU12 6LJ* ☎ *Ex Dir.*

Chester Arms, *5 Guildford Road, Ash, GU12 6BE* ☎ *01252 26602.*

Dover Arms, *31 Guildford Road, Ash, GU12 6BQ* ☎ *01252 26025.*

George Inn, *Frimley Road, Ash Vale, GU12 5PD* ☎ *01252 543500.*

Greyhound, *1 Ash Street, Ash, GU12 6LA* ☎ *01252 22012.*

Houston's, *72 Vale Road, Ash Vale, GU12 5HS* ☎ *01252 25535.*

Nightingale, *137 Guildford Road, Ash, GU12 6DF* ☎ *01252 26079.*

Old Ford, *Lynchford Road, North Camp, Ash Vale, GU12 5QA* ☎ *01252 544840.*

Standard of England, *158 Ash Hill Road, Ash Wharf, GU12 5DP* ☎ *Ex Dir.*

Swan, *Hutton Road, Ash Vale, GU12 5HA* ☎ *01252 25212.*

Sports & Leisure Centre

Ash Manor Sports Centre, *Manor Road, Ash, GU12 6QH* ☎ *01252 25484.*

Water Sports

Willow Park Windsurfing Centre, *Youngs Drive, off Shawfield Road, Ash, GU12 6RE* ☎ *01483 723757.*

See also Badshot Lea, Heath End, Mytchett, Normandy, Puttenham, Runfold, The Sands, Seale, Tongham, Wanborough. On the Hampshire boundary.

```
NOTES



```

Ashford

Noted mainly for its hospital, little remains of the old village, the area being almost entirely suburban.

ROWLAND HILL ALMSHOUSES. Almshouses founded in 1811 by the Rev Rowland Hill.
ST MATTHEW'S CHURCH. A church built on the site of a saxon church demolished in 1858. A 16th century brass survives, and a floor slab marks the site of the earlier Norman chancel.

Pubs
Ash Tree, *Convent Road, Ashford, TW15 2HW* ☎ *01784 252362.*
Black Dog, *337 Staines Road West, Ashford, TW15 1RP* ☎ *01784 254348.*
District Arms, *180 Woodthorpe Road, Ashford, TW15 3LQ* ☎ *01784 252160.*
Kings Head, *4 Feltham Road, Ashford, TW15 2EB* ☎ *Ex Dir.*
Links, *91 Fordbridge Road, Ashford, TW15 2SS* ☎ *01784 250068.*
Oaks, *77 Feltham Road, Ashford, TW15 1BS* ☎ *01784 252115.*
Royal Hart, *4 Church Road, Ashford, TW15 2UT* ☎ *01784 252047.*
Spelthorne, *360 Staines Road West, Ashford, TW15 1RY* ☎ *01784 248037.*
Putting Greens
Fordbridge Park, *Kingston Road, Ashford.*
Recreation Ground, *Clockhouse Lane, Ashford.*
Restaurant
Bulldog(Harvester), *London Road, Ashford, TW15 3AF* ☎ *01784 252386.*
Take-Away
Pizza Hut, *351 Staines Road West, Ashford, TW15 1RP* ☎ *01784 240506.*

See also Chertsey, Laleham, Shepperton, Staines, Stanwell, Sunbury, Thorpe, Walton on Thames. On the Greater London boundary & 3 miles from the Berkshire boundary.

Ashtead

Ashtead was important in Roman times, when it was an important tile-making site. It is now a large residential area, development having started only in the 1930s, rather later than surrounding areas.

ASHTEAD COMMON. 500 acres of common, where in 1926 the remains of a Roman villa were discovered, close to the site of a Roman tile factory.
ASHTEAD PARK. The mansion was built of yellow brick in 1790 by Joseph Bonomi(1739-1806), an Italian architect. It is now occupied by the City of London Freemen's School which was founded to educate the children of freemen of the City of London.
ST GILES'S CHURCH. The church was heavily restored in 1862 but still has its 16th century tower and an east window with 16th century Flemish stained glass.

Antique Dealers
Bumbles, *90 The Street, Ashtead, KT21 1AW* ☎ *01372 276219.*
Memory Lane Antiques, *102 The Street, Ashtead, KT21 1AW* ☎ *01372 273436.*
Garden Centres & Nurseries
Dobbe's Nurseries, *Bramley Nurseries, Epsom Road, Ashtead, KT21 1RD* ☎ *01372 273924.*
DIY Garden Centre, *Bramley Corner, Epsom Road, Ashtead, KT21 1JG* ☎ *01372 273590.*
Farm Lane Nursery, *Farm Lane, Ashtead, KT21 1LY* ☎ *01372 274400.*
Marsden Nursery, *6 Pleasure Pit Road, Ashtead, KT21 1HU* ☎ *01372 273891.*
Library
SCC Lending Library, *Woodfield Lane, Ashtead, KT21 2BQ* ☎ *01372 275875.*

Pubs
 Brewery Inn, *15 The Street, Ashtead, KT21 2AD* ☎ *01372 272405.*
 Leg of Mutton & Cauliflower, *48 The Street, Ashtead, KT21 1AZ* ☎ *01372 277124.*
 ◆Woodman, *238 Barnett Wood Lane, Ashtead, KT21 2DA* ☎ *01372 274524.*
Restaurant
 Curry House Tandoori, *61a The Street, Ashtead, KT21 1AA* ☎ *01372 277495.*
Take-Aways
 Burgerland, *21 The Street, Ashtead, KT21 1AA* ☎ *01372 276606.*
 HW Willcox, *220 Barnett Wood Lane, Ashtead, KT21 2DB* ☎ *01372 272844.*
 Superfish, *2 Woodfield Lane, Ashtead, KT21 1AA* ☎ *01372 273784.*

See also Burgh Heath, Epsom, Fetcham, Headley, Leatherhead, Mickleham, Oxshott, Tadworth, Walton on the Hill. 2 miles from the Greater London boundary.

᾽Badshot Lea

Formerly an important hop growing area as evidenced by the old kilns and oast houses.

Pubs
 Cricketers, *22 Badshot Lea Road, Badshot Lea, GU9 9LU* ☎ *01252 342326.*
 Crown Inn, *Pine View Close, Badshot Lea, GU9 9JS* ☎ *01252 20453.*

See also Ash, The Bourne, Farnham, Hale, Heath End, Runfold, The Sands, Seale, Tilford, Tongham, Wrecclesham. On the Hampshire boundary.

Bagshot

An early settlement with Saxon origins. Positioned on the main route to and from the West of England, Bagshot became an important staging post with as many as 14 inns. In more recent years the village expanded considerably and is dominated by the railway viaduct.

BAGSHOT PARK. A Tudor style mansion built by Queen Victoria for her third son Arthur, Duke of Connaught, who lived here until he died in 1942.
ROYAL ARMY CHAPLAINS' DEPARTMENT MUSEUM, BAGSHOT PARK. The museum depicts the role of the military chaplain through the centuries up to and including the Yugoslavia conflict, using photographs, diaries and other personal mementoes.
ST ANNE'S CHURCH. The church is closely associated with the Duke of Connaught, and the west window is dedicated to Queen Victoria.

Garden Centres & Nurseries
 Longacres Nursery, *London Road, Bagshot, GU19 5JB* ☎ *01276 476778.*
 Notcutts Garden Centre, *Waterers Nurseries, 150 London Road, Bagshot, GU19 5DG* ☎ *01276 472288.*
Hotels & Inns
 Fighting Cocks, *1 High Street, Bagshot, GU19 5AG* ☎ *01276 473160.*
 Park Gate Hotel, *London Road, Bagshot, GU19 5HN* ☎ *01276 453444.*
 ★Pennyhill Park Hotel, *London Road, Bagshot, GU19 5ET* ☎ *01276 471774.*
Library
 SCC Lending Library, *High Street, Bagshot, GU19 5AH* ☎ *01276 473759.*
Museum
 Royal Army Chaplains' Department Museum, *Bagshot Park, Bagshot, GU19 5PL* ☎ *01276 471717 x2845.*
   MUSEUM OPEN DAILY MONDAY TO FRIDAY BY APPOINTMENT 10.00 - 12.00 AND 14.00 - 16.00.

Pubs

Bird in Hand, *123 London Road, Bagshot, GU19 5DH* ☎ *01276 475554.*

Foresters Arms, *173 London Road, Bagshot, GU19 5DH* ☎ *01276 472038.*

Kings Arms, *42 High Street, Bagshot, GU19 5AZ* ☎ *01276 473812.*

◆Old Barn, *The Pantiles, 16 London Road, Bagshot, GU19 5HN* ☎ *01276 476673.*

Three Mariners, *56 High Street, Bagshot, GU19 5AW* ☎ *01276 473768.*

White Hart, *Guildford Road, Bagshot, GU19 5JW* ☎ *01276 473640.*

Restaurants

Bagshot Tandoori, *51 High Street, Bagshot, GU19 5AH* ☎ *01276 474524.*

Bel Vedere, *3 High Street, Bagshot, GU19 5AG* ☎ *01276 475583.*

Cricketers(Beefeater), *1 London Road, Bagshot, GU19 5HR* ☎ *01276 473196.*

Sultans Pleasure, *13 London Road, Bagshot, GU19 5HJ* ☎ *01276 475114.*

Take-Aways

Bagshot Chippy, *8 Guildford Road, Bagshot, GU19 5JH* ☎ *01276 472388.*

Breadwinners, *13 High Street, Bagshot, GU19 5AG* ☎ *01276 473578.*

Hong Kong 97, *15 High Street, Bagshot, GU19 5AG* ☎ *01276 473835.*

Jack's of Bagshot, *44 London Road, Bagshot, GU19 5HL* ☎ *01276 473193.*

See also Bisley, Camberley, Lightwater, West End, Windlesham. 1 mile from the Berkshire boundary.

Banstead

Although now a large suburban residential area, there are various links with the past. In 1952 a 12th century house was excavated on Banstead Downs, and in the middle of Park Road is a medieval well. Close to Banstead Wood an area has been reserved as a wildlife park.

ALL SAINTS' CHURCH. A small church built in the 12th and 13th centuries of flint and stone and restored in 1861 by G E Street(1824-1881), designer of the London Law Courts. It has a sturdy tower and a shingled spire.

Art Galleries

Mackies, *35 Nork Way, Banstead, SM7 1PB* ☎ *01737 361011.*

Sporting Gallery, *7 Nork Way, Banstead, SM7 1PB* ☎ *01737 351949.*

Book Shop

Ibis Bookshop, *109 High Street, Banstead, SM7 2NL* ☎ *01737 353260.*

Garden Centre & Nursery

Seasons Garden Centre, *21 Croydon Lane, Banstead, SM7 3BW* ☎ *0181-770 7250.*

Golf Course

Cuddington Golf Club, *Banstead Road, Banstead, SM7 1RD* ☎ *0181-393 0952.*

Information Centre

Banstead Information Centre, *Bolters Lane, Banstead, SM7 2AW* ☎ *01737 352958.*

Library

SCC Lending Library, *The Horseshoe, Bolters Lane, Banstead, SM7 2AW* ☎ *01737 351271.*

Pubs

★Mint, *Park Road, Banstead, SM7 3DS* ☎ *01737 358538.*

Victoria Hotel, *High Street, Banstead, SM7 2LY* ☎ *01737 359821.*

Wheatsheaf, *Brighton Road, Banstead, SM7 1AT* ☎ *01737 354817.*

Woodman, *Woodmansterne Street, Banstead, SM7 3NL* ☎ *01737 354438.*

★Woolpack, *High Street, Banstead, SM7 2NZ* ☎ *01737 354560.*

Restaurants

Indus, *13 Nork Way, Banstead, SM7 1PB* ☎ *01737 371065.*

Lotus Room, *44 High Street, Banstead, SM7 2LX* ☎ *01737 351354.*

Oriental Palace, *51 Nork Way, Banstead, SM7 1PE* ☎ *01737 350515.*

Royal China, *129 High Street, Banstead, SM7 2NS* ☎ *01737 373411.*

Spaghetti Tree No 3, *Nork Way, Banstead, SM7 1PB* ☎ *01737 354470.*

Sports & Leisure Centre
Banstead Sports Centre - See under Tadworth.

Take-Aways
Al-Amin, *9 Woodmansterne Street, Banstead, SM7 3NW* ☎ *01737 371112.*
Banstead Cottage, *137 High Street, Banstead, SM7 2NS* ☎ *01737 371228.*
Flame Grill, *171 High Street, Banstead, SM7 2NT* ☎ *01737 371685.*
Seine Rigger, *11 Nork Way, Banstead, SM7 1PB* ☎ *01737 351168.*

Tea Room & Cafe
Panache Coffee Shop, *45 High Street, Banstead, SM7 2NH* ☎ *01737 362569.*

See also Burgh Heath, Chipstead, Epsom, Ewell, Hooley, Kingswood, Tadworth, Walton on the Hill. 1 mile from the Greater London boundary.

Beare Green

The village has expanded considerably in recent years and is now predominantly residential.

Hotel
Surrey Hills Hotel, *Horsham Road, Beare Green, RH5 4PG* ☎ *01306 711522.*

Pub
★Dukes Head, *Horsham Road, Beare Green, RH5 4QP* ☎ *01306 711778.*

Tea Room & Cafe
Copperfields, *10 Beare Green Court, Old Horsham Road, Beare Green, RH5 4QU*
☎ *01306 712728.*

See also Capel, Coldharbour, Holmwood, Newdigate, Ockley.

Betchworth

A village that has been split in half by its own by-pass. To the north is the railway station; to the south St Michael's Church which forms the centre of the village, with several buildings dating from the 15th, 16th and 17th centuries. These include the Dolphin Inn, with its semicircle of clipped elms, and the Forge which is still functioning. The River Mole runs past the south of the village, and is crossed by a single lane brick bridge recently rebuilt exactly as it had been before.

BROCKHAM LIME WORKS. This 110 acre site was last used for the extraction of chalk in 1936. The chalk was burnt for lime in the patented 'Bishop' lime kilns. Purchased by Surrey County Council in 1977, the kilns are now listed buildings and, overgrown by scrub, are an important home to wildlife.

ST MICHAEL'S CHURCH. Probably Saxon in origin, the church is mainly 13th century but was renovated in Victorian times. The tower is unusual, having been built half way along

9

the south side of the church, instead of centrally, and there is an elaborate lychgate. The church was used in the film 'Four Weddings and a Funeral'.

Garden Centre & Nursery
  Michael Seymour Garden Centre, *Station Road, Betchworth, RH3 7DF ☎ 01737 842099.*
Pubs
★Dolphin, *The Street, Betchworth, RH3 7DW ☎ 01737 842288.*
★Red Lion, *Old Road, Betchworth, RH3 7DS ☎ 01737 843336.*
Restaurants
  Arkle Manor(Harvester), *Reigate Road, Betchworth, RH3 7HB ☎ 01737 842110.*
  Happy Eater, *Reigate Road, Betchworth, RH3 7HB ☎ 01737 843585.*

See also Box Hill, Brockham, Buckland, Dorking, Headley, Holmwood, Leigh, Mickleham, Reigate, Sidlow Bridge, Walton on the Hill.

Bisley

CHURCH OF ST JOHN THE BAPTIST. An isolated church with a shingled belfry and a 14th century porch overshadowed by a huge yew tree.
NATIONAL RIFLE ASSOCIATION RANGES. Formed in 1890, the NRA hold events and competitions throughout the year, but particularly for two weeks in July each year top marksmen meet here from all over the world.

Garden Centres & Nurseries
  Lincluden Nursery, *Bisley Green, Bisley, GU24 9EN ☎ 01483 797005.*
Pubs
  Fox Inn, *Guildford Road, Bisley, GU24 9AB ☎ 01483 473175.*

THE HONOURABLE ARTILLERY COMPANY

BISLEY SHOOTING LODGE

PAVILION HISTORY

The Shooting Lodge was built in 1928 and designed in Tudor style of the period of the foundation of the Regiment (1537).

It was built as a memorial to the members of HAC who died in the First World War. The HAC has used the Lodge for both military and social events over the past sixty years. It has now been opened for commercial use. The attractive two floored Lodge is set in an acre of gardens suitable for barbecues and picnics, there is also ample parking space within the grounds.

FACILITIES

The dining room is 56 by 20 feet, oak panelled beneath an oak-beam ceiling and will seat one hundred people with ease.

The bar is fully licensed and is at one end of the dining room. It stocks a selection of wines and spirits.

Classrooms are available in the gardens of the Lodge and provide facilities for conferences or seminars.

The accommodation is dormitory style and can sleep up to eighty. There are two individual rooms on the verandah and double bunk rooms next to the dormitory.

Baths, shower and toilets are on the ground floor and there are both ladies and gentlemen's facilities.

BOOKING

The steward of the Lodge who lives on site will be happy to advise on the facilities and design a function to meet your needs.

BOOKING AND ENQUIRIES

The Honourable Artillery Company
Bisley Camp
Brrokwood, Woking
Surrey, GU24 0NY
Tel: 01483 472376
Fax: 01483 487940

Hen & Chickens, *200 Guildford Road, Bisley, GU24 9DJ* ☎ *01483 473184.*

See also Bagshot, Brookwood, Chobham, Deepcut, Horsell, Knaphill, Lightwater, Pirbright, West End, Windlesham, Woking.

Blackheath

A Victorian village largely unchanged since the first commuters moved here in the 1870s, and Blackheath Cricket Club has flourished ever since.

ST MARTIN'S CHURCH. Built in the Spanish style by C H Townsend in 1895, and commissioned by Sir William Roberts-Austen(1843-1902), metallurgist and Assayer of the Royal Mint.
Pub
Villagers, *Blackheath Lane, Blackheath, GU4 8RB* ☎ *01483 893152.*

See also Albury, Bramley, Burpham, Chilworth, Clandon, Gomshall, Loseley, Merrow, Newlands Corner, Shalford, Shamley Green, Shere, Wonersh.

Bletchingley

The village was probably laid out by Lord Richard de Clare in the late 12th or 13th century. There were two hunting parks, a castle and a Tudor mansion which Henry VIII gave to Anne of Cleves. From 1294, as a rotten borough it returned two Members of Parliament, amongst the last of which were Lord Melbourne and Lord Palmerston. Bletchingley is an attractive village with many pretty tile-hung cottages and a wide and picturesque main street.

Bletchingley GOLF CLUB

Bletchingley Golf Club, par 72, Championship length, is set in 140 acres of glorious Surrey countryside, yet only a few minutes from Junction 6 on the M25.

Societies and visitors are welcome. Green Fees during the week £20, weekends after a certain time £25.

The rich sandy loam site is naturally so well drained that it will be possible to play at Bletchingley when many other courses are closed.

Church Lane
Bletchingley
Surrey RH1 4LP
Tel: (01883) 744666

BLETCHINGLEY CASTLE. The foundations of a rectangular keep on a wide flat mound are all that remains of the old Norman castle built by Richard de Tonebridge and which was demolished by Prince Edward after the Battle of Lewes in 1264. These remains are in what are now private gardens, although further out can be seen the lines of the castle moat.
PLACE FARM. This is the site of a large mansion built in 1520 and acquired by Henry VIII for Anne of Cleves. The house incorporates the fine Tudor archway of the gatehouse, discovered early this century, which is all that remains of the original mansion.
ST MARY'S CHURCH. Norman in origin, the church was altered in the 13th and 15th centuries and restored in the 19th century. The massive square tower is 12th century and once supported a tower, but this was destroyed by lightening in 1606 and was never replaced. There is a priest's room above the porch. Inside there are a number of brasses and monuments, including one in particular by Richard Crutcher of Sir Robert Clayton and his wife. He owned much of Bletchingley and Godstone in the late 17th century and was Lord Mayor of London in 1679. The pulpit dates from the 17th century.

Antique Dealers
  John Anthony Antiques, *71 High Street, Bletchingley, RH1 4LJ* ☎ *01883 743197.*
  Post House Antiques, *32 High Street, Bletchingley, RH1 4PA* ☎ *01883 743317.*
  Quill Antiques, *86 High Street, Bletchingley, RH1 4PA* ☎ *01883 743755.*

Art Gallery
  Cider House Galleries, *80 High Street, Bletchingley, RH1 4PA* ☎ *0883 742198.*

Golf Course
  Bletchingley Golf Club, *Church Lane, Bletchingley, RH1 4LP* ☎ *01883 744666.*

Hotel & Inn
★◆Whyte Harte Hotel, *11 High Street, Bletchingley, RH1 4PB* ☎ *01883 743231.*

Pubs
◆Plough, *2 High Street, Bletchingley, RH1 4PE* ☎ *01883 744938.*
◆Prince Albert, *Outwood Lane, Bletchingley, RH1 4LR* ☎ *01883 743257.*
  Red Lion, *Castle Street, Bletchingley, RH1 4NU* ☎ *01883 743342.*
★◆William IV, *Little Common Lane, Bletchingley, RH1 4QF* ☎ *01883 743278.*

Restaurant
  King Charles Cottage, *36 High Street, Bletchingley, RH1 4PA* ☎ *01883 743130.*

See also Caterham, Earlswood, Gatton, Godstone, Merstham, Nutfield, Outwood, Redhill, Tandridge.

Blindley Heath

Guest House
  Stantons Hall Farm, *Eastbourne Road, Blindley Heath, RH7 6LG* ☎ *01342 832401.*

Pub
◆Farmhouse Table, *Eastbourne Road, Blindley Heath, RH7 6JJ* ☎ *01342 832017.*

Restaurant
  Red Barn, *Tandridge Lane, Blindley Heath, RH7 6LL* ☎ *01342 834272.*

Tea Room
  Bannisters Bakery, *Eastbourne Road, Blindley Heath, RH7 6LQ* ☎ *01342 832086.*

See also Crowhurst, Godstone, Haxted, Horne, Lingfield, Newchapel, Outwood, Smallfield, Tandridge.

Bookham
(Great & Little)

Both villages have several 16th and 17th century houses, and remained small until enlarged by residential development early this century.

LITTLE BOOKHAM CHURCH. A small 12th century church with a bellcote and no known dedication. The tub font is possibly Saxon. In the churchyard is a vast yew said to be 900 years old, and the tomb of General Coote Manningham who formed the Rifle Brigade in the 19th century.

OLD RECTORY. An 18th century house rented by the Barretts of Wimpole Street for their daughter Elizabeth who, instead of staying there, eloped with Robert Browning.

ST NICHOLAS'S CHURCH, GREAT BOOKHAM. A fine church of Norman origin, the chancel was built in 1341 by John Rutherwyke, Abbot of Chertsey. The south aisle was widened in the 15th century, and the church was restored in the second half of the 19th century. The timber tower with its shingled spire, is built on a stone base. There is a Norman font of Sussex marble, and brasses and monuments of all periods.

THE HERMITAGE. Formerly called 'Fairfield', and once the home of Fanny Burney(1752-1840), the novelist and diarist.

Antique Dealer
  Bookham Antiques, *7 High Street, Bookham, KT23 4AA* ☎ *01372 457412.*
Art Gallery
  Kingsmead Art Gallery, *40 Church Road, Great Bookham, KT23 3PW* ☎ *01372 459579.*
Arts & Crafts
  Granary Crafts, *63 Church Road, Bookham, KT23 3EG* ☎ *01372 458600.*
    EXTENSIVE RANGE EMBROIDERY MATERIALS AND KITS. IN ATTRACTIVE VIRGINIA CREEPER COVERED COTTAGE.
    HALF DAY WEDNESDAY.
Garden Centre & Nursery
  Dobbe's Nurseries, *Guildford Road, Bookham, KT23 4EX* ☎ *01372 454553.*
Hotels & Inns
  Bookham Grange Hotel, *The Common, Little Bookham, KT23 3HS* ☎ *01372 452742.*
  Preston Cross Hotel, *Rectory Lane, Little Bookham, KT23 4DY* ☎ *01372 456642.*
Library
  SCC Lending Library, *Townshott Close, Bookham, KT23 4DQ* ☎ *01372 454440.*
Pubs
  Anchor, *161 Lower Road, Great Bookham, KT23 4AH* ☎ *01372 452429.*
  Old Crown, *1 High Street, Great Bookham, KT23 4AA* ☎ *01372 458119.*
  Old Windsor Castle, *25 Little Bookham Street, Little Bookham, KT23 3AA* ☎ *01372 452226.*
  Royal Oak, *16 High Street, Great Bookham, KT23 4AG* ☎ *01372 452533.*
Restaurants
  Curry Queen, *41 Church Road, Great Bookham, KT23 3PG* ☎ *01372 457241.*
  Morphou, *Guildford Road, Bookham, KT23 4BL* ☎ *01372 459256.*
Take-Away
  Michael's, *5 New Parade, Leatherhead Road, Bookham, KT23 4RL* ☎ *01372 454265.*

See also Box Hill, Downside, Effingham, Fetcham, Horsley, Leatherhead, Mickleham, Polesden Lacey, Ranmore Common, Stoke D'Abernon, Westcott, Westhumble.

The Bourne
(including Lower & Middle)

Hotel
  Eldon Hotel, *43 Frensham Road, Lower Bourne, GU10 3PZ* ☎ *01252 792745.*
Pubs
  Cricketers Inn, *39 Frensham Road, Lower Bourne, GU10 3PZ* ☎ *01252 715708.*
◆Fox Inn, *21 Frensham Road, Lower Bourne, GU10 3PH* ☎ *01252 716395.*
★◆Spotted Cow, *3 Bourne Grove, Lower Bourne, GU10 3QT* ☎ *01252 726541.*
Restaurant
  Bay Tree, *61 Frensham Road, Lower Bourne, GU10 3HL* ☎ *01252 792452.*

See also Badshot Lea, Elstead, Farnham, Frensham, Hale, Rowledge, Runfold, The Sands, Tilford, Tongham, Wrecclesham. 2 miles from the Hampshire boundary.

Box Hill

BOX HILL (National Trust). Situated on the edge of the North Downs, rising 400ft from the River Mole, there are more than 800 acres of woods and chalk downland. It has been designated a Country Park and there are magnificent views of Dorking and the South Downs. Hill top buildings include an information centre, and a derelict fort which is not open to the public.
BOX HILL FORT. One of a string of 13 forts built by the War Office in 1896 between Dartford and Guildford to protect London from a possible German invasion. General Sir George Chesney had suggested the possibility twenty five years earlier in an article entitled 'The Battle of Dorking'.

Pubs

Hand in Hand, *Box Hill Road, Box Hill, KT20 7PS* ☎ *01737 843352.*

Boxhills Tavern, *Box Hill Road, Box Hill, KT20 7LB* ☎ *01737 842338.*
SURREY'S HIGHEST TAVERN 618FT ABOVE SEA LEVEL. RECOGNISED AS BOXHILL'S EATING PLACE. REAL ALES. GOOD FOOD AND ENTERTAINMENT. TEA GARDEN. RESTAURANT. TWO NICE BARS.

See also Betchworth, Bookham, Brockham, Buckland, Headley, Holmwood, Leatherhead, Mickleham, Polesden Lacey, Ranmore Common, Walton on the Hill, Westcott, Westhumble.

Bramley

There are many listed buildings in the village, dating from the 15th to 19th centuries, among which are Bramley Mill and Snowdenham Mill. Though long since disused, the Guildford to Horsham Railway, and the Wey and Arun Canal can just be traced.

Antique Dealers

Bramley Antiques, *6 High Street, Bramley, GU5 0HB* ☎ *01483 898580.*

Memories Antiques, *High Street, Bramley, GU5 0HB* ☎ *01483 892205.*

Garden Centre & Nursery

Highbanks Nursery, *Birtley Road, Bramley, GU5 0LA* ☎ *01483 893380.*

Golf Course

Bramley Golf Club, *Bramley, GU5 0AL* ☎ *01483 892696.*

Hotels & Inns

★Bramley Grange, *281 Horsham Road, Bramley, GU5 0BL* ☎ *01483 893434.*

★◆Jolly Farmer, *High Street, Bramley, GU5 0HB* ☎ *01483 893355.*

Library

SCC Lending Library, *High Street, Bramley, GU5 0HG* ☎ *01483 892510.*

Pub

Wheatsheaf, *High Street, Bramley, GU5 0HB* ☎ *01483 892722.*

Restaurants

Champan Tandoori, *High Street, Bramley, GU5 0HB* ☎ *01483 893684.*

Garden Restaurant, *4a High Street, Bramley, GU5 0HB* ☎ *01483 894037.*

Hamiltons, *Bramley Grange Hotel* ☎ *01483 893434.*

La Baita, *5 High Street, Bramley, GU5 0HB* ☎ *01483 893392.*

See also Albury, Blackheath, Burpham, Chilworth, Compton, Farncombe, Godalming, Guildford, Hascombe, Hurtmore, Loseley, Newlands Corner, Shalford, Shamley Green, Wonersh.

Brockham

The name is derived from the badgers that once lived in the banks of the River Mole in this area. With its perfect picture postcard village green setting, surrounded by cottages, a white firestone church at the southernmost end and the slopes of Box Hill to the north, this village has the reputation as one of the prettiest in Surrey. One of the biggest Guy Fawkes bonfires in the county is held every November on the village green.

BETCHWORTH CASTLE. In Betchworth Park, now a golf course, are the remains of the castle which was built in the 15th century to defend the Downs. It was partly demolished in 1690 and finally dismantled in 1860 but the stables, which in 1799 were designed by Sir John Soane(1753-1837), have been converted into cottages and still survive.

CHRIST CHURCH. Built in 1846 in memory of Henry Goulburn, a Chancellor of the Exchequer who served both Peel and Wellington. The elaborately carved reredos dated 1885 depicts the Last Supper.

Nursery
   Wheelers Lane Nurseries, *Wheelers Lane, Brockham, RH3 7LA* ☎ *01737 844575.*
Pubs
◆Dukes Head, *The Green, Brockham, RH3 7JS* ☎ *01737 842023.*
   Royal Oak, *The Green, Brockham, RH3 7JS* ☎ *01737 843241.*
   Spotted Cow, *Middle Street, Strood Green, Brockham, RH3 7HU* ☎ *01737 842076.*
Restaurant
   Postillion, *2 Brockham Lane, Brockham, RH3 7EL* ☎ *01737 844832.*

See also Betchworth, Box Hill, Buckland, Dorking, Headley, Holmwood, Leigh, Mickleham, Ranmore Common, Reigate, Westcott, Westhumble.

Brook

HELEN ALLINGHAM. Helen Allingham(1848-1926), the water colour artist, lived at Sandhills and painted many cottages in the area.
PIRRIE HALL. Pirrie Hall serves as the pavilion for the six acre cricket ground.

Pub
◆Dog & Pheasant, *Haslemere Road, Brook, GU8 5UJ* ☎ *01428 682763.*

See also Chiddingfold, Grayswood, Hambledon, Haslemere, Hydestile, Milford, Thursley, Witley, Wormley.

Brookwood

The village grew up around the station which opened in 1864, and is bordered by the Basingstoke Canal which passes to the north.

BROOKWOOD CEMETERY. A 400 acre cemetery opened in 1854 to provide a resting place for many of London's dead. At one time it had its own purpose-built railway station in London for traffic to the cemetery, where there were three separate stations. Brookwood is the largest cemetery in the country, and nearly 240,000 people are buried here. Sir Thomas Beecham(1879-1961) the conductor and impresario, Dame Rebecca West(1892-1983) the novelist and critic, and Dennis Wheatley(1897-1977) the novelist are buried here.
BROOKWOOD MILITARY CEMETERY. Covering some 37 acres, this is the largest Commonwealth war cemetery in the United Kingdom. In 1917 an area of land was set aside from the main cemetery for the graves of 1,601 men and women of the Commonwealth and American forces who had died in the London district, many of wounds received in the Great War. This was extended to accommodate 3,474 graves of Commonwealth casualties of the Second World War, and there are also American, Belgian, Czech, Dutch, French and Polish plots containing the graves of casualties of our Allies. There are German and Italian plots where prisoners of war lie buried. Adjacent to the Military Cemetery is a plot of 900 graves of Chelsea Pensioners.

Garden Centres & Nurseries
   Blackhorse Plants, *Blackhorse Road, Brookwood, GU22 0QT* ☎ *01483 797534.*
   Wye Brothers, *The Old Gardens, Blackhorse Road, Brookwood, GU22 0QT*
   ☎ *01483 473278.*
Golf Course
   West Hill Golf Club, *Bagshot Road, Brookwood, GU24 0BH* ☎ *01483 474365.*
Inn
   Brookwood Hotel, *131 Connaught Road, Brookwood, GU24 0ER* ☎ *01483 475145.*
Restaurant
   Mogul, *142 Connaught Road, Brookwood, GU24 0AS* ☎ *01483 472610.*

Take-Aways

Golden Bamboo, *102 Connaught Road, Brookwood, GU24 0HJ* ☎ *01483 476459.*
Lucky, *116 Hermitage Road, Brookwood, GU21 1TT* ☎ *01483 476349.*
Mayo Fish Bar, *152 Connaught Road, Brookwood, GU24 0AL* ☎ *01483 473064.*

See also Bisley, Camberley, Deepcut, Horsell, Knaphill, Lightwater, Mytchett, Normandy, Pirbright, West End, Worplesdon.

Buckland

Known for its picturesque buildings and village green, complete with pond. The main road runs between the pretty church and the green, with a black barn on one side and the former village school on the other. Sand and gravel pits are a modern feature of the village.

St Mary's Church. Extensively rebuilt by Henry Woodyer in 1860, the church still retains its 15th century timber belfry and the best 14th century stained glass in Surrey.

Garden Centres & Nurseries

Buckland Nurseries, *Reigate Road, Buckland, RH2 9RE* ☎ *01737 242990.*
High Trees Nurseries, *Reigate Road, Buckland, RH2 9RE* ☎ *01737 247217.*

Pub

Jolly Farmers, *Reigate Road, Buckland, RH3 7BG* ☎ *01737 242764.*

See also Betchworth, Box Hill, Brockham, Dorking, Headley, Holmwood, Kingswood, Leigh, Mickleham, Reigate, Sidlow Bridge, Tadworth, Walton on the Hill, West Humble.

Burgh Heath

Burgh Heath has grown to fill the gap that existed between Banstead and Tadworth and has in the process become a suburb of both.

Antique Dealer

Tattenham Antiques, *1a The Parade, Tattenham Way, Burgh Heath, KT20 5NG* ☎ *01737 353937.*

Hotel

★Heathside Hotel, *Brighton Road, Burgh Heath, KT20 6BW* ☎ *01737 353355.*

Pub

Surrey Yeoman, *Reigate Road, Burgh Heath, KT20 5NT* ☎ *01737 354658.*

Restaurants

Banstead Tandoori, *6 High Street, Burgh Heath, KT20 5SD* ☎ *01737 351605.*
Royal Phoenix, *84 Dorking Road, Burgh Heath, KT20 5RX* ☎ *01737 371717.*

Take-Away

Oriental Chef, *4 The Parade, Brighton Road, Burgh Heath, KT20 6AT* ☎ *01737 352446.*

See also Ashtead, Banstead, Chipstead, Epsom, Ewell, Headley, Hooley, Kingswood, Tadworth, Walton on the Hill. 2 miles from the Greater London boundary

NOTES

Burpham

This one time rural village is now effectively a suburb of Guildford.

BURPHAM COURT FARM PARK. A conservation centre for rare and endangered breeds of farm livestock set in 77 acres of beautiful countryside by the River Wey. There are wildlife conservation areas, farm and riverside walks, fishing and an indoor pets corner.

Farm Attraction
   Burpham Court Farm Park, *Clay Lane, Burpham, GU4 7NA* ☎ *01483 576089.*
Pub
   Anchor & Horseshoes, *194 London Road, Burpham, GU1 1XR* ☎ *01483 504677.*
Restaurant
   Green Man(Harvester), *93 London Road, Burpham, GU1 1YT* ☎ *01483 68834.*
Tea Room & Cafe
   Burpham Court Farm Park ☎ *01483 576089.*

See also Albury, Blackheath, Bramley, Chilworth, Clandon, Guildford, Loseley, Merrow, Newlands Corner, Send, Shalford, Sutton Green, Wood Street, Worplesdon.

Burstow

The birthplace of the 19th century cricketer William Lambert.

BURSTOW COURT. The oldest and most important of the four manors in the area, dating from the early 10th century. Now known as Old Court, the house was built in the 16th century and the great hall and the moat have been preserved.

ST BARTHOLOMEW'S CHURCH. Like St Peter's at Newdigate, St Bartholomew's has a tower built entirely of timber. Buried here is John Flamsteed(1646-1719), the first astronomer-royal of England, who took holy orders and for 35 years until his death held the living here.

Restaurant
   Saffron Garden, *Rede Hall,*
   Redehall Road, Burstow, RH6 9RH
   ☎ *01342 844541.*

See also Copthorne, Felbridge, Hookwood, Horley, Horne, Newchapel, Outwood, Shipley Bridge, Smallfield. 1 mile from the Sussex boundary.

St Bartholomew's Church

Byfleet
(including West Byfleet)

The arrival of the railway at West Byfleet in 1887, and the building of Brooklands twenty years later, marked the start of development of the area, which has a history dating back to the 7th century. To the north of the village the Basingstoke Canal divides from the Wey Navigation.

BYFLEET MANOR. Built as a royal hunting lodge for Edward II and restored by Anne of Denmark, wife of James I. It has been considerably changed and rebuilt since then, and is now private apartments.
BYFLEET MILL. Built in 1647 and restored after a fire in 1991.
ST MARY'S CHURCH. Built in flint, the church has a 13th century nave, chancel and belfry.

Boat Hire
  Byfleet Boat Club, *Boat House, 4 Old Parvis Road, West Byfleet, KT14 6HB* ☎ *01932 340828.*
Book Shop
  Bookcase, *43 Old Woking Road, West Byfleet, KT14 6LG* ☎ *01932 344269.*
Golf Course
  West Byfleet Golf Club, *Sheerwater Road, West Byfleet, KT14 6AA* ☎ *01932 345230.*
Hotel
  Claremont, *2 Station Road, West Byfleet, KT14 6DR* ☎ *01932 345048.*
Libraries
  SCC Lending Library, *High Road, Byfleet, KT14 7QN* ☎ *01932 345274.*
  SCC Lending Library, *The Corner, West Byfleet, KT14 6NY* ☎ *01932 343955.*
Pubs
  ◆Blue Anchor, *155 High Road, Byfleet, KT14 7RL* ☎ *01932 346301.*
  Kings Head, *59 Chertsey Road, Byfleet, KT14 7AP* ☎ *01932 342671.*
  ★Plough, *104 High Road, Byfleet, KT14 7QT* ☎ *01932 353257.*
  Queens Head, *2 High Road, Byfleet, KT14 7QG* ☎ *01932 345433.*
  ◆Yeoman, *81 Old Woking Road, West Byfleet, KT14 6JA* ☎ *01932 344553.*
Restaurants
  Chu Chin Chow, *63 Old Woking Road, West Byfleet, KT14 6LF* ☎ *01932 349581.*
  Dipali Tandoori, *70 High Road, Byfleet, KT14 7QL* ☎ *01932 354551.*
  Mama Mia Pizzeria, *1 Parvis Road, West Byfleet, KT14 6LP* ☎ *01932 348989.*
  Raffaella, *39 Old Woking Road, West Byfleet, KT14 6LG* ☎ *01932 354329.*
  Regency Peking, *18 Station Approach, West Byfleet, KT14 6NF* ☎ *01932 340556.*
  Suman Tandoori, *37 Station Approach, West Byfleet, KT14 6NF* ☎ *01932 353297.*
Take-Aways
  Fryfare, *58 High Road, Byfleet, KT14 7QL* ☎ *01932 342660.*
  Jane's Upstairs, *51 Old Woking Road, West Byfleet, KT14 6LG* ☎ *01932 345789.*
  Kam Hong, *166 High Road, Byfleet, KT14 7RG* ☎ *01932 342047.*
  Kam Man, *92 High Road, Byfleet, KT14 7QT* ☎ *01932 340155.*
  Selections, *30 Station Approach, West Byfleet, KT14 6NF* ☎ *01932 353110.*
  Superfish, *51 Old Woking Road, West Byfleet, KT14 6LG* ☎ *01932 340366.*
Wine Bar & Cafe Bar
  Sidewalk Cafe, *29 Station Approach, West Byfleet, KT14 6NF* ☎ *01932 341718.*

See also Addlestone, Downside, Horsell, Mayford, New Haw, Ockham, Ottershaw, Pyrford, Ripley, Sheerwater, Weybridge, Whiteley Village, Wisley, Woking, Woodham.

Camberley

Surrounded by woods and heathland, Camberley is an important military centre, having established itself when in 1809 the Royal Military College moved to Sandhurst just across the boundary in Berkshire. Much of the town was developed by Captain C R Knight and Major R Spring, who purchased large amounts of land and laid out many of the principal roads.

CIVIC HALL. A wide program of popular music events and entertainment is offered alongside local amateur productions. Rock music, popular classics, country and western, traditional jazz, big band and tea dancing are all in the programme, along with all star wrestling, flea markets, antique fairs, etc.

St Michael's Church. Built in 1850, it has a cross made during the Second World War by prisoners of war held in Camberley.

Staff College and Museum. The museum tells the history of the Staff College and of the work of the staff officers of the British army, and is open by appointment only.

Surrey Heath Museum. A small high quality permanent exhibition of the environmental and social heritage of the local area and the heathland, including some Roman remains. There are also continuous temporary exhibitions throughout the year on subjects of local and regional interest, plus small travelling displays for outside venues.

Antique Dealers
P Ellis, *235 London Road, Camberley, GU15 3HB* ☎ *01276 24071.*
RJ Bowdery, *21 High Street, Camberley, GU15 3RB* ☎ *01276 23845.*
Pedlar, *231 London Road, Camberley, GU15 3EY* ☎ *01276 64750.*
Art & Craft Equipment
Brackendale Gallery, *1 Sparvell Way, Camberley, GU15 3SF* ☎ *01276 681344.*
Book Shops
Bygone Books, *443 London Road, Camberley, GU15 3JA* ☎ *01276 686583.*
Coles Bookstore, *2a Grace Reynolds Walk, Camberley, GU15 3SN* ☎ *01276 678688.*
Selnews Bargain Bookshop, *21 High Street, Camberley, GU15 3RB* ☎ *01276 23040.*
The Bookshop, *60 High Street, Camberley, GU15 3RS* ☎ *01276 683222.*
WH Smith, *51 High Street, Camberley, GU15 3RB* ☎ *01276 23888.*
Cinema
Cannon Cinema, *303 London Road, Camberley, GU15 3HE* ☎ *01276 63909.*
Civic Hall
Civic Hall, *Knoll Road, Camberley, GU15 3SY* ☎ *01276 26978.*
Garden Centres & Nurseries
Copped Hall Cottage Gardens, *Stonegate, Copped Hall Drive, Camberley, GU15 1PD* ☎ *01276 22468.*
Copped Hall Cottage Gardens, *145 London Road, Camberley, GU15 3JY* ☎ *01276 681126.*
Do It All, *Park Farm Ind Estate, Frimley Road, Camberley, GU15 2PN* ☎ *01276 683660.*
Golf Course
Camberley Heath Golf Club, *Golf Drive, Camberley, GU15 1JG* ☎ *01276 23258.*
Guest Houses
Hazel Lodge, *110 London Road, Camberley, GU15 3TJ* ☎ *01276 64856.*
The Camberley, *116 London Road, Camberley, GU15 3TJ* ☎ *01276 24410.*
The Guest House, *Tekels Park, Camberley, GU15 2LF* ☎ *01276 63723.*
Hotels & Inns
Burwood House Hotel, *15 London Road, Camberley, GU15 3UQ* ☎ *01276 685686.*
Cambridge Hotel, *121 London Road, Camberley, GU15 3LS* ☎ *01276 26488.*
★Frimley Hall Hotel(Forte), *Portsmouth Road, Camberley, GU15 2BG* ☎ *01276 28321.*
One Oak Hotel(Toby), *114 Portsmouth Road, Camberley, GU15 1HS* ☎ *01276 691939.*
Royal Academy Arms Hotel, *517 London Road, Camberley, GU15 3JF* ☎ *01276 62444.*
Information Centre
Camberley Information Centre, *Knoll Road, Camberley GU15 3SY* ☎ *01276 683626.*
Tourist Information Centre, *Haywood House, 1 Portesbery Road, Camberley, GU15 3SZ* ☎ *01276 692437.*
Library
SCC Lending Library, *Knoll Road, Camberley, GU15 3SY* ☎ *01276 63184.*
Museums
Staff College Museum, *The Staff College, London Road, Camberley, GU15 4NP* ☎ *01276 412602.*
Surrey Heath Museum, *Knoll Road, Camberley, GU15 3HD* ☎ *01276 686252.*
Pubs
Ancient Foresters, *23 Park Street, Camberley, GU15 3PQ* ☎ *01276 64830.*
Bridgers, *299 London Road, Camberley, GU15 3HE* ☎ *01276 21534.*
Brown Jug, *88 High Street, Camberley, GU15 3RS* ☎ *01276 21280.*

Carpenters Arms, *59 Park Street, Camberley, GU15 3PE* ☎ *01276 63676.*
Crown, *494 London Road, Camberley* ☎ *Ex Dir.*
Four Horseshoes, *75 Frimley Road, Camberley, GU15 3EQ* ☎ *01276 63842.*
Jolly Farmer, *1 London Road, Camberley, GU15 3UR* ☎ *01276 63082.*
Kings Arms, *407 London Road, Camberley, GU15 3HL* ☎ *01276 22274.*
Lamb, *593 London Road, Camberley, GU15 3JQ* ☎ *01276 33832.*
Royal Standard, *115 Frimley Road, Camberley, GU15 2PP* ☎ *01276 27641.*
Staff Hotel, *191 London Road, Camberley, GU15 3EY* ☎ *01276 28505.*
Wheatsheaf, *Heatherside Precinct, Camberley, GU15 5UQ* ☎ *01276 28744.*
William IV, *19 Frimley Road, Camberley, GU15 3EN* ☎ *01276 677654.*

Putting Greens
Recreation Ground, *London Road, Camberley.*
Watchetts Recreation Ground, *Park Road, Camberley.*

Restaurants
Athenian Taverna, *140 Frimley Road, Camberley, GU15 2QN* ☎ *01276 684919.*
Crab and Dragon, *220 Frimley Road, Camberley, GU15 2QJ* ☎ *01276 22578.*
Diwaneekach Tandoori, *365 London Road, Camberley, GU15 3HQ* ☎ *01276 66606.*
Duke of York(Harvester), *371 London Road, Camberley, GU15 3HL* ☎ *01276 63899.*
Dynasty, *9 Park Street, Camberley, GU15 3PQ* ☎ *01276 63652.*
El Picadero Tapas Bar, *177 London Road, Camberley, GU15 3JS* ☎ *01276 670670.*
Peking Inn, *124 Frimley Road, Camberley, GU15 2QN* ☎ *01276 26674.*
Pizza Express, *52 Park Street, Camberley, GU15 3PT* ☎ *01276 21846.*
Pizzaland, *69 High Street, Camberley, GU17 8HB* ☎ *01276 23652.*
Sinuessa, *41 Obelisk Way, Camberley, GU15 3SG* ☎ *01276 679000.*
Star of India, *16 Park Street, Camberley, GU15 3PL* ☎ *01276 64682.*
★Tithas, *31 High Street, Camberley, GU15 3RB* ☎ *01276 23279.*
Villa Romana, *20 Park Street, Camberley, GU15 3PL* ☎ *01276 24370.*
Wood Plate House, *3 Frimley Road, Camberley, GU15 3EN* ☎ *01276 64845.*

Sports & Leisure Centre
Arena Leisure Centre, *Grand Avenue, Camberley, GU15 3QJ* ☎ *01276 28787.*

Swimming Pool
Arena Leisure Centre ☎ *01276 28787.*

Take-Aways
Burger King, *34 High Street, Camberley, GU15 3RS* ☎ *01276 675690.*
Camberley Tandoori, *297 London Road, Camberley, GU15 3HE* ☎ *01276 28360.*
Fish King Fish Bar, *10 Dean Parade, Camberley, GU15 4DQ* ☎ *01276 21183.*
Kentucky Fried Chicken, *73 Park Street, Camberley, GU15 3PE* ☎ *01276 64197.*
McDonald's, *43 High Street, Camberley, GU15 3RB* ☎ *01276 681676.*
Mr Lau's Fish Bar, *9 Heatheridge Arcade, Heatherside, Camberley, GU15 1AX*
☎ *01276 62330.*
Tom's Fish & Chips, *113a Frimley Road, Camberley, GU15 2PP* ☎ *01276 63044.*

Theatre
Civic Hall ☎ *01276 23738.*

Wine Bars & Cafe Bars
Capers, *125 London Road, Camberley, GU15 3JY* ☎ *01276 685322.*
90 The High Street, *90 High Street, Camberley, GU15 3RN* ☎ *01276 65577.*

See also Bagshot, Brookwood, Deepcut, Frimley, Lightwater, Mytchett. 1 mile from the Berkshire boundary & 1 mile from the Hampshire boundary.

```
NOTES




```

Capel

This was once a staging post on the old London to Worthing coach route, and there remain a number of 15th to 17th century houses and farms in the area.

CHURCH OF ST JOHN THE BAPTIST. A 13th century church originally dedicated to St Lawrence, and extensively rebuilt in the Victorian period. The font is 13th century, and there is a notable 16th century alabaster monument to John Cowper, a Sergeant-at-Law in Elizabethan times.
LYNE HOUSE. Built as a farmhouse, it was purchased in 1799 by James Broadwood, the eldest son of John Broadwood(1732-1812) who founded the firm that made the famous Broadwood pianos.

Antique Dealer
  EL Pritchard, *Elusive Cottage, Station Approach, Capel, RH5 5HT* ☎ *01306 711684.*
Pub
  Crown Inn, *The Street, Capel, RH5 5JY* ☎ *01306 711130.*

See also Beare Green, Coldharbour, Holmwood, Newdigate, Oakwood Hill, Ockley. 2 miles from the Sussex boundary.

Caterham

Once a downland village, remnants of which can be seen in the main street of Caterham-on-the-Hill, the villagers lived off farming and quarrying. The modern town developed after the arrival of the railway in 1856, and the barracks which were built in the 1870s. It has many open spaces on its outskirts and Gravelly Hill (778ft), on the downs just south of the town, offers good views across the Weald.

CHURCH OF ST PETER AND ST PAUL, CHALDON. Dating from Norman times, this small, isolated church has a south tower with shingled spire. It is famous for its wall-painting, possibly of the early 13th century, showing the Ladder of Salvation and the Last Judgement. The pulpit is a rare example of the Cromwellian period. The second of two ancient bells, 'St Peter' and 'St Paul', dating from the 12th or 13th century and reputed to be the oldest bells in Surrey, was stolen from above the porch in 1970.
EAST SURREY MUSEUM. Local history with various displays and changing exhibitions.
ST JOHN'S CHURCH, CATERHAM VALLEY. A Victorian church with beautiful stained glass, now using the 13th century font and the 17th century altar table from St Lawrence's.
ST LAWRENCE'S CHURCH. The old parish church, built in 1085 and with 13th century additions, now stands empty. The shingled turret contains two bells that are 300 years old.
ST MARY'S CHURCH. Built in 1866 just across the road from St Lawrence's, which it replaces, the church has a tall tower and a 126ft spire which was added in 1883. Inside is a beautifully carved and painted reredos, and a list of vicars going back to 1310.

Antique Dealer
  Caterham Clearance Centre, *46 Chaldon Road, Caterham, CR3 5PE* ☎ *01883 347267.*
Art & Craft Equipment
  Craft Stationers, *3 Godstone Road, Caterham, CR3 6RE* ☎ *01883 342230.*
Book Shops
  Freedmans Bookshop, *10 High Street, Caterham, CR3 5AU* ☎ *01883 348881.*
  WH Smith, *16 Church Walk, Caterham, CR3 6RT* ☎ *01883 341559.*
  We Sell Books, *32 Church Walk Shopping Centre, Caterham, CR3 6RT* ☎ *01883 347196.*
Libraries
  SCC Lending Library (Caterham Hill), *Westway, Caterham, CR3 5TP* ☎ *01883 342008.*
  SCC Lending Library (Caterham Valley), *Stafford Road, Caterham, CR3 6JG*
  ☎ *01883 343580.*

Model Shop

MJ Models, *5c High Street, Caterham, CR3 5UE ☎ 01883 345080.*

Museum

East Surrey Museum, *1 Stafford Road, Caterham, CR3 6JG ☎ 01883 340275.*

Pottery

Shop on the Hill, *80 High Street, Caterham, CR3 5UD ☎ 01883 349788.*

OUR POTTERY IS HAND MADE ON THE PREMISES. WE ALSO SELL OTHER CRAFTS, JEWELLERY, PRINTS, PICTURES, ANTIQUES AND BRIC-A-BRAC.

Pubs

Blacksmiths Arms, *39 High Street, Caterham, CR3 5UE ☎ 01883 343603.*

Caterham Arms, *Coulsdon Road, Caterham, CR3 5NF ☎ Ex Dir.*

Clifton Arms, *110 Chaldon Road, Caterham, CR3 5PH ☎ 01883 343525.*

Commonwealth Tavern, *76 Croydon Road, Caterham, CR3 6QD ☎ 01883 343131.*

◆Golden Lion, *2 Town End, Caterham, CR3 5UG ☎ 01883 343934.*

Harrow, *235 Stanstead Road, Caterham, CR3 6AJ ☎ 01883 343260.*

King & Queen, *34 High Street, Caterham, CR3 5UA ☎ Ex Dir.*

Old Surrey Hounds, *1 The Square, Caterham, CR3 6QA ☎ 01883 343267.*

Royal Oak, *68 High Street, Caterham, CR3 5UB ☎ 01883 343510.*

Tally Ho Inn, *Coulsdon Road, Caterham, CR3 5ND ☎ 01883 343164.*

Putting Green

Queens Park, *Queens Park Road, Caterham.*

Restaurants

Caterham Chinese, *375 Croydon Road, Caterham, CR3 6PN ☎ 01883 345559.*

Charco's, *53 Croydon Road, Caterham, CR3 6PD ☎ 01883 345491.*

Hungry Toad, *19a Godstone Road, Caterham, CR3 6RE ☎ 01883 347136.*

Jim's, *161 Coulsdon Road, Caterham, CR3 5NG ☎ 01883 341916.*

Pizza Hut, *6 The Square, Caterham, CR3 6QA ☎ 01883 347334.*

Raja Tandoori, *4 High Street, Caterham, CR3 5UA ☎ 01883 348099.*

Rajduth Tandoori, *14 Godstone Road, Caterham, CR3 6RA ☎ 01883 348539.*

Thai House, *52 Croydon Road, Caterham, CR3 6QB ☎ 01883 345903.*

Swimming Pool

De Stafford School, *Burntwood Lane, Caterham, CR3 5YX (Enquiries ☎ 01883 722000 x454).*

Take-Aways

Capones Pizza Parlour, *177 Coulsdon Road, Caterham, CR3 5NU ☎ 01883 342466.*

Charcoal Grill, *75 High Street, Caterham, CR3 5UF ☎ 01883 343810.*

Earlswood Fish Bar, *180 Coulsdon Road, Caterham, CR3 5ND ☎ 01883 343123.*

Great Wall, *183 Coulsdon Road, Caterham, CR3 5NU ☎ 01883 343705.*

Hartleys Sandwich Bar, *17 Godstone Road, Caterham, CR3 6RE ☎ 01883 346988.*

Royal Tandoori, *169 Coulsdon Road, Caterham, CR3 5NU ☎ 01883 341156.*

Starburger, *36 Croydon Road, Caterham, CR3 6QB ☎ 01883 348305.*

Sun Hong, *36 High Street, Caterham, CR3 5UB ☎ 01883 349956.*

Taylor Fish Bar, *181 Coulsdon Road, Caterham, CR3 5NU ☎ 01883 346208.*

Wimpy, *50 Church Walk, Caterham, CR3 6RT ☎ 01883 346996.*

Tea Room & Cafe

Chequered Flag, *85 Coulsdon Road, Caterham, CR3 5NF ☎ 01883 343598.*

Gallery Tea Shop, *22 Godstone Road, Caterham, CR3 6RA ☎ 01883 342677.*

Theatre

Miller Centre, *30 Godstone Road, Caterham, CR3 6RA ☎ 01883 349850.*

See also Bletchingley, Godstone, Merstham, Nutfield, Oxted, Tandridge, Warlingham, Whyteleafe, Woldingham. 2 miles from the Greater London boundary.

NOTES

Charlwood

The village grew and prospered in medieval and Tudor times due to the local iron industry, but with the decline of this industry in the 18th century the locals turned to farming. In the 1890s, a race course was built at Gatwick Manor and shortly before the second war a small aerodrome developed next to it. During the War, the aerodrome expanded onto the racecourse and since then has developed into an international airport. The Manor House has gone and that part of the parish has since been transferred to Sussex.

GATWICK ZOO, AVIARY & TROPICAL GARDEN. 10 acres of landscaped grounds housing hundreds of rare and beautiful creatures including otters, penguins, wallabies, flamingoes, and monkeys, all displayed in large enclosures. There are many walk-through enclosures including two tropical houses containing plants, birds and butterflies from around the world.

LOWFIELD HEATH WINDMILL. An 18th century post mill which once stood at Lowfield Heath near the airport and which, in order to save it, was re-erected near Gatwick Zoo.

ST NICHOLAS'S CHURCH. One of the most interesting churches in the area, it was built around a Norman tower, and enlarged in the 13th and 15th centuries. The murals on the south wall, which tell the story of St Margaret, date from around 1300, and the screen is said to be the finest medieval screen in Surrey.

Art & Craft Equipment
   Chris Craft, *Edolphs Farm, Norwood Hill Road, Charlwood, RH6 0EB* ☎ *01293 863241.*
Hotels
   Russ Hill Hotel, *Russ Hill, Charlwood, RH6 0EL* ☎ *01293 862171.*
   ★Stanhill Court Hotel, *Stanhill Road, Charlwood, RH6 0EP* ☎ *01293 862166.*
Nursery
   Biltan Farm, *Stan Hill, Charlwood, RH6 0EP* ☎ *01293 862775.*
Pubs
   Greyhound, *12 The Street, Charlwood, RH6 0BY* ☎ *01293 862203.*
   Half Moon, *73 The Street, Charlwood, RH6 0DS* ☎ *01293 862902.*
   Rising Sun, *64 The Street, Charlwood, RH6 0DS* ☎ *01293 862338.*
Restaurant
   Limes Bistro, *The Street, Charlwood, RH6 0BY* ☎ *01293 862680.*
Tea Room & Cafe
   Gatwick Zoo & Aviaries, *Russ Hill, Charlwood, RH6 0EL* ☎ *01293 862312.*
Wildlife Park
   Gatwick Zoo & Aviaries, *Russ Hill, Charlwood, RH6 0EL* ☎ *01293 862312.*
Windmill
   Lowfield Heath Windmill, *Russ Hill, Charlwood (Enquiries* ☎ *01293 862646).*

See also Hookwood, Horley, Newdigate, Norwood Hill. On the Sussex boundary.

Chertsey

Chertsey has a substantial history due mainly to the existence of the Abbey. An old market town on the Thames, its three main streets still retain much of their 18th century architecture. The town centre lies close to the site of the old Abbey.

ABBEYFIELDS. An area which includes the ancient fishponds, the abbey wall, an arboretum, a sensory garden and a river walk.

CHERTSEY ABBEY. This huge Benedictine abbey was the first religious settlement in Surrey. It was founded in AD666, destroyed by the Danes in the 9th century, and re-founded in the 11th century, but finally the dissolution of 1537 led to its destruction. The stones were used by Henry VIII to build nearby Oatlands Palace (Weybridge) and Hampton Court (Molesey). The ancient fishponds, the irrigation system and some sections of the Abbey walls still remain.

CHERTSEY BRIDGE. Built by James Paine in the 1780s and recently restored.

CHERTSEY MEADS. 170 acres of riverside land, now a local nature reserve and area of ecological interest, with a riverside walk.

CHERTSEY MUSEUM. The museum houses excellent displays of local history and archaeology and contains the Olive Matthews collection of 18th and 19th century costume and the Micklethwaite collection of Meissen porcelain. On display are a Celtic sword and a Viking sword discovered in the silt of the Thames, and superb Chertsey tiles made between 1250 and 1310. There is also a programme of temporary exhibitions.

CURFEW HOUSE. Built in 1725 and once a school, it is one of the finest Georgian Houses in Windsor Street.

GOGMORE FARM PARK. A large riverside park along the banks of the River Bourne, with outdoor sports facilities.

ST ANN'S HILL. A delightfully wooded viewpoint and beauty spot, rising to 250 ft, where the Armada beacon is located.

ST PETER'S CHURCH. A curfew bell in the church commemorates Blanche Heriot who, at the time of the War of the Roses, knowing that her lover was to be executed at curfew, climbed the church tower, hanging on to the clapper of the bell until he was reprieved. Her courage was celebrated in the ballad 'Curfew Must Not Ring Tonight' by the American poet Rose Hartwick Thorpe.

SURREY BIRD RESCUE & CONSERVATION CENTRE. A restored barn dating from the mid 16th century houses a rescue centre for donkeys, goats, sheep, pigs, swans and flamingoes.

Antique Dealers
Bygones, *6 Windsor Street, Chertsey, KT16 8AS* ☎ *01932 568260.*
Chertsey Antiques, *8 Windsor Street, Chertsey, KT16 8AS* ☎ *01932 563565.*
Boat Hire
Chertsey Meads Marine, *The Meads, Mead Lane, Chertsey, KT16 8LN* ☎ *01932 564699.*
Harris Boatbuilders, *The Boatyard, Laleham Reach, Chertsey, KT16 8RP* ☎ *01932 563111.*
Golf Course
Laleham Golf Club, *Laleham Reach, Chertsey, KT16 8RP* ☎ *01932 564211.*
Guest House
Riverdene, *22 Bridge Road, Chertsey, KT16 8JN* ☎ *01932 565593.*
Historic Building
Chertsey Abbey, *Abbeyfields Park, Staines Lane, Chertsey.*
Hotels & Inns
Bridge Hotel(Galleon), *Bridge Road, Chertsey, KT16 8JZ* ☎ *01932 563175.*
Coach & Horses, *14a St Anns Road, Chertsey, KT16 9DG* ☎ *01932 563085.*
★◆Crown Hotel, *7 London Street, Chertsey, KT16 8AP* ☎ *01932 564657.*
Town Hall Tavern, *20 London Street, Chertsey, KT16 8AA* ☎ *01932 563045.*
Library
SCC Lending Library, *Guildford Street, Chertsey, KT16 9BE* ☎ *01932 564101.*
Museum
Chertsey Museum, *The Cedars, 33 Windsor Street, Chertsey, KT16 8AT* ☎ *01932 565764.*
OPEN: TUES-FRI 12.30-4.30, SAT 11.00-4.00. SHOP AND GARDEN. ADMISSION FREE.
Pubs
Castle, *1 Fordwater Road, Chertsey, KT16 8HW* ☎ *01932 563069.*
George, *45 Guildford Street, Chertsey, KT16 9BA* ☎ *01932 562128.*
★Golden Grove, *St Ann's Hill Road, Chertsey KT16 9EN* ☎ *01932 562132.*
Kings Arms, *2 Guildford Road, Chertsey, KT16 9BJ* ☎ *01932 569959.*
Kings Head, *103 Guildford Street, Chertsey, KT16 9AS* ☎ *01932 561541.*
Prince Regent, *126 Guildford Street, Chertsey, KT16 9AH* ☎ *01932 562015.*
Swan, *Windsor Street, Chertsey, KT16 8AY* ☎ *01932 562129.*
Victory, *49 Station Road, Chertsey, KT16 8BN* ☎ *01932 564020.*
Vine, *5 Bridge Road, Chertsey, KT16 8JH* ☎ *01932 563010.*
Putting Green
Chertsey Recreation Ground, *Guildford Road, Chertsey.*

Restaurants
Ali's Tandoori, *9 Guildford Street, Chertsey, KT16 9BG* ☎ *01932 567876.*
Dilshad Tandoori, *38 Guildford Street, Chertsey, KT16 9BE* ☎ *01932 560906.*
Tintoretto, *65 Guildford Street, Chertsey, KT16 9AU* ☎ *01932 561726.*
Twynersh House(Beefeater), *St Ann's Road, Chertsey, KT16 9EG* ☎ *01932 568231.*
Take-Aways
Clauds Burger & Fish Bar, *5 Guildford Street, Chertsey, KT16 9BG* ☎ *01932 562021.*
Relish The Thought One, *119 Guildford Street, Chertsey, KT16 9AS* ☎ *01932 566669.*
Simpsons Fried Chicken, *3 Windsor Street, Chertsey, KT16 8AY* ☎ *01932 562546.*
Sincere House, *127 Guildford Street, Chertsey, KT16 9AL* ☎ *01932 562533.*
Trawlers, *110 Guildford Street, Chertsey, KT16 9AH* ☎ *01932 561081.*
Tea Rooms & Cafes
Bridge Cafe, *108 Bridge Street, Chertsey, KT16 8LA* ☎ *01932 562928.*
Relish The Thought Two, *Gogmore Farm Park, Curfew Bell Road, Chertsey, KT16 9HE*
☎ *01932 570605.*
Water Sports
Chertsey Windsurfing, *Old Littleton Lane, off Bridge Road, Chertsey* ☎ *01932 560125.*
Wine Bar & Cafe Bar
Windsors, *23 Windsor Street, Chertsey, KT16 8AY* ☎ *01932 560745.*

See also Addlestone, Ashford, Laleham, Lyne, New Haw, Ottershaw, Shepperton, Thorpe,
Virginia Water, Walton on Thames, Weybridge, Wisley, Woodham.

Chessington

Chessington comprises large areas of inter war and post war housing and light
industry. The original Burnt Stub Zoo has been transformed into Chessington World
of Adventures.

CHESSINGTON WORLD OF ADVENTURES. A theme park divided into separate areas each with their own
rides - the Forbidden Kingdom, Calamity Canyon, Toytown, Transylvania, Smugglers Cove and
the Mystic East. The zoo is divided into three separate animal lands and there is also a Circus
World. At the centre is Market Square which incorporates Burnt Stub mansion.

Garden Centre & Nursery
Chessington Nurseries, *Leatherhead Road, Chessington, KT9 2NG* ☎ *01372 725638.*
Golf Course & Driving Range
Chessington Golf Centre, *Garrison Lane, Chessington, KT9 2LW* ☎ *0181-391 0948.*
Library
SCC Lending Library, *Hook Road, Chessington, KT9 1EJ* ☎ *0181-397 4931.*
Pubs
Blackamoors Head, *116 Moor Lane, Chessington, KT9 1HX* ☎ *0181-397 5646.*
Bonesgate, *273 Moor Lane, Chessington, KT9 2BQ* ☎ *0181-391 4316.*
Fox & Hounds, *423 Leatherhead Road, Chessington, KT9 2NQ* ☎ *01372 722232.*
Lucky Rover, *312 Hook Road, Chessington, KT9 1NY* ☎ *0181-397 3227.*
North Star, *271 Hook Road, Chessington, KT9 1EQ* ☎ *0181-397 4227.*
Port of Call, *Cox Lane, Chessington, KT9 1SG* ☎ *0181-397 3529.*
White Hart, *378 Hook Road, Chessington, KT9 1NA* ☎ *0181-397 3257.*
Restaurants
Harrow(Harvester), *Leatherhead Road, Chessington, KT9 2HS* ☎ *0181-397 5582.*
Harrison's Bistro, *4 Ace Parade, Hook Rise South, Chessington, KT9 1DR* ☎ *0181-397 0708.*
Monkey Puzzle(Beefeater), *Leatherhead Road, Chessington, KT9 2NE* ☎ *01372 744060.*
Pizza Hut, *377 Hook Road, Chessington, KT9 1EL* ☎ *0181-974 1522.*
Red Rose, *334 Hook Road, Chessington, KT9 1NU* ☎ *0181-391 5530.*
Regent, *7 Ace Parade, Hook Road, Chessington, KT9 1DR* ☎ *0181-397 3957.*

Take-Aways

Barry's Fish & Chips, *Chessington North Station, Bridge Road, Chessington, KT9 2RT* ☎ *0181-391 9077.*

Mr Chips, *344 Hook Road, Chessington, KT9 1NU* ☎ *0181-397 1976.*

Lunchbox, *Chessington South Station, Garrison Lane, Chessington, KT9 2JR* ☎ *0181-974 2264.*

Theme Park

Chessington World of Adventures, *Leatherhead Road, Chessington, KT9 2NE* ☎ *01372 727227.*

See also Claygate, Epsom, Esher, Ewell, Hinchley Wood, Oxshott, Thames Ditton, Worcester Park. Situated within Greater London, but surrounded by Surrey.

Chiddingfold

This is the first place in Britain where glass making was carried out by Flemish craftsmen. There were 11 glass works on the village green during the reign of Elizabeth I, but manufacture ceased in the early 17th century by royal command. Glass from here was used in the windows of St George's Chapel at Windsor and St Stephen's Chapel at Westminster. Chiddingfold has the largest concentration of listed buildings anywhere in the country. It is a typical early English village with a traditional village green complete with pond and surrounded by 14th and 15th century houses, and a forge which is still working. The forge stands on the site of the original Market House and has the village lock-up attached. In the footpath to the north of the forge is embedded the original iron template for fashioning waggon wheels, last used in the late 1920s. Since the mid 1800s the village has been famous for its Guy Fawkes bonfire and fireworks, celebrations which in 1929 gave rise to the Riot Act being read at the Swan and the Winterton Arms, for the last time anywhere in England.

CROWN INN. Dating from 1285 when the building was a rest home for Cistercian monks on pilgrimage, it is one of the oldest and most picturesque inns in the County. Edward VI is said to have stayed here 400 years ago. It has some fine timbering and a great hall.

RAMSTER GARDENS. A 20 acre woodland garden of exceptional interest with fine rhododendrons, azaleas, camellias, magnolias, trees and shrubs laid out in the early years of this century by Gauntlett Nurseries of Chiddingfold. The house is based on a Jacobean farmhouse and is not open to the public.

ST MARY'S CHURCH. The church may well date from before the 12th century. The chancel has an interesting priest's door and five 13th century lancet windows in the south wall. To the right of the font is a small lancet window containing 427 pieces of Chiddingfold glass. The minute bell dates from 1489.

Antique Dealer
  Crown Antiques, *The Green, Chiddingfold, GU8 4TU* ☎ *01428 685995.*
Gardens
  Ramster Gardens, Petworth Road, Chiddingfold, GU8 4SN ☎ 01428 644422
Golf Course & Driving Range
  Shillinglee Park Golf Course, *Chiddingfold, GU8 4TA* ☎ *01428 653237.*
Inn
  ★◆Crown Inn, *The Green, Petworth Road, Chiddingfold, GU8 4TX* ☎ *01428 682255.*
Pubs
  Rams Nest Inn, *Petworth Road, Chiddingfold, GU8 4SS* ☎ *01428 644460.*
  ★◆Swan Hotel, *Petworth Road, Chiddingfold, GU8 4TY* ☎ *01428 682073.*
  ◆Winterton Arms, *Petworth Road, Chiddingfold, GU8 4UU* ☎ *01428 683221.*

See also Brook, Dunsfold, Grayswood, Hambledon, Hydestile, Witley, Wormley. 2 miles from the Sussex boundary.

Chilworth

Gunpowder was made here as early as 1580 and although there were some serious explosions, manufacture continued until 1920. The protective mounds of earth built around some of the buildings came to be known as 'Chilworth Mounds'.

CHILWORTH MANOR. A 17th century house with an 18th century wing on the site of an 11th century monastery recorded in the Domesday Book. Stewponds in the garden date from the monastic period. The garden was laid out in the 17th century and the walled garden was added by Sarah, Duchess of Marlborough in the 18th century. The gardens are open to visitors only as part of the National Gardens Scheme.
GUNPOWDER MILLS. Now owned and maintained by Guildford Borough Council, the old grinding stones and mill race can still be seen.
ST MARTHA'S. A Norman church on the summit of a wooded greensand hill (573ft). It was damaged in the 18th century by an explosion at the nearby gunpowder mill, and rebuilt in the 19th century using carstone, course sand and iron which occurs on the hill. Yvonne Arnaud, the actress, is buried here.

Pub
  Percy Arms, *Dorking Road, Chilworth, GU4 8NP* ☎ *01483 61765.*

See also Albury, Blackheath, Bramley, Burpham, Clandon, Guildford, Loseley, Merrow, Newlands Corner, Shalford, Shamley Green, Shere, Wonersh.

Chipstead

ST MARGARET'S CHURCH. A large 13th century cruciform church with a central tower added in 1631, and an aisle added in 1883 by R Norman Shaw(1831-1912). The screen is 15th century, the pulpit 17th century, and there are fragments of medieval glass still to be seen. Sir Edward Banks, the builder of the old London Bridge is commemorated here.

Pubs
  Midday Sun, *Outwood Lane, Chipstead, CR5 3NA* ☎ *01737 552644.*
  ★Well House Inn, *Chipstead Lane, Chipstead, CR5 3SQ* ☎ *01737 832233.*
  White Hart, *Hazelwood Lane, Chipstead, CR5 3QW* ☎ *01737 552708.*

Restaurants
Kashmir Valley, *32 Station Approach, Chipstead, CR5 3TD* ☎ *01737 556401.*
Ramblers Rest, *Outwood Lane, Chipstead, CR5 3NP* ☎ *01737 552661.*
Take-Away
Simply Delicious, *18 Station Approach, Chipstead, CR5 3TD* ☎ *01737 553381.*

See also Banstead, Burgh Heath, Hooley, Kingswood, Merstham, Whyteleafe. On the Greater London boundary.

Chobham

CHOBHAM COMMON. This is the largest area of heathland in South East England, being some 2,000 acres in size. Queen Victoria reviewed her troops here before they left for the Crimea, and a commemorative stone stands near Chobham Clump. Parts of the common are still used for military training.
JUBILEE MOUNT. Once used as allotments for ex-servicemen after the Crimean War, it is now planted with ornamental shrubs and conifers.
ST LAWRENCE'S CHURCH. A heavily restored 11th century church with a wooden porch reputed to be from Chertsey Abbey.

Antique Dealers
Chobham Antiques, *65 High Street, Chobham, GU24 8AF* ☎ *01276 855443.*
Tarrystone Antique Centre, *40 High Street, Chobham, GU24 8AA* ☎ *01276 855950.*
What-Not Antiques, *Park Gallery, Station Road, Chobham* ☎ *01276 856766.*
Farm Shop
White Lodge Farm, *Station Road, Chobham, GU24 8AR* ☎ *01276 858628.*
MEMBER OF 'A TASTE OF SURREY' - SUPPLIERS OF HOME CURED PORK PRODUCTS.
Garden Centres & Nurseries
Chobham Nurseries, *Bagshot Road, Chobham, GU24 8DE* ☎ *01276 858252.*
Mimbridge Garden Centre, *Station Road, Chobham, GU24 8AS* ☎ *01276 858237.*
Plant Centre, *Bagshot Road, Chobham, GU24 8SJ* ☎ *01276 855408.*
Riverside Nurseries, *Philpot Lane, Chobham, GU24 8HE* ☎ *01276 857687.*
T Hilling & Co, *The Nurseries, Bagshot Road, Chobham* ☎ *01276 855387.*
Tenaker Nurseries, *Scotts Grove Road, Chobham, GU24 8DT* ☎ *01276 858523.*
Pubs
Castle Grove, *Scotts Grove Road, Chobham, GU24 8DY* ☎ *01276 858196.*
Cricketers, *160 Windsor Road, Chobham, GU24 8QX* ☎ *01276 858304.*
Four Horseshoes, *13 Windsor Road, Chobham, GU24 8NA* ☎ *01276 857581.*
Red Lion, *15 Red Lion Road, Chobham, GU24 8RG* ☎ *01276 858813.*
Sun Inn, *High Street, Chobham, GU24 8AF* ☎ *01276 857112.*
Restaurants
Cloche Hat, *Burrowhill, Chobham, GU24 8QS* ☎ *01276 858000.*
Four Seasons, *14 High Street, Chobham, GU24 8AA* ☎ *01276 857238.*
Frascati, *2 Station Road, Chobham, GU24 8AQ* ☎ *01276 858114.*
★Quails, *1 Bagshot Road, Chobham, GU24 8BP* ☎ *01276 858491.*
White Hart(Blubeckers), *High Street, Chobham, GU24 8AA* ☎ *01276 857580.*
Tea Room
Saddlers Halt Tea Rooms, *86 High Street, Chobham, GU24 8LZ* ☎ *01276 855808.*

See also Addlestone, Bisley, Horsell, Knaphill, Lightwater, Sheerwater, West End, Windlesham, Woking. 3 miles from the Berkshire boundary.

Churt

Only ever a small village, some of the buildings in Churt date from medieval times. David Lloyd George(1863-1945) came to live here in 1921. He occupied two homes, Bron-y-De and Avalon, and although the former house which he built has been demolished, the apple orchards he planted still exist.

THE DEVIL'S JUMPS. One of Surrey's most spectacular viewpoints, these three curious conical hills are associated with pagan legend. The devil used to hop from one summit to another roaring with glee until the god Thor grew tired of the noise and threw a slab of stone which came to rest on Stony Jump. Stony Jump is the largest of these hills and now belongs to the National Trust. Borrow Jump was the site of an observatory.

Garden Centres & Nurseries
Avalon Farm, *Tilford Road, Churt, GU10 2LL* ☎ *01428 604842.*
Landscape Centre, *Barford Court Farm, Lampard Lane, Churt, GU10 2HU* ☎ *01428 712610.*
Millais Nurseries, *Crosswater Lane, Churt, GU10 2JN* ☎ *01252 792698.*
Hotel
Pride of the Valley Hotel, *Jumps Road, Churt, GU10 2LE* ☎ *01428 605799.*
Pick Your Own
Avalon Farms, *Packhouse Farm, Tilford Road, Churt, GU10 2LL* ☎ *01428 605161.*
Pub
Crossways Inn, *Churt Road, Churt, GU10 2JE* ☎ *01428 714323.*
Restaurants
Miravalle, *Pride of the Valley Hotel* ☎ *01428 605799.*
Pipasha Tandoori, *The Crossways, Churt, GU10 2JE* ☎ *01428 712080.*

See also Frensham, Hindhead, Rowledge, Thursley. On the Hampshire boundary.

Clandon
(East & West)

Both villages were feudal manors until the 16th century when they became part of the large landed estates of Clandon Park and Hatchlands Park.

CHURCH OF ST THOMAS OF CANTERBURY, EAST CLANDON. A 12th century Grade 1 listed building, restored in 1900. It was a Benedictine monastery under the patronage of Chertsey Abbey until the reformation, and was a stopping place for pilgrims travelling to Canterbury.
CLANDON PARK (National Trust). Built by the Venetian architect, Giacomo Leoni in the early 1730s, for the 2nd Lord Onslow. It has a magnificent two-storeyed marble hall, and houses the Onslow family pictures and the Gubbay collection of furniture, pictures, porcelain and needlework. The old kitchens are open to visitors. There is a parterre garden, grotto and Maori House.
HATCHLANDS PARK (National Trust). This handsome red-brick Georgian house was built in 1758 by Stiff Leadbetter for Admiral Edward Boscawen(1711-1761), hero of the Battle of Louisberg. The splendid interior is by Robert Adam(1728-1792) with additional work by tenant and artist Alec Cobbe. In 1988 the house was extensively redecorated and the Cobbe collection of fine keyboard instruments, paintings and furniture was installed. The garden, by Humphrey Repton(1752-1818) and Gertrude Jekyll(1843-1942), has been restored and new walks opened in the park.
QUEEN'S ROYAL SURREY REGIMENTAL MUSEUM. The museum contains the relics and artifacts of the two Surrey infantry regiments. Admission is through the National Trust house at Clandon Park.

Aquatic Centre
Surrey Water Gardens, *Clandon Park Garden Centre* ☎ *01483 224822.*

Garden Centres & Nurseries
Clandon Park Garden Centre, *Clandon Park, West Clandon, GU4 7RQ* ☎ *01483 222925.*
RN Whapshott, *West Clandon Nursery, Lime Grove, West Clandon, GU4 7UH*
☎ *01483 222443.*
Historic Buildings
Clandon Park, *West Clandon, GU4 7RQ* ☎ *01483 222482.*
Hatchlands Park, *East Clandon, GU4 7RT* ☎ *01483 222482.*
Museum
Queens Royal Surrey Regiment Museum, *Clandon Park* ☎ *01483 223419.*
Pubs
★Bulls Head, *The Street, West Clandon, GU4 7ST* ☎ *01483 222444.*
★◆Onslow Arms, *The Street, West Clandon, GU4 7TE* ☎ *01483 222447.*
★Queens Head, *The Street, East Clandon, GU4 7RY* ☎ *01483 222332.*
Restaurants
Clandon Park ☎ *01483 222502.*
Hatchlands ☎ *01483 211120.*

See also Albury, Blackheath, Burpham, Chilworth, Gomshall, Horsley, Merrow, Newlands Corner, Ockham, Ripley, Send, Shere, Sutton Green.

Claygate

A tiny hamlet in the 1830s, the village built its own church in 1840 and quickly grew after the arrival of the railway in 1885 into what is now a large suburban area. Claygate is renowned for its fireplaces built of miniature bricks, but the brick works are now long gone.

RUXLEY TOWERS. Originally built as a country house in the 1830s, it became the headquarters of the NAAFI when they were evacuated from London during the Second World War.
TELEGRAPH HILL. The name of the hill is derived from the semaphore tower built in 1822 as part of a chain which enabled messages to be sent between London and Portsmouth. (See Ockham).

Art & Craft Equipment
Craft & Hobby Shop, *2 The Green, Claygate, KT10 0JL* ☎ *01372 468289.*
Garden Centre & Nursery
Kennedy's Garden Centre, *Oaken Lane, Claygate, KT10 0RH* ☎ *0181-398 0047.*
Pubs
Foley Arms, *Foley Road, Claygate, KT10 0XX* ☎ *01372 463431.*
Griffin, *58 Common Road, Claygate, KT10 0HW* ☎ *01372 463799.*
Hare & Hounds, *The Green, Claygate, KT10 0JL* ☎ *01372 465149.*
★◆Swan, *2 Hare Lane, Claygate, KT10 9BS* ☎ *01372 462582.*
Winning Horse, *35 Coverts Road, Claygate, KT10 0JY* ☎ *01372 462793.*
Restaurants
Claygate Tandoori, *10 The Parade, Claygate, KT10 0NU* ☎ *01372 462920.*
Greek Vine, *The Green, Claygate, KT10 0JQ* ☎ *01372 465125.*
Green Cottage, *29 The Parade, Claygate, KT10 0PD* ☎ *01372 464648.*
Le Petit Pierrot, *4 The Parade, Claygate, KT10 0NU* ☎ *01372 465105.*
★Les Alouettes, *7 High Street, Claygate, KT10 0JW* ☎ *01372 464882.*

See also Chessington, Esher, Hersham, Hinchley Wood, Oxshott, Stoke D'Abernon, Thames Ditton. 1 mile from the Greater London boundary.

NOTES

Cobham

The town is set beside an attractive stretch of the River Mole. A bridge over the river is known to have been in existence in 1351 and rebuilt in 1782 to the design of George Gwilt, the County Surveyor of the time. Matthew Arnold(1822-1888), the poet and critic lived in Cobham.

COBHAM BUS MUSEUM. A private collection of 40 vehicles dating from the 1930s to the present day, owned by the London Bus Preservation Trust and housed in a working garage environment.
COBHAM MILL. The present water mill was rebuilt in 1822. It is now fully restored and there are demonstrations of grinding.
PAINSHILL PARK. A great ornamental landscape garden created by The Hon Charles Hamilton, plantsman and painter, between 1738 and 1773. Here he transformed 200 acres of barren heathland into dramatic parkland with a 14 acre lake, Gothic temple, Chinese bridge, ruined abbey, grotto and spectacular working water wheel, all of which has been restored since 1981, after sinking into dereliction after the Second World War.
ST ANDREW'S CHURCH. The 12th century flint church was renovated in Victorian times. The oldest part is the Norman tower, and the chancel and north chapel date from around 1200. There are many interesting monuments including some 16th century brasses.

Antique Dealers
   Cobham Galleries, *65 Portsmouth Road, Cobham, KT11 1JQ* ☎ *01932 867909.*
   Past Caring, *10 High Street, Cobham, KT11 3DY* ☎ *01932 863191.*
Book Shop
   Bookmark, *12a Anyards Road, Cobham, KT11 2JZ* ☎ *01932 862903.*
Farm Shop
   Maxted & Steele, *Mays Green, Old Lane, Cobham, KT11 1MJ* ☎ *01932 868028.*
   MEMBER OF 'A TASTE OF SURREY' - FREE RANGE EGG PRODUCER.
Garden Centres & Nurseries
   Barbeque Shop, *46a Portsmouth Road, Cobham, KT11 1HY* ☎ *01932 866044.*
   Cedar Nursery, *Horsley Road, Cobham, KT11 3JX* ☎ *01932 862473.*
Golf Course & Driving Range
   Silvermere Golf & Leisure Complex, *Redhill Road, Cobham, KT11 1EF* ☎ *01932 867275.*
Golf Driving Range
   Fairmile Golf Range, *Portsmouth Road, Cobham, KT11 1BQ* ☎ *01932 864419.*
Hotels & Inns
   Cedar House Hotel, *Mill Road, Cobham, KT11 3AN* ☎ *01932 863424.*
   ★Hilton National, *Seven Hills Road South, Cobham, KT11 1EW* ☎ *01932 864471.*
Library
   SCC Lending Library, *Cedar Road, Cobham, KT11 2AE* ☎ *01932 863292.*
Museum
   Cobham Bus Museum, *Redhill Road, Cobham, KT11 1EF* ☎ *01932 864078.*
Park & Gardens
   Painshill Park, *Portsmouth Road, Cobham, KT11 1JE* ☎ *01932 868113.*
Pubs
   ◆Old Bear, *High Street, Cobham, KT11 3DX* ☎ *01932 862840.*
   Running Mare, *45 Tilt Road, Cobham, KT11 3EZ* ☎ *01932 862007.*
   ◆Snail, *17 Portsmouth Road, Cobham, KT11 1JF* ☎ *01932 862409.*
   ◆Vermont Exchange, *46 Portsmouth Road, Cobham, KT11 1HY* ☎ *01932 864213.*
Restaurants
   Alfredo's, *40 Portsmouth Road, Cobham, KT11 1HZ* ☎ *01932 863666.*
   Cobham Tandoori, *12c Anyards Road, Cobham, KT11 2JZ* ☎ *01932 863842.*
   Giardino, *221 Portsmouth Road, Cobham, KT11 1JR* ☎ *01932 863973.*
   Homestead, *19 Anyards Road, Cobham, KT11 2LW* ☎ *01932 865005.*
   La Capanna, *48 High Street, Cobham, KT11 3EF* ☎ *01932 862121.*
   Wings Garden, *41 Oakdene Parade, High Street, Cobham, KT11 2LR* ☎ *01932 864390.*

Special Pursuits

Flying Colours (Paintball), *The Courtyard, Pound Farm, Old Lane, Cobham, KT11 1NH* ☎ *01932 865788.*

Take-Aways

Big Fry, *15 Anyards Road, Cobham, KT11 2LW* ☎ *01932 865409.*

Po On, *38 High Street, Cobham, KT11 3EB* ☎ *01932 865746.*

Water Mill

Cobham Mill, *Mill Road, Cobham (Enquiries* ☎ *01932 864393).*

Wine Bar & Cafe Bar

Rocky's, *212 Portsmouth Road, Cobham, KT11 1HS* ☎ *01932 867243.*

See also Downside, Hersham, Ockham, Oxshott, Stoke D'Abernon, Walton on Thames, Weybridge, Whiteley Village, Wisley.

Coldharbour

The village is set 700ft up on the greensand ridge and from here paths lead across Coldharbour Common to Leith Hill.

ANSTIEBURY CAMP. An oval iron age fort dating from the 2nd century BC. Plans were made to shelter the women and children of Dorking here in the event of a Napoleonic invasion in the mid 1800s.

LEITH HILL. Much of the land around here including Leith Hill Woods is owned by the National Trust. At 965ft this is the highest point in South East England. The 64ft tower at the top of the hill can be reached by a steep climb from the road immediately below it, or a gentler approach from the Abinger road. From the top there is a spectacular panorama of woods and farmland. The beautiful Rhododendron Wood (much of which was swept away in the storm of 1987) is a little way to the south-west and is at its best in April and May.

LEITH HILL PLACE. Once the home of Richard Hull who built the Leith Hill Tower, and of Ralph Vaughan Williams(1872-1958), the composer who lived here for many years and created with E M Forster(1879-1970) and others the annual Leith Hill Festival, which is held in Dorking Halls in early April.

LEITH HILL TOWER (National Trust). Built in 1766 by Richard Hull on the highest point in south-east England allegedly to increase the height of the hill to allow it to be classified as a mountain. The top of the tower is 1,029ft above sea level and provides magnificent views to the North and South Downs. On a clear day it is possible to see 12 counties, and the sea is visible through the Shoreham Gap. Richard Hull lived at nearby Leith Hill Place and is buried beneath the tower.

Inn

★Plough Inn, *Coldharbour Lane, Coldharbour, RH5 6HD* ☎ *01306 711793.*

FOOD AVAILABLE. CHILDREN WELCOME. GARDEN. NO SMOKING AREA. GOOD BEER GUIDE 1995.

See also Beare Green, Capel, Holmwood, Newdigate, Ockley. 3 miles from the Sussex boundary.

Compton

The Victorian artist George Frederick Watts made his home here and his work can be seen in the Watts Gallery.

MARY WONDRAUSCH POTTERY CENTRE. A member of the Craftsman Potters Association, Mary Wondrausch works mainly in 17th century style earthenware. Most of this finely detailed slipware pottery in Fremington clay is individually commissioned and includes commemorative plates, owl jugs, salt kips, egg stands and pitchers.

St Nicholas's Church. The church has several fascinating and unique features, and is historically the most important in Surrey. The tower, crowned with a 14th century spire, is thought to be of a Saxon construction, while the nave and chancel are classic Norman. A unique feature is the two-storey sanctuary, dating from about 1180, which retains its original Norman woodwork. The church has whitewashed walls and arches carved from chalk. There is a scratched carving on a chancel pillar of a soldier straight from the Bayeux Tapestry. Aldous Huxley(1894-1963), the novelist and essayist, is buried in the cemetery.

Watts Gallery. A memorial to George Frederick Watts, OM RA (1817-1904), the famous and prolific Victorian painter and sculptor who produced over 2,000 paintings during his lifetime, was nicknamed `England's Michelangelo', and who lived nearby. The gallery was purpose built in 1903 to house over 250 of his works, including fascinating portraits of Lily Langtry, Edward VII and Florence Nightingale.

Watts Mortuary Chapel. This extraordinary art nouveau circular chapel was designed by Watts's second wife Mary, who was also an artist, for the new village cemetery, and was decorated with tiles made by the villagers. Both husband and wife are buried here.

Art Gallery
  Watts Gallery, *Down Lane, Compton, GU3 1DQ* ☎ *01483 810235.*
Craft Centre
  Mary Wondrausch, *The Pottery, Brickfields, Compton, GU3 1HZ* ☎ *01483 414097.*
Inn
★◆Harrow Inn, *The Street, Compton, GU3 1EG* ☎ *01483 810379.*
Nursery
  Compton Nurseries, *The Street, Compton, GU3 1DT* ☎ *01483 811387.*
Pub
★◆Withies Inn, *Withies Lane, Compton, GU3 1JA* ☎ *01483 421158.*
Tea Room
  Tea Shop, *The Old Pottery, Down Lane, Compton, GU3 1DQ* ☎ *01483 811030.*

See also Bramley, Eashing, Elstead, Farncombe, Godalming, Guildford, Hurtmore, Loseley, Milford, Normandy, Peper Harow, Puttenham, Seale, Shackleford, Shalford, The Sands, Wanborough, Wood Street.

Copthorne

Antique Dealer
  Copthorne Group Antiques, *Briars, Copthorne Bank, Copthorne, RH10 3QZ*
  ☎ *01342 712802.*
Garden Centre & Nursery
  Snowhill Garden Centre, *Snowhill Lane, Copthorne, RH10 3EY* ☎ *01342 712545.*
Golf Course
  Effingham Park Hotel Golf Centre, *West Park Road, Copthorne, RH10 3EU* ☎ *01342 716528.*
Guest House
  Oakleigh House, *West Park Road, Copthorne, RH10 3HG* ☎ *01342 712703.*
Hotels & Inns
★Effingham Park Hotel(Copthorne), *West Park Road, Copthorne, RH10 3EU*
  ☎ *01342 714994.*
◆Hunters Moon Inn, *Copthorne Bank, Copthorne, RH10 3JF* ☎ *01342 713309.*
Pubs
  Abergavenny Arms, *Common Road, Copthorne, RH10 3LB* ☎ *01342 714177.*
  Cherry Tree, *Copthorne Bank, Copthorne, RH10 3JG* ☎ *01342 712427.*
◆Hedgehog Inn, *Effingham Road, Copthorne, RH10 3HY* ☎ *01342 716202.*
  Prince Albert, *Copthorne Bank, Copthorne, RH10 3QU* ☎ *01342 712702.*

Restaurant
Wellingtonia, *Effingham Park Hotel* ☎ *01342 717559.*

See also Burstow, Felbridge, Hookwood, Horne, Shipley Bridge, Smallfield. On the Sussex boundary.

Cranleigh

Charcoal was made in this area from Roman days and the industry became important once again for the manufacture of gas masks during the Great War. In the 15th and 16th centuries Cranleigh shared in the neighbouring industries of iron and glass. It was also a centre for hawking and hunting in the middle ages, when it was called Craneley, deriving its name from the craneries of Vachery and Baynards, but this was eventually changed to Cranleigh in 1867 to avoid postal confusion with Crawley. The railway arrived in 1865 and was axed in 1965. Inspite of this, the village expanded rapidly after the closure of the railway, but is still claimed to be a village, the largest in England. Although the brick yards closed in 1962, tile making still continues.

COTTAGE HOSPITAL. Founded in a 14th century timbered cottage in 1859, it is claimed to be the first village hospital in England.
CRANLEIGH SCHOOL. Founded in 1865 for wealthy farmers' sons half a mile north of the village. The school opened with 22 boarders and 4 day boys and now has over 500 children. The main building is in red brick with a central courtyard. There is a neo Queen Anne block and many newer buildings have been added recently.
ST NICHOLAS'S CHURCH. A 13th century church much restored in 1846. It still possesses a 14th century screen to the south transept.
SMITHBROOK KILNS. Over 60 small businesses including craft workshops are now located here and the original brick kilns are being used as a wine cellar.
THE OBELISK. The obelisk commemorates the opening of a turnpike road from Guildford to Horsham in 1794, and gave the distances to Brighton and Windsor.

Antique Dealers
Keith's Treasure Chest, *Western House, High Street, Cranleigh, GU6 8RL* ☎ *01483 274799.*
What-Not Antiques, *56 Smithbrook Kilns, Horsham Road, Cranleigh, GU6 8JJ* ☎ *01483 271796.*
Art & Craft Equipment
Cranleigh Gallery, *High Street, Cranleigh, GU6 8RL* ☎ *01483 274691.*
Arts Centre
Cranleigh Arts Centre, *High Street, Cranleigh, GU6 8AS* ☎ *01483 278001.*
Book Shops
Books & Bits, *The Common, Cranleigh, GU6 8NS* ☎ *01483 275895.*
The Bookshop, *High Street, Cranleigh, GU6 8AZ* ☎ *01483 274265.*
Cinema
Regal Cinema, *High Street, Cranleigh, GU6 8RT* ☎ *01483 272373.*
Garden Centres & Nurseries
Cranleigh Nurseries, *Guildford Road, Cranleigh, GU6 8PG* ☎ *01483 271234.*
Homeleigh Nursery, *Coombe Lea, Guildford Road, Cranleigh, GU6 8PP* ☎ *01483 274182.*
Norther Lane Nursery, *Guildford Road, Cranleigh, GU6 8LT* ☎ *01483 271611.*
Notcutts Garden Centre, *Guildford Road, Cranleigh, GU6 8LT* ☎ *01483 274222.*
Golf Course
Fernfell Golf & Country Club, *Barhatch Lane, Cranleigh, GU6 7NG* ☎ *01483 268855.*
Hotels & Inns
Cranley Hotel, *The Common, Cranleigh, GU6 8SQ* ☎ *01483 272827.*
White Hart Hotel, *Ewhurst Road, Cranleigh, GU6 7AE* ☎ *01483 268647.*

Library
   SCC Lending Library, *High Street, Cranleigh, GU6 8AS* ☎ *01483 272413.*
Model Shop
   Roxley Models, *19 Smithbrook Kilns, Horsham Road(A281), Nr Cranleigh, GU6 8JJ*
   ☎ *01483 271931.*
      CORGI, EFE, LLEDO, ETC. HORNBY RAILWAYS, REVELL AIRCRAFT, TRANSPORT BOOKS AND VIDEOS, POST
      OFFICE AND BT POSTCARDS. OPEN MONDAY TO FRIDAY 10.00 TO 1.00: 2.00 TO 5.00.
Pubs
◆Boy & Donkey, *Knowle Lane, Cranleigh, GU6 8JW* ☎ *01483 274423.*
◆Four Elms, *Smithwood Common Road, Cranleigh, GU6 8QP* ☎ *01483 272539.*
   Leathern Bottle, *Horsham-Guildford Road, Cranleigh, GU6 8LH* ☎ *01483 274117.*
   Little Park Hatch, *Bookhurst Road, Cranleigh, GU6 7DN* ☎ *01483 274374.*
   Onslow Arms, *High Street, Cranleigh, GU6 8AU* ☎ *01483 273929.*
   Three Horseshoes, *4 High Street, Cranleigh, GU6 8AE* ☎ *01483 276978.*
Restaurants
   Curry Inn Tandoori, *High Street, Cranleigh, GU6 8RL* ☎ *01483 273992.*
   Golden Palace, *Stockland Square, High Street, Cranleigh, GU6 8RG* ☎ *01483 275276.*
   La Scala, *High Street, Cranleigh, GU6 8RF* ☎ *01483 274900.*
   La Barbe Encore, *Freeland House, High Street, Cranleigh, GU6 8AE* ☎ *01483 273889.*
   New Lotus House, *4 Bank Buildings, High Street, Cranleigh, GU6 8BB* ☎ *01483 275233.*
   Zio'Toto, *60 High Street, Cranleigh, GU6 8RN* ☎ *01483 271272.*
Sports & Leisure Centres
   Cranleigh Recreation Centre, *Village Way, Cranleigh, GU6 8AE* ☎ *01483 274400.*
   Glebelands Centre, *Parsonage Road, Cranleigh, GU6 7AN* ☎ *01483 271117.*
Swimming Pool
   Cranleigh Recreation Centre ☎ *01483 274400.*
Take-Away
   Mini Fishbar, *Ewhurst Road, Cranleigh, GU6 7AE* ☎ *01483 274534.*
Tea Rooms & Cafes
   Bricks, *Smithbrook Kilns, Smithbrook, Cranleigh, GU6 8JJ* ☎ *01483 276780.*
   Cromwell Coffee Rooms, *High Street, Cranleigh, GU6 8AU* ☎ *01483 273783.*
   Notcutts Garden Centre ☎ *01483 274222.*
   Tiffins, *6 Bank Buildings, High Street, Cranleigh, GU6 8BB* ☎ *01483 272320.*
Wine Bar & Cafe Bar
   Natasha's, *Ewhurst Road, Cranleigh, GU6 7EF* ☎ *01483 275797.*

See also Ellen's Green, Ewhurst, Forest Green. 3 miles from the Sussex boundary.

Crowhurst

CROWHURST PLACE. Built for the Gaynesford family, this moated Tudor manor house is one of the best examples of domestic architecture in Surrey.
MANSION HOUSE FARM. A late medieval half-timbered house with a brick and tile front elevation.
ST GEORGE'S CHURCH. Partly Norman, partly 13th century and restored several times since the 17th century. Set in the floor close to the altar is the only Sussex iron tombstone in Surrey. In the churchyard are several ancient yew trees, including one reputed to be over a thousand years old.

Pub
★◆Brickmakers Arms, *Tandridge Lane, Crowhurst Lane End, RH8 9NS* ☎ *01342 893042.*

See also Blindley Heath, Godstone, Haxted, Limpsfield, Lingfield, Newchapel, Oxted, Tandridge. 2 miles from the Kent boundary.

Deepcut

The village is surrounded by open heathland and woods which are owned mostly by the Ministry of Defence. The Royal Logistic Corps have a training centre here at Blackdown Barracks.

ROYAL LOGISTIC CORPS MUSEUM - The museum displays the collections of the Royal Corps of Transport, the Royal Army Ordnance Corps, the Royal Pioneer Corps, the Army Catering Corps and the Postal & Courier Service (Royal Engineers). The museum has a large archive and photographic collection, and shows the developments in clothing, ammunition, rations, transport and communications.

ST BARBARA'S CHURCH. Built in 1901 largely from corrugated iron, it is dedicated to the patron saint of arsenals and powder magazines.

Cafe
   Keys Cafe, *61 Deepcut Bridge Road, Deepcut, GU16 6QP* ☎ *01252 835670.*
Museum
   Royal Logistic Corps Museum, *Princess Royal Barracks, Deepcut, GU16 6RW*
   ☎ *01252 340871.*
Take-Away
   Dragon House, *67 Deepcut Bridge Road, Deepcut, GU16 6QP* ☎ *01252 835289.*

See also Bisley, Brookwood, Camberley, Frimley, Knaphill, Mytchett, Pirbright. 3 miles from the Berkshire boundary & 2 miles from the Hampshire boundary.

Dorking

Dorking is situated in a gap between the North Downs and the greensand ridge, and was inhabited by settlers in both the stone age and the iron age. The High Street follows the line of Stane Street built by the Romans to connect London with Chichester. Dorking's early prosperity came from the production of charcoal and iron, later developing as a market town, and now ancient West Street has become an internationally known centre for antique dealers. Built on sand, the town has many caves under the buildings, the deepest of which is 75ft down and can be visited on application to the Dorking museum.

BURFORD BRIDGE HOTEL. Called the Hare & Hounds in the 12th century, this is where Lord Nelson(1758-1805) finally separated from Lady Nelson in 1800, and where in 1805 he is reputed to have stopped on his way to the Battle of Trafalgar. Here also in 1818 and in failing health John Keats(1795-1821), the poet completed `Endymion'.

COTMANDENE. An open space which was as famous for cricket as the Oval in the mid 19th century.

DENBIES VINEYARD. Set in 250 acres of beautiful countryside with views of Box Hill, this is the largest vineyard in Britain with some seven million vines. Every year over one million bottles of wine are produced at the imposing flint-clad chateau complex, which incorporates a visitor centre. There are tours of the winery on a special train, and tasting of wines in the cellars.

DORKING & DISTRICT MUSEUM. A museum reflecting the history of Dorking and its surroundings. There are oil and water colour paintings of the town and its surroundings by local artists, natural history displays, and a small collection of period costume. There is also a local history reference library.

DORKING HALLS. A three hall complex used for drama, music, dinner dances, films and children's shows. The Halls were built in 1931 for the Leith Hill Music Festival, which was founded by Ralph Vaughan Williams in 1904, and which is still held here each year.

OLD KING'S HEAD COURT. Charles Dickens, who had associations with Dorking placed the home of

Sam Weller here, and wrote that the 'Marquis of Granby' in the `Pickwick Papers' was based upon the old Kings Head, a coaching inn that has since been converted into a shopping precinct.

ST MARTIN'S CHURCH. One of the finer large 19th century churches in the county. Designed by Henry Woodyer, whose most important work it is, it has one of the tallest parish church spires in England, which at 210 feet dominates the town.

STEPPING STONES. A lane off the main road just south of the Burford Bridge Hotel leads to the famous stepping stones across the River Mole onto the slopes of Box Hill.

UNITED REFORMED CHURCH. This stands on the site of the oldest non-conformist chapel in Surrey, and houses the organ from Brighton's Royal Pavilion.

WHITE HORSE INN. Charles Dickens stayed at this 400-year-old inn which now has an 18th and 19th century frontage.

Antique Dealers

Dorking Antique Centre, *17 West Street, Dorking, RH4 1BL* ☎ *01306 740915.*

Dorking Desk Shop, *41 West Street, Dorking, RH4 1BU* ☎ *01306 883327.*

Dorking Emporium, *1a West Street, Dorking, RH4 1BL* ☎ *01306 876646.*

Elaine Saunderson, *18 Church Street, Dorking, RH4 1DW* ☎ *01306 881231.*

Hampshires of Dorking, *52 West Street, Dorking, RH4 1BU* ☎ *01306 887076.*

Harman's Antique Centre, *19 West Street, Dorking, RH4 1QH* ☎ *01306 743330.*

Harveys Period Decor, *5 West Street, Dorking, RH4 1BL* ☎ *01306 877767.*

Hebeco, *47 West Street, Dorking, RH4 1BU* ☎ *01306 875396.*

J&M Coombes, *44 West Street, Dorking, RH4 1BU* ☎ *01306 885479.*

John Lang Antiques, *6 Old Kings Head Court, 11 High Street, Dorking, RH4 1AR* ☎ *01306 882203.*

Malthouse, *49 West Street, Dorking, RH4 1BU* ☎ *01306 886169.*

Mayfair Antiques, *43 West Street, Dorking, RH4 1BU* ☎ *01306 885007.*

Norfolk House Galleries, *48 West Street, Dorking, RH4 1BU* ☎ *01306 881028.*

Oriental Carpets & Decorative Arts, *37 West Street, Dorking, RH4 1BU* ☎ *01306 876370.*

Patrick Worth, *11 West Street, Dorking, RH4 1BL* ☎ *01306 884484.*

Pilgrims Antique Centre, *7 West Street, Dorking, RH4 1BL* ☎ *01306 875028.*

Sean James Antiques, *14 Reigate Road, Dorking, RH4 1SG* ☎ *01306 887720.*

Thorpe & Foster, *51 West Street, Dorking, RH4 1BU* ☎ *01306 881029.*

Victoria & Edward Antique Centre, *61 West Street, Dorking, RH4 1BS* ☎ *01306 889645.* TWENTY FIVE DEALERS UNDER ONE ROOF. WE BUY AND SELL.

Vinery, *55 West Street, Dorking, RH4 1BS* ☎ *01306 743440.*

West Street Antiques, *63 West Street, Dorking, RH4 1BS* ☎ *01306 883487.*

Art Galleries

King's Court Galleries, *54 West Street, Dorking, RH4 1BS* ☎ *01306 881757.*

Spectrum Gallery, *268 High Street, Dorking, RH4 1QT* ☎ *01306 886088.*

Art & Craft Equipment

Quilt Room, *20 West Street, Dorking, RH4 1BL* ☎ *01306 740739.*

Book Shops

Bookends, *37 High Street, Dorking, RH4 1AR* ☎ *01306 889055.*

Fowler's Guides

The editors are always pleased to hear of any new establishments, or existing ones which have been omitted, for inclusion in future editions.

Books, Bits & Bobs, *20 South Street, Dorking, RH4 2HG* ☎ *01306 743119.*
Dorking Christian Bookshop, *22 West Street, Dorking, RH4 1BY* ☎ *01306 880722.*
TS Hill Books, *122 South Street, Dorking, RH4 2EU* ☎ *01306 886468.*
WH Smith, *101 High Street, Dorking, RH4 1AL* ☎ *01306 882194.*
Waterstone's, *54 South Street, Dorking, RH4 2HQ* ☎ *01306 886884.*

Cinema
Dorking Halls, *Reigate Road, Dorking, RH4 1SG* ☎ *01306 889694.*

Garden Centres & Nurseries
Dorking Garden Centre, *Reigate Road, Dorking, RH4 1NP* ☎ *01306 884845.*
Pixholme Court Gardens, *Pixham Lane, Dorking, RH4 1PG* ☎ *01306 743041.*

Golf Courses
Betchworth Park Golf Club, *Reigate Road, Dorking, RH4 1NZ* ☎ *01306 882052.*
Dorking Golf Club, *Chart Park, Dorking, RH5 4BX* ☎ *01306 886917.*

Guest Houses
Fairdene, *Moores Road, Dorking, RH4 2BG* ☎ *01306 888337.*
Torridon, *Longfield Road, Dorking, RH4 3DF* ☎ *01306 883724.*

Historic Building
Polesden Lacey - See under Polesden Lacey.

Hotels & Inns
★Burford Bridge Hotel(Forte), *Old London Road, Burford Bridge, Dorking, RH5 6BX*
☎ *01306 884561.*
Forte Travelodge, *Reigate Road, Dorking, RH4 1QB* ☎ *01306 740361.*
Pilgrim, *Station Road, Dorking, RH4 1HF* ☎ *01306 889951.*
A PLEASANT TRADITIONAL PUB ON THE EDGE OF TOWN OFFERING SIMPLE B & B ACCOMMODATION WITH GOOD
COOKING, FINE ALES AND A WARM FRIENDLY ATMOSPHERE.
◆Star & Garter Hotel, *Station Approach, Dorking, RH4 1TF* ☎ *01306 882820.*
★White Horse Hotel(Forte), *High Street, Dorking, RH4 1BE* ☎ *01306 881138.*

Libraries
SCC Lending Library, *Pippbrook House, Reigate Road, Dorking, RH4 1SH* ☎ *01306 882948.*
Performing Arts, *Vaughan-Williams House, West Street, Dorking, RH4 1DA*
☎ *01306 887509.*

Model Shops
Dorking Dolls House Gallery, *23 West Street, Dorking, RH4 1BY* ☎ *01306 885785.*
Dorking Model Centre, *13 West Street, Dorking, RH4 1BL* ☎ *01306 881747.*

Museum
Dorking & District Museum, *Old Foundry, 62a West Street, Dorking, RH4 1BS*
☎ *01306 883429.*

Pubs
Bulls Head, *11 South Street, Dorking, RH4 2DY* ☎ *01306 885720.*
Bush, *10 Horsham Road, Dorking, RH4 2JL* ☎ *01306 889830.*
★Cricketers, *81 South Street, Dorking, RH4 2JU* ☎ *01306 889938.*
Jolly Butchers, *45 Dene Street, Dorking, RH4 2DW* ☎ *01306 881722.*
Kings Arms, *45 West Street, Dorking, RH4 1BU* ☎ *01306 883361.*
Malthouse, *Mill Lane, Dorking, RH4 1DX* ☎ *01306 882393.*
Old House at Home, *24 West Street, Dorking, RH4 1BY* ☎ *01306 889664.*
Prince of Wales, *55 Hampstead Road, Dorking, RH4 3AH* ☎ *01306 889925.*
Queens Head, *Horsham Road, Dorking, RH4 2JS* ☎ *01306 883041.*
Spotted Dog, *42 South Street, Dorking, RH4 2HQ* ☎ *01306 883729.*
Star, *36 West Street, Dorking, RH4 1BU* ☎ *01306 889734.*
Surrey Yeoman, *220 High Street, Dorking, RH4 1QR* ☎ *01306 889748.*
White Hart, *5 Dene Street, Dorking, RH4 2DR* ☎ *01306 881960.*
Windmill Inn, *Flint Hill, Dorking, RH4 2LL* ☎ *01306 885729.*

Restaurants
Amalfi, *Allen Court, 56a High Street, Dorking, RH4 1AY* ☎ *01306 743980.*
Bali, *5 High Street, Dorking, RH4 1AR* ☎ *01306 886412.*
Belle Epoque, *84 South Street, Dorking, RH4 2EW* ☎ *01306 883239.*
Curry Garden, *41 South Street, Dorking, RH4 2JX* ☎ *01306 889648.*

Denbies Wine Estate, *London Road, Dorking, RH5 6AA* ☎ *01306 876616.*
Dorking Cantonese, *96 South Street, Dorking, RH4 2EW* ☎ *01306 883143.*
Fountain Garden, *16 West Street, Dorking, RH4 1BL* ☎ *01306 876788.*
High Island, *8 Reigate Road, Dorking, RH4 1SG* ☎ *01306 889918.*
Highland Cottage, *Junction Road, Dorking, RH4 3HB* ☎ *01306 742448.*
Khyber Pass, *304 High Street, Dorking, RH4 1QX* ☎ *01306 889006.*
Lane's Brasserie, *112 High Street, Dorking, RH4 1BA* ☎ *01306 887306.*
Little Chef, *Reigate Road, Dorking, RH4 1QB* ☎ *01306 740251.*
★Partners West Street, *2 West Street, Dorking, RH4 1BL* ☎ *01306 882826.*
Pickwick's, *Old Kings Head Court, 11 High Street, Dorking, RH4 1AR* ☎ *01306 888849.*
Pizza Express, *235 High Street, Dorking, RH4 1RT* ☎ *01306 888236.*
Pizza Piazza, *77 South Street, Dorking, RH4 2JU* ☎ *01306 889790.*
Poppins, *40 High Street, Dorking, RH4 1AY* ☎ *01306 889009.*
River Kwai, *274 High Street, Dorking, RH4 1QT* ☎ *01306 889053.*
Rue St Germain, *170 High Street, Dorking, RH4 1BG* ☎ *01306 888996.*
Watermill, *Reigate Road, Dorking, RH4 1NN* ☎ *01306 887831.*

Swimming Pool
Dorking Swimming & Sports Centre, *Reigate Road, Dorking, RH4 1SW* ☎ *01306 887722.*

Take-Aways
Between the Slices, *38 West Street, Dorking, RH4 1BU* ☎ *01306 886619.*
Dorking Kebab, *195 High Street, Dorking, RH4 1RU* ☎ *01306 881723.*
Kentucky Fried Chicken, *350 High Street, Dorking, RH4 1QX* ☎ *01306 889980.*
Ryka's, *Old London Road, Burford Bridge, Dorking, RH5 6BY* ☎ *01306 884454.*
Seven Seas Fish Bar, *59 Dene Street, Dorking, RH4 2DP* ☎ *01306 889672.*
Starburger, *40 High Street, Dorking, RH4 1AY* ☎ *01306 889009.*
Superdish, *245 High Street, Dorking, RH4 1RT* ☎ *01306 889600.*
Wimpy, *203 High Street, Dorking, RH4 1RU* ☎ *01306 889862.*
Yicken Chinese Meals, *104 South Street, Dorking, RH4 2EW* ☎ *01306 884076.*

Tea Rooms & Cafes
Haskett's Tea & Coffee Rooms, *86b South Street, Dorking, RH4 2EW* ☎ *01306 885833.*
Patio, *68 High Street, Dorking, RH4 1AY* ☎ *01306 883991.*
Queens Cafe, *Horsham Road, Dorking, RH4 2JR* ☎ *01306 883000.*

Theatre
Dorking Halls, *Reigate Road, Dorking, RH4 1SG* ☎ *01306 889694.*

Vineyard
Denbies Wine Estate, *London Road, Dorking, RH5 6AA* ☎ *01306 876616.*
MEMBER OF 'A TASTE OF SURREY' - WINE PRODUCER.

Wine Bar & Cafe Bar
Whynots, *Allen Court, 56a High Street, Dorking, RH4 1AY* ☎ *01306 743222.*

See also Betchworth, Brockham, Buckland, Holmwood, Leigh, Mickleham, Ranmore Common,
Westcott, Westhumble, Wotton.

Dormansland
(including Dormans Park)

The village developed after the local commons were enclosed in 1815 and was
much expanded after the railway arrived in 1884. Dormans Park developed similarly
on the other side of the line nearer to the station.

DRY HILL. There is considerable evidence here of an ancient British iron-age fort covering 26
acres and defended by three ditches, although the greater part of these has vanished.
GREATHED MANOR. A Victorian manor house built in 1868 by Robert Kerr. Named Ford Manor
when it was built, it was previously the home of the Spender-Clay family. It was purchased in
1959 by the Country Houses Association who changed the name in memory of their founder,
Rear Admiral Greathed. The house is divided into private apartments, but some parts are

occasionally open to the public.

OLD SURREY HALL. A large moated manor house built around a 15th century farmhouse in 1922.

Historic Building
   Greathed Manor, *Dormansland, RH7 6PA* ☎ *01342 832577*.
Pubs
   Coach House, *Wilderwick Road, Dormans Park, RH19 3NT* ☎ *01342 870448*.
◆Old House at Home, *63 West Street, Dormansland, RH7 6QT* ☎ *01342 832117*.
◆Plough, *Plough Road, Dormansland, RH7 6PS* ☎ *01342 832933*.
   Prince of Wales, *Lingfield Road, Baldwins Hill, Dormans Park, RH19 2EQ* ☎ *01342 325703*.
   Royal Oak, *High Street, Dormansland, RH7 6NN* ☎ *01342 832383*.
Special Pursuits
   Skirmish (paintball), *The Oast House, Ladycross Farm, Hollow Lane, Dormansland, RH7 6PB*
   ☎ *01342 870870*.

See also Felbridge, Haxted, Lingfield, Newchapel. 2 miles from the Sussex boundary & 2 miles from the Kent boundary.

Downside

Attractive cottages surround the large open green, on one side of which is a small chapel with a pump in front.

Nursery
   Cobham Park Nurseries, *Plough Lane, Downside, KT11 3LT* ☎ *01932 863933*.
Pubs
★Cricketers, *Downside Common, off Downside Road, Downside KT11 3NX* ☎ *01932 862105*.
★Plough, *Plough Lane, Downside, KT11 3LT* ☎ *01932 862514*.

See also Bookham, Byfleet, Cobham, Effingham, Fetcham, Horsley, Leatherhead, Ockham, Oxshott, Stoke D'Abernon, Whiteley Village, Wisley.

Dunsfold

The main village is built around an open common and a number of houses date from the 15th and 16th centuries. The old ironworks and hammer ponds, where cannon balls were cast, can still be seen by the river at Furnace Bridge. Dunsfold Aerodrome was constructed during the second World War.

CHURCH OF ST MARY & ALL SAINTS. This is a rare example of an almost complete 13th century building. All the original furniture survives and the oak pews are amongst the oldest in the country. The font is carved from Sussex marble, and in the churchyard is a yew which is nearly 1,000 years old.

Pub
★◆Sun, *The Common, Dunsfold, GU8 4LE* ☎ *01483 200242*.

See also Alfold, Chiddingfold, Hambledon, Hascombe. 2 miles from the Sussex boundary.

Earlswood

EARLSWOOD HOSPITAL. An impressive Victorian building designed as a mental hospital.
EARLSWOOD LAKES. Set in common land and popular for boating and fishing.

Antique Dealers
  FG Lawrence & Sons, *89 Brighton Road, Earlswood, RH1 6PS* ☎ *01737 764196.*
  Wakeman Bros, *43 Woodlands Road, Earlswood, RH1 6HB* ☎ *01737 761895.*
Boat Hire
  Earlswood Lakes, *Woodhatch Road, Earlswood.*
Golf Driving Range
  Redhill Golf Centre, *Canada Ave, Three Arch Road, Earlswood, RH1 5RH* ☎ *01737 770204.*
Inn
  Nags Head, *1 Horley Road, Earlswood, RH1 5AL* ☎ *01737 762822.*
Nursery
  Hillside Shrubs & Plants, *109 Horley Road, Earlswood, RH1 5AS* ☎ *01737 765645.*
Pubs
  Albatross, *30 Common Road, Earlswood, RH1 6HG* ☎ *01737 773922.*
  Flying Scud, *90 Woodlands Road, Earlswood, RH1 6HB* ☎ *01737 763652.*
  Prince Albert, *108 Horley Road, Earlswood, RH1 5AA* ☎ *01737 764479.*
Restaurants
  Da Maria, *77 Horley Road, Earlswood, RH1 5AS* ☎ *01737 769444.*
  Oaklands, *Haigh Crescent, Earlswood, RH1 6RA* ☎ *01737 771866.*
  Ruchita Tandoori, *8 Station Approach, Earlswood, RH1 6JH* ☎ *01737 764125.*
Special Pursuits
  Commando War Games, *75 Brambletye Park Road, Earlswood, RH1 6EN* ☎ *01737 763061.*
Take-Aways
  Albert Fish Bar, *81 Horley Road, Earlswood, RH1 5AS* ☎ *01737 764061.*
  Earlswood Tandoori, *96 Earlswood Road, Earlswood, RH1 6HW* ☎ *01737 778122.*
  Redhill Fish Bar, *63 Earlswood Road, Earlswood, RH1 6HJ* ☎ *01737 762610.*
  Spices Indian Take Away, *7 The Brow, Spencer Way, Earlswood, RH1 5SP* ☎ *01737 763203.*

See also Bletchingley, Gatton, Merstham, Nutfield, Outwood, Redhill, Reigate, Salfords, Sidlow
Bridge.

Eashing

EASHING BRIDGE. The old seven arch bargate stone bridge across the River Wey was probably built
by the Cistercian monks of Waverley Abbey in about 1200. Together with Elstead and Tilford, it
is one of three medieval bridges crossing the Wey and is now owned by the National Trust.

Pub
★◆Stag, *The Hollow, Eashing, GU7 2QG* ☎ *01483 421568.*

See also Compton, Elstead, Farncombe, Godalming, Hurtmore, Hydestile, Loseley, Milford, Peper
Harow, Puttenham, Shackleford, Wanborough, Witley, Wormley.

```
NOTES



```

Effingham
(including Effingham Junction)

Effingham is noted for the number and beauty of its trees and particularly Beech Avenue, a long avenue of beech trees now designated as a public open space. Charles, Lord Howard of Effingham(1536-1624), created Lord High Admiral by Elizabeth I in 1585, and Drake's commander in chief in 1588 at the time of the Armada, lived close by and took his title from the village.

Golf Course
Effingham Golf Club, *Guildford Road, Effingham, KT24 5PZ* ☎ *01372 452203.*
Guest House
Crosslands, *Guildford Road, Effingham, KT24 5PE* ☎ *01372 453479.*
Hotel
★Sir Douglas Haig Hotel, *The Street, Effingham, KT24 5LU* ☎ *01372 456886.*
Pubs
Lord Howard, *Forest Road, Effingham Junction, KT24 5HL* ☎ *01483 282572.*
Plough Inn, *Orestan Lane, Effingham, KT24 5SW* ☎ *01372 458121.*

See also Bookham, Downside, Fetcham, Horsley, Ockham, Polesden Lacey, Ranmore Common, Westhumble.

Egham

A small town close to the Thames with a long history dating back to the Magna Carta.

AIR FORCES MEMORIAL. The Air Forces Memorial, at the top of Cooper's Hill, commemorates 20,000 airmen who died in the Second World War with no known grave. It commands a magnificent view of Windsor Castle and seven counties.

CHURCH OF ST JOHN THE BAPTIST. Built in 1820 on the site of the 11th century Runnymede parish church, and has an unusual tower with an oval cupola. Inside are the coats of arms of the 25 rebellious barons responsible for the Magna Carta. The 15th century lych gate was originally the porch of an earlier church.

EGHAM MUSEUM. A collection and display of objects of local interest illustrating the history of Egham and of the surrounding districts.

GREAT FOSTERS. The property stands on the site of a Tudor hunting lodge, and was constructed by a courtier of Elizabeth I.

HIGH STREET. A Magna Carta fountain and a King John sculpture and tableau panel were unveiled in 1994 and stand in the pedestrianised high street.

KENNEDY MEMORIAL. Beside the meadows at Runnymede stands the John F Kennedy Memorial on an acre of ground given to the United States.

MAGNA CARTA MEMORIAL. The domed Classical temple at the foot of Cooper's Hill, was built by the American Bar Association as a monument to mark the signing of the Magna Carta by King John in 1215, here on the broad meadow at Runnymede beside the River Thames.

ROYAL HOLLOWAY & BEDFORD NEW COLLEGE. This gigantic building, in the style of a French château, was built between 1879 and 1887 of stone and brilliant red brick, as one of the first women's colleges in the country. Its companion piece, the Holloway Sanatorium in Virginia Water was built in 1884. Both buildings were designed by W H Crossland for Thomas Holloway(1800-1883), a manufacturer of patent medicines.The College picture gallery contains a fine collection of Victorian paintings, which include works by Millais, Landseer, Fildes, Frith, Holl and Maclise. The theatre is used for a wide programme of events including lunchtime and evening concerts, lectures, drama and recitals.

RUNNYMEDE. 188 acres of historic meadows where King John sealed the Magna Carta, together with 110 acres of wooded slopes of Cooper's Hill overlooking the meadows, which now belong to the National Trust.

RUNNYMEDE PLEASURE GROUNDS. A large play and picnic area by the river.

SWAN SANCTUARY. Originally set up by an Egham resident in her back garden, the sanctuary is now on a permanent site provided by the council and can handle over a hundred swans.

Animal Sanctuary
  Swan Sanctuary, *Field View, Egham, TW20 8AT* ☎ *01784 431667.*
Art Gallery - Public
  University of London, *Royal Holloway College, Egham Hill, Egham, TW20 0EX*
  ☎ *01784 443004.*
Art & Craft Equipment
  Craftline, *7 The Precinct, High Street, Egham, TW20 9HN* ☎ *01784 436115.*
Boat Hire
  Nicholes Boatyard, *Yardmead, Windsor Road, Egham, TW20 0AB* ☎ *01784 432342.*
Book Shops
  Blacklocks, *8 Victoria Street, Egham, TW20 0QY* ☎ *01784 438025.*
  Dillons, *Royal Holloway College, Egham Hill, Egham, TW20 0EX* ☎ *01784 471272.*
Garden Centres & Nurseries
  Egham Garden Centre, *Vicarage Road, Egham, TW20 8NT* ☎ *01784 433388.*
  HJ Pearcey & Sons, *41 Clarence Street, Egham, TW20 9QY* ☎ *01784 432805.*
  Mayflower Nurseries, *Thorpe Lea Road, Egham, TW20 8JL* ☎ *01784 432945.*
Guest Houses
  Venture, *18 Riverside, Egham, TW20 0AA* ☎ *01784 433313.*
  Wildings, *44 Grange Road, Egham, TW20 9QP* ☎ *01784 435115.*
Hotels
  ★Great Fosters Hotel, *Stroude Road, Egham, TW20 9UR* ☎ *01784 433822.*
  ★Runnymede Hotel, *Windsor Road, Egham, TW20 0AG* ☎ *01784 436171.*
Libraries
  SCC Lending Library, *High Street, Egham, TW20 9EA* ☎ *01784 433904.*
  University of London, *Spring Rise, Egham, TW20 9PP* ☎ *01784 434560.*
Museum
  Egham Museum, *Literary Institute, 51 High Street, Egham, TW20 9EW*
  (Enquiries ☎ *01344 843047).*
Pubs
  Compasses, *158 Thorpe Lea Road, Egham, TW20 8HA* ☎ *01784 454354.*
  Crown, *38 High Street, Egham, TW20 9DP* ☎ *01784 432608.*
  Eclipse, *Egham Hill, Egham, TW20 0AY* ☎ *01784 432989.*
  Foresters Arms, *1 North Street, Egham, TW20 9RP* ☎ *01784 432625.*
  Next Door, *6 High Street, Egham, TW20 9EA* ☎ *01784 439496.*
  Prince Alfred, *196 Thorpe Lea Road, Egham, TW20 8HP* ☎ *01784 454996.*
  Railway Hotel, *40 Station Road, Egham, TW20 9LF* ☎ *01784 473443.*
  Red Lion, *52 High Street, Egham, TW20 9EW* ☎ *01784 432314.*
  Robin Hood, *142 Thorpe Lea Road, Egham, TW20 8HA* ☎ *01784 453914.*
  Royal Ascot, *Egham Hill, Egham, TW20 0BQ* ☎ *01784 432164.*
  Sun Inn, *Wick Lane, Egham, TW20 0UF* ☎ *01784 432515.*
  Victoria Hotel, *19 The Avenue, Egham, TW20 9AB* ☎ *01784 432183.*
  White Lion, *115 High Street, Egham, TW20 9HQ* ☎ *01784 432498.*
Restaurants
  Bengal Brasserie, *70 High Street, Egham, TW20 9EY* ☎ *01784 436007.*
  Blue Sky, *17 High Street, Egham, TW20 9DT* ☎ *01784 432329.*
  Bonne Franquette, *5 High Street, Egham, TW20 9EA* ☎ *01784 439494.*
  Charcoals, *Skytes Meadow, Windsor Road, Egham, TW20 0AE* ☎ *01784 432244.*
  Egham Tandoori, *231 Pooley Green Road, Egham, TW20 8AS* ☎ *01784 451856.*
  Portico, *15 The Precinct, High Street, Egham, TW20 9HN* ☎ *01784 473133.*
  Silk Thai, *67 High Street, Egham, TW20 9EY* ☎ *01784 438682.*

Sports & Leisure Centre
   Sports Centre, *Vicarage Road, Egham, TW20 8NL* ☎ *01784 437695.*
Take-Aways
   Chef Hong Kong, *16 Victoria Street, Egham, TW20 0QY* ☎ *01784 473682.*
   Fryfare, *1 Limes Road, Egham, TW20 9QT* ☎ *01784 432817.*
   Jack's, *106 Thorpe Lea Road, Egham, TW20 8BL* ☎ *01784 455393.*
   Jack's Famous Fish & Chips, *19 High Street, Egham, TW20 9DT* ☎ *01784 435492.*
   Just Good Food, *102 High Street, Egham, TW20 9HQ* ☎ *01784 434578.*
   Thorpe Take Away, *102 Thorpe Lea Road, Egham, TW20 8BN* ☎ *01784 453211.*
   Tophat Take Away, *44a High Street, Egham, TW20 9DP* ☎ *01784 436066.*
Theatre
   University of London, *Royal Holloway College, Egham Hill, Egham, TW20 0EX*
   ☎ *01784 443004.*
Wine Bars & Cafe Bars
★Bar 163, *163 High Street, Egham, TW20 9HP* ☎ *01784 432344.*
   Langham Place, *6 High Street, Egham, TW20 9EA* ☎ *01784 439496.*
   Star Cafe, *223 Pooley Green Road, Egham, TW20 8AS* ☎ *01784 451071.*

See also Englefield Green, Lyne, Staines, Sunningdale, Thorpe, Virginia Water. 1 mile from the Berkshire boundary & 1 mile from the Greater London boundary.

Ellen's Green

A hamlet which dates from Elizabethan days.

Inn
★Thurlow Arms, *off Baynards Lane, Ellen's Green, RH12 3AD* ☎ *01403 822459.*
Pub
◆Wheatsheaf Inn, *Horsham Road, Ellen's Green, RH12 3AS* ☎ *01403 822155.*

See also Cranleigh, Ewhurst, Oakwood Hill. On the Sussex boundary.

Elstead

Formerly a small but prosperous centre of the woollen trade, and now a charming old village beside the River Wey, with some notable buildings around the small green.

ELSTEAD BRIDGE. A five-arched bridge which, together with Eashing and Tilford, is one of three medieval bridges over the Wey.
ELSTEAD MILL. Almost certainly built on the site of an earlier mill which was one of the six mills of Farnham mentioned in the Domesday Book, this Georgian water mill is generally considered to be the finest brick built mill in Surrey. It was at one time used as a paper mill.
ST JAMES'S CHURCH. A 14th century church greatly renovated by the Victorians.

Pubs
   Golden Fleece, *Farnham Road, Elstead, GU8 6DB* ☎ *01252 702349.*
◆Nellie Dene's, *Elstead Mill, Farnham Road, Elstead, GU8 6LE* ☎ *01252 703333.*
   Star Inn, *Milford Road, Elstead, GU8 6HE* ☎ *01252 703305.*
★Woolpack Inn, *The Green, Milford Road, Elstead, GU8 6HD* ☎ *01252 703106.*
Restaurants
   Elstead Mill, *Farnham Road, Elstead, GU8 6LE* ☎ *01252 703333.*
   Pangs Lodge, *172 Thursley Road, Elstead, GU8 6DH* ☎ *01252 702323.*

Take-Away
 Superfryer, *1 Parkview, Milford Road, Elstead, GU8 6HP* ☎ *01252 702528.*

See also The Bourne, Compton, Eashing, Hurtmore, Milford, Peper Harow, Puttenham, Runfold,
The Sands, Seale, Shackleford, Thursley, Tilford, Tongham, Witley.

Englefield Green

ST JUDE'S CHURCH. A colourful church built in 1859 by Edward Lamb for John Monsell(1811-1875),
then vicar of Egham and writer of popular hymns such as 'Fight the good fight'.
SAVILL GARDEN. Situated in Windsor Great Park, construction of the garden began in 1932 and it is
now considered to be one of the finest of its type in the temperate region of the world. It covers
some 35 acres of woodland and offers a great display of colour throughout the seasons, and
particularly in spring and summer, with a fine range of rhododendrons, camellias, magnolias and
many other trees and shrubs. There are adjoining formal rose gardens and herbaceous borders.

Hotel
 Anugraha Hotel, *Wick Lane, Englefield Green, TW20 0XN* ☎ *01784 434355.*
Park & Garden
 Savill Garden, *Wick Lane, Englefield Green (Enquiries* ☎ *01753 860222).*
Pubs
 Armstrong Gun, *49 Victoria Street, Englefield Green, TW20 0QX* ☎ *01784 433000.*
 Barley Mow, *Barley Mow Road, Englefield Green, TW20 0NX* ☎ *01784 431857.*
 Beehive, *34 Middle Hill, Englefield Green, TW20 0JQ* ☎ *01784 431621.*
 Fox & Hounds, *Bishopsgate Road, Englefield Green, TW20 0XU* ☎ *01784 433098.*
 Happy Man, *12 Harvest Road, Englefield Green, TW20 0QS* ☎ *01784 433265.*
 Holly Tree, *5 St Judes Road, Englefield Green, TW20 0DB* ☎ *01784 433045.*
 Sun, *81 Bishopsgate Road, Englefield Green, TW20 0UF* ☎ *01784 432515.*
Restaurants
 Magna Carta Tandoori, *2 St Judes Road, Englefield Green, TW20 0DB* ☎ *01784 437397.*
 Savill Garden Restaurant, *Wick Lane, Englefield Green, TW20 0UU* ☎ *01753 860222.*

See also Egham, Lyne, Staines, Sunningdale, Thorpe, Virginia Water. On the Berkshire boundary.

Epsom
(including Epsom Downs)

Originally a farming community, which between the 1620s and 1720s found fame
and grew rapidly as one of Britain's first spa towns based on its medicinal spring,
and which reverted to agriculture when the fashion passed. Prosperity revived in the
days of the stage coach, and further expansion started with the arrival of the railway
in 1847. Epsom is still a market town and has the widest high street in Surrey. The
buildings in Church Street recall the town's heyday in the 18th century. Today
Epsom is best known as the home of the Derby.

DERBY DAY EXPERIENCE. A dramatic presentation using film, video, spectacular theatrical effects
and specially composed music describing one of England's greatest social and sporting events,
from pre-Derby preparations to the thrilling climax at the winning post. Also here is Mrs
Beeton's Boutique, named after Mrs Isabella Beeton(1836-1865) who for thirteen years lived in
the old Epsom grandstand and where she assembled much of her legendry Book of Household
Management, which was published in parts during 1859 and 1860.
EPSOM COLLEGE. Founded for the sons of doctors in 1853, the school is just north of the town, in
Gothic style red-brick Victorian buildings.

EPSOM DOWNS. Racing has taken place on the Downs south east of the town since the time of James I. The Oaks was first run in 1779, and the Derby in 1780. Both races are run in early June, and there are other meetings at Epsom in April and August.

EPSOM PLAYHOUSE. One of Surrey's leading theatres, the main auditorium is used for both theatre and concerts, and for a regular season of films. Myers Hall is used for jazz, children's events, small scale plays, recitals and other events.

HORTON PARK CHILDRENS' FARM. A farm for the under 8s where the emphasis is on doing and touching. There are lots of friendly animals and play areas both inside and out.

ST MARTIN'S CHURCH. A very large church dating mainly from 1825, but the flint tower remains from the original medieval church, as does the 15th century font.

Antique Dealer
Fogg Antiques, *75b South Street, Epsom, KT18 7PY* ☎ *01372 726931.*
Art Gallery
Eagle Gallery, *8 Spread Eagle Walk, High Street, Epsom, KT18 8DN* ☎ *01372 744336.*
Art & Craft Equipment
OW Annetts & Sons, *22a Upper High Street, Epsom, KT17 4QJ* ☎ *01372 720323.*
Book Shops
Hammicks, *18 Ashley Centre, Epsom, KT18 5DA* ☎ *01372 742533.*
John Menzies, *36 Ashley Centre, Epsom, KT18 5DB* ☎ *01372 728292.*
Low Price Books, *21 High Street, Epsom, KT19 8DD* ☎ *01372 743165.*
Surrey Bookshop, *11 Kings Shade Walk, High Street, Epsom, KT19 8EB* ☎ *01372 740272.*
Farm Attraction
Horton Park Childrens' Farm, *Horton Lane, Epsom, KT19 8QG* ☎ *01372 743984.*
Golf Course
Epsom Golf Club, *Longdown Lane South, Epsom, KT17 4JR* ☎ *01372 721666.*
Golf Course & Driving Range
Horton Park Country Club, *Hook Road, Epsom, KT19 8QG* ☎ *0181-393 8400.*
Guest House
Angleside, *27 Ashley Road, Epsom, KT18 5BD* ☎ *01372 724303.*
Hotels & Inns
Chalk Lane Hotel, *Chalk Lane, Epsom, KT18 7BB* ☎ *01372 721179.*
★Drift Bridge Hotel(Toby), *Reigate Road, Epsom, KT17 3JZ* ☎ *01737 352163.*
Epsom Downs Hotel, *9 Longdown Road, Epsom, KT17 3PT* ☎ *01372 740643.*
White House Hotel, *Downs Hill Road, Epsom, KT18 5HW* ☎ *01372 722472.*
Information Centre
County Information Centre, *Epsom Library, 12 Waterloo Road, Epsom, KT19 8AX* ☎ *01372 744224.*
Libraries
SCC Lending Library (Epsom), *12 Waterloo Road, Epsom, KT19 8AX* ☎ *01372 721707.*
SCC Lending Library (Tattenhams), *Tattenham Crescent, Epsom, KT18 5NU* ☎ *01737 354144.*
Model Shop
Masters Models, *29 Tattenham Crescent, Epsom, KT18 5QJ* ☎ *01737 356867.*
Museum
Derby Day Experience, *Queen's Stand, The Racecourse, Epsom Downs, KT18 5LQ* ☎ *01372 726311.*
TELEPHONE FOR OPEN DAYS OR TO ARRANGE FOR A PRIVATE VISIT FOR GROUPS OF 20 OR MORE.
Pubs
Albion, *134 High Street, Epsom, KT19 8BT* ☎ *01372 727317.*
Amato, *18 Chalk Lane, Epsom, KT18 7AS* ☎ *01372 721085.*
Barley Mow, *12 Pikes Hill, Epsom, KT17 4EA* ☎ *01372 721044.*
Blenheim, *7 Manor Green Road, Epsom, KT19 8RA* ☎ *01372 720073.*
Cricketers, *1 Stamford Green Road, Epsom, KT18 7SR* ☎ *01372 740420.*
Derby Arms, *Derby Arms Road, Epsom Downs, KT18 5LE* ☎ *01372 722330.*
Jolly Coopers, *84 Wheelers Lane, Epsom, KT18 7SD* ☎ *01372 723222.*
Kings Arms, *144 East Street, Epsom, KT17 1EY* ☎ *01372 723892.*

Ladas, *13 Woodcote Road, Epsom, KT18 7QS* ☎ *01372 723780.*
Legends, *1a Waterloo Road, Epsom, KT19 8AY* ☎ *01372 739366.*
Magpie, *30 South Street, Epsom, KT18 7PF* ☎ *01372 721374.*
Marquis of Granby, *4 West Street, Epsom, KT18 7RG* ☎ *01372 723676.*
Olde Kings Head, *26 Church Street, Epsom, KT17 4QB* ☎ *Ex Dir.*
Plough & Harrow, *27 East Street, Epsom, KT17 1BD* ☎ *01372 740518.*
Queens Head, *77 South Street, Epsom, KT18 7PY* ☎ *01372 720332.*
Railway Guard, *48 Church Road, Epsom, KT17 4DZ* ☎ *01372 721143.*
Rifleman, *5 East Street, Epsom, KT17 1BB* ☎ *01372 726079.*
Rising Sun, *14 Heathcote Road, Epsom, KT18 5DX* ☎ *01372 723700.*
Rubbing House, *Vale Road, Epsom Downs, KT18 5LJ* ☎ *01372 723245.*
Sefton Arms, *Sefton Road, Epsom, KT19 9HG* ☎ *Ex Dir.*
Wellington, *High Street, Epsom* ☎ *Ex Dir.*
White Horse, *63 Dorking Road, Epsom, KT18 7JU* ☎ *01372 720759.*

Race Course
Epsom Racecourse, *The Grandstand, Epsom Downs, KT18 5LQ* ☎ *01372 726311.*

Restaurants
Cafe Conservatory, *14 Ashley Centre, Epsom, KT18 5DA* ☎ *01372 727988.*
Clock Tower Patisserie, *129 High Street, Epsom, KT19 8EF* ☎ *01372 743573.*
Hing Yip, *14 East Street, Epsom, KT17 1HH* ☎ *01372 723792.*
India Garden, *132 High Street, Epsom, KT19 8BT* ☎ *01372 722617.*
Mamma Giulia, *96 High Street, Epsom, KT19 8BJ* ☎ *01372 725505.*
Pizza Express, *8 South Street, Epsom, KT18 7PF* ☎ *01372 729618.*
Pizza Hut, *7 High Street, Epsom, KT19 8DA* ☎ *01372 727272.*
Pizza Piazza, *34 South Street, Epsom, KT18 7PF* ☎ *01372 724049.*
Raj, *211 Firtree Road, Epsom, KT17 3LB* ☎ *01737 371067.*
Rincon, *16 Highview House, Tattenham Crescent, Epsom Downs, KT18 5QJ*
☎ *01737 373647.*
River Kwai, *4 East Street, Epsom, KT17 1HH* ☎ *01372 741475.*
Saqui Tandoori, *14 Highview House, Tattenham Crescent, Epsom Downs, KT18 5QJ*
☎ *01737 362147.*
Tattenham Corner(Beefeater), *Tattenham Crescent, Epsom Downs, KT18 5NY*
☎ *01737 351454.*

Sports & Leisure Centres
Court Room Gym, *Court Recreation Ground, off Pound Lane, Epsom, KT19 8SB*
☎ *01372 749280.*
Rainbow Centre, *39 East Street, Epsom, KT17 1BN* ☎ *01372 749606.*

Swimming Pool
Rainbow Centre, *39 East Street, Epsom, KT17 1BN* ☎ *01372 749606.*

Take-Aways
Botan Kebabs, *32a Waterloo Road, Epsom, KT19 8EX* ☎ *01372 749561.*
Burgerland, *78 East Street, Epsom, KT17 1HF* ☎ *01372 739677.*
Dinner Box, *25 Pound Lane, Epsom, KT19 8RY* ☎ *01372 740829.*
Golden Bull, *195a Kingston Road, Epsom, KT19 0AB* ☎ *0181-393 5199.*
Grants Fish Bar, *14 Upper High Street, Epsom, KT17 4QJ* ☎ *01372 729880.*
Hollymoor Fish Bar, *111 Hollymoor Lane, Epsom, KT19 9JZ* ☎ *01372 722574.*
Jade Garden, *69 Poole Road, Epsom, KT19 9SQ* ☎ *0181-393 3947.*
Just A Crust, *8 East Street, Epsom, KT17 1HH* ☎ *01372 744237.*
Manning Fish & Chips, *21 Pound Lane, Epsom, KT19 8RY* ☎ *01372 721655.*
McDonald's, *36 High Street, Epsom, KT19 8AH* ☎ *01372 741962.*
Tasty Kitchen, *123 East Street, Epsom, KT17 1EJ* ☎ *01372 721386.*
Yum Yums, *26 West Street, Epsom, KT18 7RJ* ☎ *01372 748577.*

Tea Rooms & Cafes
Courtneys Cafe & Bistro, *7 Spreadeagle Walk, High Street, Epsom, KT19 8DN*
☎ *01372 739873.*
Harringtons, *5 Waterloo Road, Epsom, KT19 8AY* ☎ *01372 720238.*
Touchdown, *Epsom Station, Epsom, KT19 8EU* ☎ *01372 742025.*

Theatre
  Epsom Playhouse, *Ashley Avenue, Epsom, KT18 5AL* ☎ *01372 742555.*
Wine Bar & Cafe Bar
  Caspers, *11 Upper High Street, Epsom, KT17 4QY* ☎ *01372 727752.*

See also Ashtead, Banstead, Burgh Heath, Chessington, Ewell, Leatherhead, Tadworth, Worcester Park. 2 miles from the Greater London boundary.

Esher

Esher has been inhabited since prehistoric times. In medieval times the area was divided into three manors, the remnants of which are Claremont, Sandown and Wayneflete. Because of her connection with Claremont, Queen Victoria was often to be seen in Esher. Esher is still a small town with an attractive tree-lined High Street, and is surrounded by open countryside.

BEAR. An old coaching inn built in the early 1800s, it was an important stop on the London to Portsmouth road.

CHRIST CHURCH. Built in 1854 to replace St George's, it has a tall spire and a fine reredos in the Lady Chapel.

CLAREMONT. The present mansion dates in part from the late 18th century although it has been much altered since. Built by Lancelot 'Capability' Brown(1715-1783) to replace a house built by Sir John Vanbrugh(1664-1726) for himself, the house was owned successively by Clive of India, Princess Charlotte(daughter of George IV), Queen Victoria, her youngest son the Duke of Albany, and his son Prince Leopold who was brought up as a German. In 1914 his interests were vested in the Public Trustee and the property was eventually sold at auction. It is now a girls' school.

CLAREMONT LANDSCAPE GARDEN (National Trust). One of the earliest surviving English landscape gardens, restored by the National Trust. The gardens were begun by Sir John Vanbrugh and Charles Bridgeman prior to 1720, and extended and naturalised by William Kent(1684-1748). Capability Brown made improvements. The grounds extend to 50 acres, with a lake with an island and pavilion, a grotto, turf amphitheatre, viewpoints and avenues.

ESHER PLACE. The present building is the last in a series built in the grounds of what was the medieval manor of Esher-Episcopi. The French Renaissance style mansion was built in the 1890s, incorporating parts of an earlier house dating from 1805, and is now a trades union education and training base. Only the gatehouse remains of an earlier grand red brick mansion built on lower ground in the 1470s by William of Wayneflete, Bishop of Winchester (see below).

ST GEORGE'S CHURCH. A delightful 16th century church, with additions of the 18th and 19th centuries. St George's was closed up when Christ Church was built on Esher Green in 1854, and it therefore escaped the renovations of the Victorian restorers. The church has a splendid collection of monuments and fittings, including a marble monument commemorating Princess Charlotte, who died at Claremont in 1817.

SANDOWN PARK RACECOURSE. Laid out in 1875, Sandown is undoubtedly one of the most popular racecourses in the country with racing throughout the year except in August. The Leisure Complex offers golf, snooker, ski school and squash.

WAYNEFLETE TOWER. This gatehouse is all that remains of a grand manor house built in the 1470s by William of Wayneflete, Bishop of Winchester from 1447 to 1486.

Art Gallery
  West End Galleries, *6 Winterdown Road, Esher, KT10 8LJ* ☎ *01372 464493.*
Cinema
  Cannon Cinema, *22 High Street, Esher, KT10 9RL* ☎ *01372 463362.*
Farm Shop
  Garson Farm, *Winterdown Road, Esher, KT10 8LS* ☎ *01372 464389.*
    MEMBER OF 'A TASTE OF SURREY' - TRADITIONAL & EXCLUSIVE FOODS.

FOWLER'S GUIDE TO SURREY

Garden Centre & Nursery
  Garson Farm, *Winterdown Road, Esher, KT10 8LS* ☎ *01372 460181.*
Golf Course
  Thames Ditton & Esher Golf Club, *Portsmouth Road, Esher, KT10 9AL* ☎ *0181-398 1551.*
Golf Course - Public
  Moore Place, *Portsmouth Road, Esher, KT10 9AL* ☎ *01372 463533.*
Golf Course & Driving Range
  Sandown Golf Centre, *Sandown Park, More Lane, Esher, KT10 8AN* ☎ *01372 463340.*
Hotel
  ★Haven Hotel, *Portsmouth Road, Esher KT10 9AR* ☎ *0181-398 0023.*
Library
  SCC Lending Library, *Old Church Path, Esher, KT10 9NS* ☎ *01372 465036.*
Park & Garden
  Claremont Landscape Garden, *Portsmouth Road, Esher, KT10 9JG* ☎ *01372 469421.*
Pick Your Own
  Garson Farm, *Winterdown Road, Esher, KT10 8LS* ☎ *01372 460181.*
Pubs
  Albert Arms, *82 High Street, Esher, KT10 9QS* ☎ *0372 465290.*
  Alma Arms, *Alma Road, Esher, KT10 8JN* ☎ *0181-398 4444.*
  Bear, *71 High Street, Esher, KT10 9RQ* ☎ *01372 469786.*
  Claremont Arms, *2 Church Street, Esher, KT10 8QS* ☎ *01372 464083.*
  Prince of Wales, *West End Lane, West End, Esher, KT10 8LA* ☎ *01372 465483.*
  Wheatsheaf, *40 Esher Green, Esher, KT10 8AG* ☎ *01372 464014.*
  White Lion, *110 High Street, Esher, KT10 9QJ* ☎ *01372 464557.*
Race Course
  Sandown Park, *Portsmouth Road, Esher, KT10 9AJ* ☎ *01372 463072.*
Restaurants
  Boulevard Saint Michel, *45 High Street, Esher, KT10 9RL* ☎ *01372 467241.*
  Cafe Piccolo, *10 High Street, Esher, KT10 9RT* ☎ *01372 465596.*
  Conservatory, *Garson Farm, Winterdown Road, Esher, KT10 8LS* ☎ *01372 470957.*
  Esher Chop Suey, *11 Church Street, Esher, KT10 8QS* ☎ *01372 466143.*
  ★Good Earth, *14 High Street, Esher, KT10 9RT* ☎ *01372 462489.*
  Greek Vine, *104 High Street, Esher, KT10 9RT* ☎ *01372 468888.*
  Marquis of Granby(Chef & Brewer), *Portsmouth Road, Esher, KT10 9AL* ☎ *0181-398 3815.*
  Moore Place(Beefeater), *Portsmouth Road, Esher, KT10 9AL* ☎ *01372 463532.*
  Orient, *63 High Street, Esher, KT10 9RQ* ☎ *01372 466628.*
  Panahar Tandoori, *124 High Street, Esher, KT10 9QJ* ☎ *01372 463081.*
  Wan Fu Rendezvous, *66 High Street, Esher, KT10 9QS* ☎ *01372 466450.*
Special Pursuits
  Go Karting at Sandown, *More Lane, Esher, KT10 8AN* ☎ *01372 471312.*
  Sandown Ski School, *More Lane, Esher, KT10 8AN* ☎ *01372 467132.*
Take-Away
  Chop, *100 High Street, Esher, KT10 9QJ* ☎ *01372 460243.*

See also Chessington, Claygate, Hersham, Hinchley Wood, Molesey, Oxshott, Thames Ditton, Walton on Thames. 2 miles from the Greater London boundary.

NOTES

Ewell
(including West Ewell)

Ewell was Surrey's largest Roman town, growing up around natural springs, and was still inhabited in Saxon times. The church was rebuilt in the 13th century, and at the end of the middle ages there were three mills and a smithy. Many houses were rebuilt in Tudor times, and weekly markets were introduced in 1618, but the houses built in the 17th century and before have now mostly gone. Ewell is at the source of the River Hogsmill and in Victorian times its waters supplied the brewery and powered the corn grinding, paper making and gunpowder mills. There was also a brickyard.

ADRIAN MANN THEATRE. The theatre stages a programme of plays and dance by touring companies as well as providing opportunities for students. The public are welcome.

BOURNE HALL. Named after the old house which was demolished to make way for this remarkable 1960s building concealed amongst rambling gardens in the heart of Ewell village. The main and minor halls and rooms play host to many professional and local concerts, drama and children's events.

BOURNE HALL MUSEUM. The museum occupies the upper floor of Bourne Hall and has displays on stone age hunters, Roman travellers, medieval peasants, Henry VIII at Nonsuch Palace and Samuel Pepys at Epsom Wells. Georgian and Edwardian memorabilia is displayed alongside more modern exhibits, particularly items of local interest. There is also an archive of old photographs and pictures.

CHURCH OF ST MARY THE VIRGIN. A large church built in 1848 to replace the old medieval church, the flint tower of which was left standing as a monument in the churchyard.

EWELL CASTLE. An 18th century mansion with battlements, which is now a school.

NONSUCH PALACE. Intended as a magnificent royal palace to rival Hampton Court, a palace like no palace a king had ever built before, it was begun in 1538 and was nearly finished when Henry VIII died nine years later. Acquired by the Earl of Arundel, it was finished ten years after that and was eventually bought by Elizabeth I. Charles II gave it to his mistress, Barbara Villiers, Duchess of Cleveland(1640-1709) who allowed it to fall into ruins.

NONSUCH PARK. 300 acres of woods and parkland which was once part of the Nonsuch Palace estate, and which now surrounds Nonsuch Manor House.

Antique Dealers
AE Booth & Son, *9 High Street, Ewell, KT17 1SG* ☎ *0181-393 5245.*
Max Robertson, *15 Corner House Parade, Epsom Road, Ewell, KT17 1NX* ☎ *0181-786 7877.*
Token House, *7 Market Parade, High Street, Ewell, KT17 1SL* ☎ *0181-393 9654.*
Art Gallery
Les Galeries des Beaux Arts, *30 High Street, Ewell, KT17 1RW* ☎ *0181-393 2128.*
Book Shops
JW McKenzie, *12 Stoneleigh Park Road, Ewell, KT19 0QT* ☎ *0181-393 7700.*
Peters Books, *54 High Street, Ewell, KT19 8DS* ☎ *0181-393 8048.*
Cinema
MGM Cinema, *Kingston Road, Ewell, KT19 0SA* ☎ *0181-394 0760.*
Civic Centre
Bourne Hall, *Spring Street, Ewell, KT17 1UD* ☎ *0181-393 9571.*
Garden Centres & Nurseries
Beechcroft Nursery, *127 Reigate Road, Ewell, KT17 3DE* ☎ *0181-393 4265.*
Seymours Garden Centre, *Ewell By-Pass, Ewell, KT17 1PS* ☎ *0181-393 0111.*
Hotel
Nonsuch Park Hotel, *355 London Road, Ewell, KT17 2DE* ☎ *0181-393 0771.*
Information Centre
Ewell Information Centre, *Bourne Hall Library, Spring Street, Ewell KT17 1TG* ☎ *0181-394 0372.*

Libraries
  SCC Lending Library (Ewell Court House), *Lakehurst Road, Ewell, KT19 0EB*
  ☎ *0181-393 1069.*
  SCC Lending Library (Bourne Hall), *Spring Street, Ewell KT17 1TG* ☎ *0181-394 0951.*
  SCC Lending Library (Stoneleigh), *1 The Broadway, Stoneleigh, Ewell, KT17 2JA*
  ☎ *0181-394 0328.*
Model Shops
  Harts Models & Accessories, *176 Kingston Road, Ewell, KT19 0SF* ☎ *0181-786 7575.*
  Mick Charles Models, *192 Kingston Road, Ewell, KT19 0SF* ☎ *0181-393 3232.*
Museum
  Bourne Hall Museum, *Bourne Hall, Spring Street, Ewell, KT17 1UF* ☎ *0181-394 1734.*
Park
  Nonsuch Park, *London Road, Ewell (Enquiries* ☎ *0181-393 2676).*
Pubs
  Eight Bells, *78 Kingston Road, Ewell, KT17 2DU* ☎ *0181-393 9973.*
◆Green Man, *71 High Street, Ewell, KT17 1RX* ☎ *0181-394 2923.*
  Jolly Waggoners, *112 Beggars Hill, Ewell, KT17 2EQ* ☎ *0181-393 5728.*
  King William IV, *17 High Street, Ewell, KT17 1SB* ☎ *0181-393 2063.*
  Kingfisher, *Ruxley Lane, West Ewell, KT19 9JS* ☎ *0181-397 5297.*
  Organ Inn, *65 London Road, Ewell, KT17 2BL* ☎ *0181-393 2242.*
◆Plough Inn, *Plough Road, Ewell, KT19 9RA* ☎ *0181-394 2885.*
  Spring Hotel, *1 London Road, Ewell, KT17 2AY* ☎ *0181-393 1061.*
  Stoneleigh Inn, *The Broadway, Stoneleigh, Ewell, KT17 2JA* ☎ *0181-393 2765.*
  Wheatsheaf, *34 Kingston Road, Ewell, KT17 2AA* ☎ *0181-393 2879.*
Restaurants
  A Roma, *67 High Street, Ewell, KT17 1RX* ☎ *0181-393 8810.*
  C'est la Vie, *17 High Street, Ewell, KT17 1SB* ☎ *0181-394 2933.*
  Curry House, *1 Cheam Road, Ewell, KT17 1SP* ☎ *0181-393 5528.*
  Il Capriccio, *47 High Street, Ewell, KT17 1RX* ☎ *0181-786 8160.*
  Marianna's, *397 Kingston Road, Ewell, KT19 0BT* ☎ *0181-394 0926.*
  Monihar Tandoori, *1 Castle Parade, Ewell, KT17 2PR* ☎ *0181-393 3605.*
  Peking Chef, *399a Kingston Road, Ewell, KT19 0BT* ☎ *0181-393 2061.*
  Pulau Pinang, *52 High Street, Ewell, KT19 8AJ* ☎ *0181-394 0897.*
  Queen Adelaide(Chef & Brewer), *272 Kingston Road, Ewell, KT19 0SH* ☎ *0181-393 2666.*
  Sapphire, *56 High Street, Ewell, KT17 1RW* ☎ *0181-393 3959.*
  Surrey Palace, *207 Kingston Road, Ewell, KT19 0AB* ☎ *0181-393 6733.*
  Universal Chinese, *12 Castle Parade, Ewell By Pass, Ewell KT17 2PR* ☎ *0181-394 0564.*
Take-Aways
  Fortune House, *218 Chessington Road, West Ewell, KT19 9XA* ☎ *0181-394 0635.*
  New Taion, *417 Kingston Road, Ewell, KT19 0BT* ☎ *0181-393 5751.*
  Sunhing, *213 Kingston Road, Ewell, KT19 0AB* ☎ *0181-393 8478.*
  Superfish, *9 Castle Parade, Ewell, KT17 2PR* ☎ *0181-393 3674.*
Tea Rooms & Cafes
  Blue Boy Cafe, *228 Chessington Road, West Ewell, KT19 9XF* ☎ *0181-393 2636.*
  DJ's Cafe, *188a Kingston Road, Ewell, KT19 0SF* ☎ *0181-393 9280.*
Theatres
  Adrian Mann Theatre, *NESCOT, Reigate Road, Ewell, KT17 3DS* ☎ *0181-393 6660.*
  Bourne Hall Theatre, *Bourne Hall, Spring Street, Ewell, KT17 1UD* ☎ *0181-393 9571.*
Wine Bar & Cafe Bar
  Marbles, *2 Cheam Road, Ewell, KT17 1SN* ☎ *0181-393 8522.*

See also Banstead, Burgh Heath, Chessington, Epsom, Worcester Park. 1 mile from the Greater
London boundary.

```
NOTES



```

Ewhurst

An attractive village below the Surrey hills with some old houses and an unusual
village sign erected to mark the Coronation in 1953.

CHURCH OF ST PETER & ST PAUL. A Norman church with medieval windows and a spire which was
added in 1838 to the central tower. It has a fine Norman doorway, an ancient font and a
Jacobean pulpit. A giant yew tree stands in the churchyard.

Inn
  Bulls Head, *The Street, Ewhurst, GU6 7QD* ☎ *01483 277447.*
Pub
★◆Windmill Inn, *Pitch Hill, Ewhurst, GU6 7NN* ☎ *01483 277566.*

See also Cranleigh, Ellen's Green, Forest Green, Holmbury St Mary, Oakwood Hill, Ockley,
Peaslake.

Farncombe

Separated by the River Wey but otherwise closely adjoining the town of Godalming,
the few older buildings indicate that before the arrival of the railway this was a
pleasant little riverside village.

LAMMAS LANDS. Riverside meadows where for centuries cattle have grazed.
WYATT ALMSHOUSES. Ten red brick cottages and a small chapel donated by Richard Wyatt in 1622.

Antique Dealers
  Copperfield Antiques, *9 Farncombe Street, Farncombe, GU7 3BA* ☎ *01483 861454.*
  Curio Corner, *2 Summers Road, Farncombe, GU7 3BB* ☎ *01483 426076.*
  Heath-Bullock Antiques, *8 Meadrow, Farncombe, GU7 3HN* ☎ *01483 422562.*
Golf Course & Driving Range
  Broadwater Park Golf Club, *Guildford Road, Farncombe, GU7 3DD* ☎ *01483 429955.*
Hotel
  Meads Hotel, *65 Meadrow, Farncombe, GU7 3HS* ☎ *01483 421800.*
Model Shop
  Mainly Models, *14 Farncombe Street, Farncombe, GU7 3LH* ☎ *01483 427181.*
Park
  Broadwater Park, *Farncombe.*
Pubs
  Duke of Wellington, *Farncombe Street, Farncombe, GU7 3LH* ☎ *01483 417548.*
  Freeholder, *St Johns Street, Farncombe, GU7 3EJ* ☎ *01483 425827.*
  Leathern Bottle, *77 Meadrow, Farncombe, GU7 3HN* ☎ *01483 425642.*
  Three Lions, *55 Meadrow, Farncombe, GU7 3HS* ☎ *01483 417880.*
  Wey Inn, *1 Meadrow, Farncombe, GU7 3HJ* ☎ *01483 416680.*
  White Hart, *Bourne Road, Farncombe, GU7 3NQ* ☎ *01483 421430.*
Restaurants
  Farncombe Tandoori, *18 Farncombe Street, Farncombe, GU7 3LH* ☎ *01483 423131.*
  Manor Inn(Beefeater), *Meadrow, Farncombe, GU7 3BX* ☎ *01483 427134.*
Sports & Leisure Centre
  Godalming Leisure Centre, *Summers Road, Farncombe, GU7 3BH* ☎ *01483 417282.*
Swimming Pool
  Godalming Leisure Centre, *Summers Road, Farncombe, GU7 3BH* ☎ *01483 417282.*
Take-Aways
  Brotherwoods, *Lower Manor Road, Farncombe, GU7 3EG* ☎ *01483 416663.*
  Cathay House, *57 St Johns Street, Farncombe, GU7 3EH* ☎ *01483 417620.*

Rina's Fish Bar, *Kings Road, Farncombe, GU7 3ES* ☎ *01483 415269.*

See also Bramley, Compton, Eashing, Godalming, Guildford, Hascombe, Hurtmore, Hydestile, Loseley, Milford, Peper Harow, Puttenham, Shackleford, Shalford, Wanborough, Witley, Wonersh.

Farnham

The most westerly town in Surrey, and now one of the finest Georgian towns in England. The town's history goes back to a much earlier period, as palaeolithic, neolithic, bronze and iron-age finds have been made here. In addition there are half-timbered Tudor buildings and gabled 17th century almshouses. The River Wey flows past the south of the town, and there is a park of 308 acres.

CASTLE STREET. A wide and elegant street, with many gracious Georgian houses, designed to hold fairs and markets. The old Market House was demolished in 1864 after 300 years and stood on the cobbled area of the street now used as a market place.

FARNHAM CASTLE. The building of Farnham Castle was begun in 1129 by Henry of Blois, Bishop of Winchester, and destroyed in 1155 by order of Henry II. Building resumed soon after and, although both the court and the wall date from the late 12th and early 13th centuries, the main buildings have been extensively repaired and altered. Farnham castle was continuously occupied, apart from a short period during the civil war, by the Bishops of Winchester until 1927, and then by the Bishop of Guildford until 1956. Many kings and queens, from Edward I to Queen Victoria, have been entertained in the Castle, which is owned by the Church Commissioners and now used as a training centre. Parts of the castle are open to the public on a limited basis.

Farnham Castle

FARNHAM CASTLE KEEP. The foundations of the original massive central tower of Farnham Castle still remain and are maintained by English Heritage This impressive Norman keep on top of the artificial mound provides a suitable point from where the rest of the medieval buildings can be seen.

JAMES HOCKEY GALLERY. The gallery puts on exhibitions by contemporary artists, designers and degree and diploma students.

LUDLAM'S CAVE. A benevolent witch known as Mother Ludlam is reputed to have lived here. By tradition she would lend any item so long as the borrower kept his word to return it within an agreed time. A cauldron, with the trivet, was borrowed but returned late. She would not take it back, and thereafter lent nothing further. The cauldron is now in St Mary's church, Frensham.

MOOR PARK. Formerly known as Compton Hall, it was bought in 1680 by Sir William Temple(1628-1699), the diplomatist and essay writer, whose secretary was Jonathan Swift(1667-1745), the satirist. The house and gardens were redesigned in 1680 and again in the 18th century.

MUSEUM OF FARNHAM. Located in Willmer House, the museum collections cover life in the district from earliest times and include archaeological finds, 17th and 18th century furniture and clocks, costumes, folk material, and items associated with local artists, architects and inventors. There is also a collection of 19th century English and French glass paperweights.

NEW ASHGATE GALLERY. Monthly exhibitions of work by contemporary artists and craftsmen. There is a jewellery workshop and craft shop.

REDGRAVE THEATRE. A lively family theatre named after Sir Michael Redgrave(1908-1985) which has an enviable reputation for artistic excellence.

ST ANDREW'S CHURCH. This is one of the largest churches in Surrey and although most of the present structure is 15th century it was originally a Norman church. The top half of the tower and all the glass is Victorian, and the most recent restoration work was done in 1959. William Cobbett is buried here.

SC JOHNSON GALLERY & STUDIO. Diverse exhibitions of contemporary arts and crafts by local and professional artists. There is an active workshop programme and occasional guided tours and demonstrations.

THE BUSH HOTEL. Farnham's oldest hotel, it was already ancient when first recorded in 1603, and some 17th century timbers still survive in the present building. On the ceiling of the lounge is a very unusual sundial which used to be lit by the reflection from an outside pool.

THE MALTINGS. Originally a tannery and then a brewery, this delightful 18th century riverside building is now a leading arts centre and meeting place. It regularly features jazz, dance, classical music, drama events and a wide range of crafts and antique markets and other exhibitions. The art gallery has an extensive visual arts programme and also craft and design studios.

WAVERLEY ABBEY. Beside the river are the ruins of this the first Cistercian Abbey in England, founded in the 12th century and dissolved by Henry VIII 400 years later.

WEST STREET. West Street has two fine Georgian houses, Willmer House of 1718, and Sandford House of 1757. Willmer House, which houses the museum, was built in 1718 and is an outstanding example of an early Georgian town house. The hand-cut brick façade is regarded as one of the finest in the country. It has a walled garden and contains fine carving and panelling.

WILLIAM COBBETT. The politician and writer William Cobbett(1763-1835) was born in what is now the William Cobbett pub. His 'Rural Rides', published in 1830, gives an excellent account of life in early 19th century England.

Antique Dealers
Annie's Antiques, *1 Ridgeway Parade, Farnham, GU9 8UZ* ☎ *01252 713447*.
Bits & Pieces Antiques, *82 West Street, Farnham, GU9 7EN* ☎ *01252 715043*.
Bourne Mill Antiques, *39 Guildford Road, Farnham, GU9 9QB* ☎ *01252 716663*.
Christopher's Antiques, *39 West Street, Farnham, GU9 7DX* ☎ *01252 713794*.
Farnham Antique Centre, *27 South Street, Farnham, GU9 7QU* ☎ *01252 724475*.
Georgian House Antiques, *90 West Street, Farnham, GU9 7EN* ☎ *01252 718148*.
Treasury, *61a Downing Street, Farnham, GU9 7PN* ☎ *01252 722199*.

Art Gallery - Public
SC Johnson Gallery & Studio, *Farnham Maltings* ☎ *01252 726234*.

Art Galleries
Andrew Lloyd Gallery, *17 Castle Street, Farnham, GU9 7JA* ☎ *01252 724333*.
CCA Galleries, *13 Lion & Lamb Yard, West Street, Farnham, GU9 7LL* ☎ *01252 722231*.
Lion & Lamb Gallery, *West Street, Farnham, GU9 7HH* ☎ *01252 714154*.
New Ashgate Gallery, *Wagon Yard, Lower Church Lane, Farnham, GU9 7PS*
☎ *01252 713208*.

Art & Craft Equipment
Herald Art Shop, *114 West Street, Farnham, GU9 7HL* ☎ *01252 725224*.

Arts Centre
Farnham Maltings, *Bridge Square, Farnham, GU9 7QR* ☎ *01252 726234*.

Book Shops
Bookshelf Bargains, *25 The Borough, Farnham, GU9 7NJ* ☎ *01252 714811*.
Cobweb Books, *29 The Woolmead, East Street, Farnham, GU9 7TT* ☎ *01252 734531*.
Hammicks, *11 Lion & Lamb Yard, Farnham, GU9 7LL* ☎ *01252 724666*.
WH Smith, *14 The Borough, Farnham, GU9 7NF* ☎ *01252 715304*.

Garden Centre
Bourne Mill Garden Centre, *39 Guildford Road, Farnham, GU9 9PY* ☎ *01252 734293*.

Golf Course
Farnham Park Par Three, *Folly Hill, Farnham, GU9 0AU* ☎ *01252 715216*.

Historic Building
  Farnham Castle Keep, *Castle Hill, Farnham, GU9 0AE* ☎ *01252 713393.*
Hotels & Inns
  Albion, *2 Hale Road, Farnham, GU9 9QH* ☎ *01252 716602.*
  ★Bishops Table Hotel, *27 West Street, Farnham, GU9 7DR* ☎ *01252 710222.*
  Blue Boy Hotel, *Station Hill, Farnham, GU9 8AD* ☎ *01252 715198.*
  ★Bush Hotel(Forte), *The Borough, Farnham, GU9 7NN* ☎ *01252 715237.*
  Duke of Cambridge, *East Street, Farnham, GU9 7TH* ☎ *01252 716584.*
  Stafford House Hotel, *22 Firgrove Hill, Farnham, GU9 8LQ* ☎ *01252 724336.*
  Wellingtons, *Folly Hill, Farnham, GU9 0BB* ☎ *01252 715549.*
Information Centre
  Tourist Information Centre, *Vernon House, 28 West Street, Farnham, GU9 7DR*
  ☎ *01252 715109.*
Library
  SCC Lending Library, *28 West Street, Farnham, GU9 7DR* ☎ *01252 716021.*
Model Shop
  Models of Distinction, *23 The Woolmead, Farnham, GU9 7TT* ☎ *01252 716981.*
Museum
  Museum of Farnham, *Willmer House, 38 West Street, Farnham, GU9 7DX* ☎ *01252 715094.*
Pubs
  Bricklayers Arms, *36 Weydon Lane, Farnham, GU9 8UP* ☎ *01252 726214.*
  Coach & Horses, *2 Castle Street, Farnham, GU9 7HR* ☎ *01252 726523.*
  Hop Blossom, *Long Garden Walk, Castle Street, Farnham, GU9 7HX* ☎ *01252 710770.*
  Jolly Sailor, *64 West Street, Farnham, GU9 7EN* ☎ *01252 713001.*
  Lamb, *43 Abbey Street, Farnham, GU9 7RJ* ☎ *01252 714133.*
  Marlborough Head Hotel, *East Street, Farnham, GU9 7RX* ☎ *01252 724297.*
  Nelson Arms, *50 Castle Street, Farnham, GU9 7JQ* ☎ *01252 716078.*
  Plough, *74 West Street, Farnham, GU9 7EH* ☎ *01252 716332.*
  Queens Head, *9 The Borough, Farnham, GU9 7NA* ☎ *01252 726524.*
  Seven Stars, *88 East Street, Farnham, GU9 7TP* ☎ *01252 714814.*
  ◆Shepherd & Flock, *22 Moor Park Lane, Farnham, GU9 9JB* ☎ *01252 716675.*
  Six Bells Inn, *55 Hale Road, Farnham, GU9 9QZ* ☎ *01252 716697.*
  Waverley Arms, *Waverley Lane, Farnham, GU9 8BQ* ☎ *01252 715221.*
  Wheatsheaf Inn, *19 West Street, Farnham, GU9 7EH* ☎ *01252 725132.*
  William Cobbett, *4 Bridge Square, Farnham, GU9 7QR* ☎ *01252 726281.*
Restaurants
  Antonios, *2 Lion & Lamb Yard, Farnham, GU9 7LL* ☎ *01252 715156.*
  Banaras, *40 Downing Street, Farnham, GU9 7PH* ☎ *01252 734081.*
  Colony, *68 Castle Street, Farnham, GU9 7LN* ☎ *01252 725108.*
  Darjeeling, *25 South Street, Farnham, GU9 7QU* ☎ *01252 714322.*
  Farnham Tandoori, *47 West Street, Farnham, GU9 7DX* ☎ *01252 716853.*
  Garden Restaurant, *Redgrave Theatre* ☎ *01252 716601.*
  Gorge, *10 The Woolmead, Farnham, GU9 7TX* ☎ *01252 726070.*
  Kar Ling Kwong, *48 East Street, Farnham, GU9 7SW* ☎ *01252 714854.*
  ★Krugs, *84 West Street, Farnham, GU9 7EN* ☎ *01252 723277.*
  Pizza Piazza, *68 Castle Street, Farnham, GU9 7LN* ☎ *01252 721383.*
  Sinuessa, *62a East Street, Farnham, GU9 7TJ* ☎ *01252 726038.*
  Vienna, *112 West Street, Farnham, GU9 7EN* ☎ *01252 722978.*
Sports & Leisure Centre
  Farnham Sports Centre, *Dogflud Way, Farnham, GU9 7UD* ☎ *01252 723208.*
Swimming Pool
  Farnham Sports Centre ☎ *01252 723208.*
Take-Aways
  Heath End Fisheries, *43 Farnborough Road, Heath End, Farnham, GU9 9AQ*
  ☎ *01252 716482.*
  Kim Lau Fish Bar, *468 Trimmers Close, Farnham, GU9 0ET* ☎ *01252 725442.*
  Tai-Shun, *39 South Street, Farnham, GU9 7RE* ☎ *01252 725056.*

Tasty House, *1 Station Hill, Farnham, GU9 8AA* ☎ *01252 716706.*
Wimpy, *13 East Street, Farnham, GU9 7RX* ☎ *01252 726483.*
Tea Rooms & Cafes
Farnham Maltings, *Bridge Square, Farnham, GU9 7QR* ☎ *01252 718098.*
Lion & Lamb Coffee Shop, *2 Lion & Lamb Yard, Farnham, GU9 7LL* ☎ *01252 715156.*
Whistling Jacks, *28b Downing Street, Farnham, GU9 7PD* ☎ *01252 715744.*
Theatres
Farnham Maltings, *Bridge Square, Farnham, GU9 7QR* ☎ *01252 726234.*
Redgrave Theatre, *East Street, Farnham, GU9 7SB* ☎ *01252 715301.*
Wine Bars & Cafe Bars
Borelli's, *Borelli Yard, The Borough, Farnham, GU9 7NJ* ☎ *01252 735254.*
Sevens, *7 The Borough, Farnham, GU9 7NA* ☎ *01252 715345.*

See also Badshot Lea, The Bourne, Frensham, Hale, Heath End, Rowledge, Runfold, The Sands, Seale, Tilford, Tongham, Wrecclesham. 2 miles from the Hampshire boundary.

Felbridge

Local mill ponds suggest that the iron industry once flourished in the area. Generous benefactors of Felbridge were the Evelyn family who once lived in Felbridge Place, which is now demolished.

Inn
★◆Woodcock, *Woodcock Hill, Felbridge, RH19 2RE* ☎ *01342 325859.*
COUNTRY INN AND RESTAURANT. EGON RONAY RECOMMENDED. BARS OPEN ALL DAY. OVERNIGHT ACCOMMODATION AVAILABLE. EXCELLENT RESTAURANT & BAR FOOD. REAL ALES.
Pub
Star Inn, *London Road, Felbridge, RH19 2QR* ☎ *01342 323239.*

See also Burstow, Copthorne, Dormansland, Horne, Lingfield, Newchapel, Shipley Bridge, Smallfield. On the Sussex boundary.

Fetcham

Fetcham has been inhabited since Saxon times, but relatively few old properties have survived as the area has been developed. The River Mole now forms an effective boundary between Fetcham and Leatherhead.

BOCKETTS FARM PARK. Set in an area of outstanding natural beauty on the edge of the North Downs, this is a working family farm with historic buildings and many interesting breeds of farm animals and poultry. There are outdoor paddocks and large covered areas with many friendly animals. There are displays of agricultural bygones and craft demonstrations, and trailer rides are usually available. The tea room is in an 18th century barn.
FETCHAM PARK. Once part of the original Norman manor, the present house was built in 1705 for Arthur Moore, a director of the South Sea Company, and transformed in 1870 into a Victorian red brick mansion.
ST MARY'S CHURCH. The walls contain Roman bricks and other pre-Conquest masonry, although the church dates mainly from the 13th to 15th centuries.

Farm Attraction
Bocketts Farm Park, *Young Street, Fetcham, KT22 9DA* ☎ *01372 363764.*
Garden Centre
Fetcham Garden Centre, *81 The Street, Fetcham, KT22 9RD* ☎ *01372 375673.*

Pub
  Bell Inn, *Bell Lane, Fetcham, KT22 9QN* ☎ *01372 372624.*
Restaurants
  Fetcham Tandoori, *248 Cobham Road, Fetcham, KT22 9JF* ☎ *01372 374927.*
  Rising Sun(Harvester), *Hawks Hill, Fetcham, KT22 9DJ* ☎ *01372 379872.*
Take-Aways
  Domino's Pizza, *2 Sunmead Parade, Guildford Road, Fetcham, KT22 9AL* ☎ *01372 379000.*
  Fetcham Fish Bar, *85 The Street, Fetcham, KT22 9RD* ☎ *01372 374321.*
  Wings Garden, *83 The Street, Fetcham, KT22 9RD* ☎ *01372 379307.*
Tea Rooms & Cafes
  Clarks Cafe, *1 Sunmead Parade, Fetcham, KT22 9AL* ☎ *01372 375780.*
  Old Barn Tea Room, *Bocketts Farm Park* ☎ *01372 363764.*

See also Ashtead, Bookham, Downside, Effingham, Horsley, Leatherhead, Mickleham, Oxshott, Polesden Lacey, Ranmore Common, Stoke D'Abernon, Westhumble. 3 miles from the Greater London boundary.

Forest Green

THE FORGE. A working forge renovated in 1985 and now specialising in traditional wrought iron work. A museum and gallery is planned for the 16th century barn that has recently been re-assembled next door.

Pub
  ★◆Parrot Inn, *Horsham Road, Forest Green, RH5 5RZ* ☎ *01306 621339.*

See also Abinger Common, Cranleigh, Ewhurst, Holmbury St Mary, Oakwood Hill, Ockley, Peaslake. 3 miles from the Sussex boundary.

Frensham

FRENSHAM COUNTRY PARK. 1,000 acres of woods and heath, which include the famous ponds and their sandy beaches. The Great Pond is almost two miles in circumference and is one of the largest lakes in southern England. Originally a natural pool, it was subsequently enlarged in the middle ages to supply fish for the Bishop of Winchester. In 1913 the first seaplane was successfully tested here. The Little Pond is far from little, and both are used for sailing, fishing and bird watching, for many rare wild-fowl visit them.
FRENSHAM MILL. The dam, bridge and water channels associated with the old water mill which ceased working in 1926 are still visible to the south west of the village.
ST MARY'S CHURCH. Dating from 1239, the church houses the legendary witch's cauldron, 3 ft in diameter, used by a Mother Ludlam who in the Middle Ages lived in a cave near Waverley Abbey (see under Farnham). Of more religious significance is the 13th century font made of Purbeck marble, and the west window which is probably one of the earliest perpendicular windows in the country.

Garden Centres & Nurseries
  Frensham Garden Centre, *The Reeds, Frensham, GU10 3BP* ☎ *01252 792545.*
Hotels & Inns
  ★Frensham Pond Hotel, *Pond Lane, Frensham, GU10 2QB* ☎ *01252 795161.*
  Mariners Hotel, *Millbridge, Frensham, GU10 3DJ* ☎ *01252 792050.*
Park
  Frensham Country Park, *Frensham (Enquiries* ☎ *01252 792416).*

Pubs
★Blue Bell Inn, *Batts Corner, Dockenfield, Frensham, GU10 4EX* ☎ *01252 792801.*
 Holly Bush, *Shortfield Common, Frensham, GU10 3BJ* ☎ *01252 793593.*
Tea Room & Cafe
 Frensham Coffee Shop, *Frensham Garden Centre* ☎ *01252 794562.*

See also The Bourne, Churt, Farnham, Hindhead, Rowledge, Tilford, Wrecclesham. 1 mile from
the Hampshire boundary.

Frimley
(including Frimley Green)

An early settlement with Saxon origins, Frimley was a predominantly farming
community until well into this century. To the south of the village, the Basingstoke
Canal goes over the London to Southampton railway on an impressive four-arch
aqueduct.

BLACKWATER VALLEY VISITOR CENTRE. A centre providing information on activities and places to visit
in the Blackwater Valley.
FRIMLEY LODGE PARK. An excellent all round park facility, located in beautiful mature woodlands
next to the Basingstoke Canal. There are canal side and woodland walks as well as many
sporting facilities, and the park is also used for festivals and fairs.

Art & Craft Equipment
 Fordham-Barnett Trust, *29 Stonehouse Rise, Frimley, GU15 5DP* ☎ *01276 24264.*
Golf Course
 Frimley Lodge Park, *Sturt Road, Frimley Green* ☎ *01276 686252.*
Golf Course & Driving Range
 Pine Ridge Golf Centre, *Old Bisley Road, Frimley, GU16 5NX* ☎ *01276 20770.*
Hotels & Inns
 Kingfisher Inn, *Wharf Road, Frimley Green, GU16 6PT* ☎ *01252 836648.*
★Lakeside Hotel, *Wharf Road, Frimley Green, GU16 6JR* ☎ *01252 838000.*
Library
 SCC Lending Library, *4 Beech Road, Frimley Green, GU16 6LQ* ☎ *01252 835530.*
Model Shop
 Surrey & Hants Models, *84 High Street, Frimley, GU16 5JE* ☎ *01276 27311.*
Park
 Frimley Lodge Park, *Sturt Road, Frimley Green.*
Pubs
 Old Wheatsheaf, *205 Frimley Green Road, Frimley Green, GU16 6LA* ☎ *01252 835074.*
 Railway Arms, *78 High Street, Frimley, GU16 5JE* ☎ *01276 23544.*
 Rose & Thistle, *1 Sturt Road, Frimley Green, GU16 6HT* ☎ *01252 835524.*
 White Hart Hotel, *High Street, Frimley, GU16 5HU* ☎ *Ex Dir.*
Railway
 Frimley & Ascot Locomotive Club, *Frimley Lodge Park (Enquiries* ☎ *01276 475902).*
Restaurants
 Ancient Raj, *9 The Parade, High Street, Frimley, GU16 5HY* ☎ *01276 21503.*
 Gallant Chinese, *2 The Parade, High Street, Frimley, GU16 5HY* ☎ *01276 681321.*
 Kings Head(Harvester), *Guildford Road, Frimley Green, GU16 6NR* ☎ *01252 835431.*
 Villa Bianca, *58 High Street, Frimley, GU16 5JE* ☎ *01276 62879.*
Sports & Leisure Centre
 Tomlinscote Sport Centre, *Tomlinscote Way, Frimley, GU16 5PY* ☎ *01276 670316.*
Take-Aways
 Frimley Tandoori, *47 Frimley High Street, Frimley, GU16 5HJ* ☎ *01276 24637.*

Herbies, *5 Beaumaris Parade, Balmoral Drive, Frimley, GU16 5UR* ☎ *01252 838200.*
Hong Kong 97, *19 Farm Road, Frimley, GU16 5TH* ☎ *01276 676888.*
Lemon Plaice, *68 High Street, Frimley, GU16 5JE* ☎ *01276 64577.*
Silver Sea Fish Bar, *15 Guildford Road, Frimley Green, GU16 6NL* ☎ *01252 835262.*
Starburger, *29 High Street, Frimley, GU16 5HJ* ☎ *01276 24380.*
Tasty Eater, *10 The Parade, High Street, Frimley, GU16 5HY* ☎ *01276 20525.*
Wing Lee, *220 Frimley Green Road, Frimley Green, GU16 6LL* ☎ *01252 835952.*
Yum Yum, *82 High Street, Frimley, GU15 3RS* ☎ *01276 63280.*

See also Camberley, Deepcut, Mytchett. 2 miles from the Berkshire boundary & 1 mile from the Hampshire boundary.

Gatton

Roman and Saxon remains have been found at Gatton. It was mentioned in the Domesday Book and Henry VIII gave the land to Anne of Cleves. Gatton was a rotten borough until 1832, returning two Members of Parliament inspite of its tiny electorate. It had always been a farming community, and most of the houses were swallowed up when the park was landscaped.

GATTON HALL. An impressive building set amid trees on top of the North Downs. The park was landscaped in 1751 by Capability Brown, who also dug the 40 acre lake at this time, and the pillared portico was added by Sir Jeremiah Colman in 1891. In the early 19th century the Hall was owned by Lord Monson who was a collector of ecclesiastical furniture. Gatton Hall is now a school.
GATTON TOWN HALL. The so-called town hall is a tiny Classical temple built in 1765.
ST ANDREW'S CHURCH. A Victorian church with Saxon origins which contains a wealth of ancient furniture collected from all over Europe by Lord Monson.

Farm Shop
Fanny's Farm Shop, *Lodge Farm, Markedge Lane, Gatton, RH1 3AN* ☎ *01737 554444.*
MEMBER OF 'A TASTE OF SURREY' - FRESH FARM FOOD & UNUSUAL PLANTS.
Tea Room
Fanny's Farm Shop ☎ *01737 554444.*

See also Bletchingley, Earlswood, Kingswood, Merstham, Nutfield, Redhill, Reigate, Tadworth.

Godalming

An old wool town and once a centre of the cloth trade, Godalming was an important coaching stop on the London to Portsmouth road in stagecoach days. It is full of narrow streets and interesting half timbered houses and inns of Tudor and Stuart days. The polygonal white market hall, with its arcades and cupola, is the focal point of the long street. In 1881 the town became the first in the world to have a public electricity supply.

BUSBRIDGE LAKES. Forty acres of lakes and parkland with 120 species of exotic birds and ornamental waterfowl from all over the world. Around the three lakes, the follies, grottoes and caves are nature trails and picnic spots.
CHARTERHOUSE SCHOOL. Charterhouse School is north west of the town. The school was founded in 1611 by Thomas Sutton and moved here from London in 1872. The Victorian buildings with their turrets and Gothic brickwork, by Philip Hardwick(1792-1870), are dominated by the 150ft Founder's Tower, and the chapel was built in the 1920s by Sir Giles Gilbert Scott(1880-1960).
CHARTERHOUSE SCHOOL MUSEUM. The school's collection of local antiquities, classical pottery, ancient Peruvian pottery, natural history, and relics of the school, are housed in two Victorian Gothic halls, built in 1890.

CHURCH OF ST PETER AND ST PAUL. The church has a central medieval tower and leaded spire. It stands on a Saxon site and contains work of all periods, from Norman times to the restorations of the 19th century.

GODALMING MUSEUM. The museum shows the story of the town and the Godalming Hundred from prehistoric to modern times. There is a special display commemorating the architect Sir Edwin Lutyens(1869-1944) and the museum has a Gertrude Jekyll(1843-1932) style walled garden. There is also a local history library.

KING'S ARMS HOTEL. An old coaching inn bearing the date 1753, but in fact built much earlier. Peter the Great stayed as a paying guest in 1698, and Tsar Alexander I of Russia and King Frederick William of Prussia dined in 1816.

OLD TOWN HALL. Built in 1814 on the site of an earlier market hall, and known also as the Hundred House or Pepperpot. The site was a centre of local government for over 1,000 years.

RED LION. Once part of the original grammar school.

RIVER WEY & GODALMING NAVIGATIONS. See entry under this heading in Guildford.

Godalming old Town Hall

Antique Dealers
Church Street Antiques, *15 Church Street, Godalming, GU7 1EL* ☎ *01483 860894.*
Olde Curiosity Shoppe, *99 High Street, Godalming, GU7 1AQ* ☎ *01483 415889.*
Priory Antiques, *29 Church Street, Godalming, GU7 1EL* ☎ *01483 421804.*

Art Gallery
Godalming Galleries, *3 Wharf Street, Godalming, GU7 1NN* ☎ *01483 422254.*

Art & Craft Equipment
Arts & Artists, *45 Bridge Street, Godalming, GU7 1HL* ☎ *01483 423432.*

Boat Hire
Farncombe Boat House, *Catteshall Lock, Catteshall Road, Godalming, GU7 1NH* ☎ *01483 421306.*
Godalming Packetboat Co, *The Wharf, Godalming (Enquiries* ☎ *01483 425397).*

Book Shops
Bookshelf Bargains, *111 High Street, Godalming, GU7 1AQ* ☎ *01483 424252.*
Church Street Bookshop, *26 Church Street, Godalming, GU7 1EW* ☎ *01483 418878.*
Eureka Bookroom, *19a Church Street, Godalming, GU7 1EL* ☎ *01483 426968.*
WH Smith, *82 High Street, Godalming, GU7 1DU* ☎ *01483 417090.*

Entertainment Complex
Borough Hall, *The Burys, Godalming, GU7 1HR* ☎ *01483 869071.*
GODALMING'S VERY POPULAR MULTI-PURPOSE COMPLEX. USED FOR CINEMA, DINNER DANCES, WEDDING RECEPTIONS, BARN DANCES, BLOOD DONORS, OPERATICS, MUSIC FESTIVALS, CHURCH, NURSERY SCHOOL, MATHS FRENCH AND DRAMA TUITION, AEROBICS, MARTIAL ARTS, SADDLERY, FLEA MARKETS, FLOWER CLUBS. TIERED SEATING 250 CAPACITY.

Garden Centre
Scats, *Farmers Centre, Brighton Road, Godalming, GU7 1NS* ☎ *01483 415101.*

Hotels & Inns
★Inn on The Lake, *Ockford Road, Godalming, GU7 1RH* ☎ *01483 415575.*
Kings Arms & Royal Hotel, *24 High Street, Godalming, GU7 1EB* ☎ *01483 421545.*

Library
SCC Lending Library, *Bridge Street, Godalming, GU7 1HT* ☎ *01483 422743.*

Model Shop
Godalming Radio Controlled Models, *3 Bridge Street, Godalming, GU7 1HY* ☎ *01483 421425.*

Museum
 Godalming Museum, *109a High Street, Godalming, GU7 1AQ* ☎ *01483 426510.*
Pubs
 Anchor Inn, *110 Ockford Road, Godalming, GU7 1RG* ☎ *01483 417085.*
 Charterhouse Arms, *Deanery Road, Godalming, GU7 2PQ* ☎ *01483 861291.*
 Cricketers, *37 Nightingale Road, Godalming, GU7 2HU* ☎ *01483 420273.*
 King Alfred, *18 Quarry Hill, Godalming, GU7 2NW* ☎ *01483 421467.*
 Ram Cider House, *Catteshall Lane, Godalming, GU7 1LW* ☎ *01483 421093.*
 Red Lion Hotel, *1 Mill Lane, Godalming, GU7 1DT* ☎ *01483 415207.*
 Richmond Arms, *149 High Street, Godalming, GU7 1AF* ☎ *01483 416515.*
 Rose & Crown, *4 Mill Lane, Godalming, GU7 1HF* ☎ *01483 417764.*
 Star Inn, *17 Church Street, Godalming, GU7 1EL* ☎ *01483 417717.*
 Woolpack, *28 High Street, Godalming, GU7 1DZ* ☎ *01483 414003.*
Restaurants
 Godalming Tandoori, *143 High Street, Godalming, GU7 1AF* ☎ *01483 426084.*
 Mongolian, *10 Wharf Street, Godalming, GU7 1NN* ☎ *01483 414155.*
  DELICIOUS BARBECUED FOOD - EAT AS MUCH AS YOU LIKE FOR £8.95 - INFORMAL ATMOSPHERE.
 Pizza Piazza, *78 High Street, Godalming, GU7 1DU* ☎ *01483 429191.*
 Pizzavino, *131 High Street, Godalming, GU7 1AF* ☎ *01483 422685.*
 Slim Jim's, *62 High Street, Godalming, GU7 1DU* ☎ *01483 416439.*
 Supreme Tandoori, *6 Bridge Street, Godalming, GU7 1HY* ☎ *01483 417434.*
Sports & Leisure Centre
 Godalming Leisure Centre - See under Farncombe.
Tea Rooms & Cafes
 By The Wey, *Farncombe Boat House, Catteshall Road, Godalming, GU7 1NH*
 ☎ *01483 418769.*
 Cellar, *42 High Street, Godalming, GU7 1DY* ☎ *01483 417097.*
 G Bassani, *142 High Street, Godalming, GU7 1AB* ☎ *01483 416538.*
 Piggies, *Station Approach, Godalming, GU7 1EU* ☎ *01483 421022.*
Wildlife Park
 Busbridge Lakes, *Hambledon Road, Godalming, GU8 4AY* ☎ *01483 421955.*
Wine Bars & Cafe Bars
 Aitch's Bar Cafe, *1 Angel Court, High Street, Godalming, GU7 1DT* ☎ *01483 861052.*
 Piggies, *14a Church Street, Godalming, GU7 1EW* ☎ *01483 416669.*

See also Bramley, Compton, Eashing, Farncombe, Hambledon, Hascombe, Hurtmore, Hydestile, Loseley, Milford, Peper Harow, Shackleford, Shalford, Wanborough, Witley, Wonersh, Wormley.

Godstone
(including South Godstone)

In Elizabethan days Godstone was a centre for the leather trade, and later on of the gunpowder industry. Being just one day's travel from London, most of the notable buildings of that period were inns. From the 17th to the 19th century stone was mined from under the North Downs, and there are some 300 miles of uncharted tunnels and galleries between Godstone and Reigate. High quality sand has since been quarried, and more recently there has been drilling for oil. Today Godstone is a pretty village in unspoilt North Downs country, with a large village green and a pond. The railway station is two miles south of Godstone at South Godstone.

BAY POND. A nature reserve between the White Hart and the Church, run by the Surrey Wildlife Trust.
GODSTONE FARM. A farm set in 40 acres, where children are encouraged to climb into the pens and touch many of the young animals. There is a nature trail, an adventure playground and a picnic area.

HUNDRED'S KNOLL. On the A25 just over a mile to the west of the village stands a monument to the Saxon tithingmen from the surrounding villages of the Hundred of Tandridge, who met on that hill as the first local government and court in the Godstone Rural District.

LEIGH MILL. On the site of a mill mentioned in the Domesday Book, it was owned by the Evelyn family and used as a gunpowder mill at the time of the Spanish armada in 1588. Sir John Evelyn founded several powder mills in Surrey, and gunpowder was supplied to the Crown from here until 1636. After gunpowder production ceased, the mill was used as a corn mill up until World War I.

ST MARY'S ALMSHOUSES. Eight tudor-style almshouses in Church Lane designed by Sir George Gilbert Scott(1811-1878) and built in 1872.

ST NICHOLAS'S CHURCH. Originally 12th century, it was almost entirely rebuilt in 1872 by Sir George Gilbert Scott(1811-1878), although the structure of the 13th century tower remains. The church contains fine stained glass windows, and the 17th century black & white marble tomb of Sir John Evelyn, and his wife.

WHITE HART. Built in the 1300s during the reign of Edward II, visited by Richard II and licensed since his reign, it was altered in Elizabethan times. It was known for a time as the Clayton Arms, after Sir Robert Clayton who was Lord Mayor of London in 1679 and who, by the time he died, was the biggest landowner in the district of Godstone & Bletchingley. The Czar of Russia stayed here in 1815, as did Queen Victoria on her way to Brighton.

Book Shop
Latter-Day Book Store, *11 High Street, Godstone, RH9 8LS* ☎ *01883 744060.*
Farm Attraction
Godstone Farm, *Tilburstow Hill Road, Godstone, RH9 8LX* ☎ *01883 742546.*
Garden Centres & Nurseries
Brook Nursery Garden Centre, *Eastbourne Road, South Godstone, RH9 8JB*
☎ *01342 893265.*
Knights Garden Centre, *Nags Hall Nursery, Oxted Road, Godstone, RH9 8DB*
☎ *01883 742275.*
Nettleton Nurseries, *Ivy Mill Lane, Godstone, RH9 8NF* ☎ *01883 742426.*
Walkers Garden Centre, *Anglefield Corner, Eastbourne Road, South Godstone, RH9 8JG*
☎ *01342 893109.*
Windsor Farm Nursery, *Bletchingley Road, Godstone, RH9 8NB* ☎ *01883 742284.*
Woodham Nursery, *Eastbourne Road, South Godstone, RH9 8EZ* ☎ *01342 892331.*
Hotels & Inns
★◆Bell Hotel, *128 High Street, Godstone, RH9 8DX* ☎ *01883 743133.*
Godstone Hotel, *87 High Street, Godstone, RH9 8DT* ☎ *01883 742461.*
◆Old Surrey, *Godstone Hill, Godstone, RH9 8AP* ☎ *01883 743480.*
Nature Reserve
Bay Pond *(Enquiries* ☎ *01372 379509).*
Pick Your Own
Flower Farm, *Flower Lane, Godstone, RH9 8DE* ☎ *01883 743636.*
OPEN MAY TO OCTOBER; ENTRANCE ON A25, 1/2 MILE EAST OF VILLAGE.
Pubs
★Fox & Hounds, *Tilburstow Hill Road, South Godstone, RH9 8LY* ☎ *01342 893474.*
Hare & Hounds, *Bletchingley Road, Godstone, RH9 8LN* ☎ *01883 742296.*
Railway Hotel, *Eastbourne Road, South Godstone, RH9 8EZ* ☎ *01342 892104.*
Restaurants
Coach House, *Godstone Hotel* ☎ *01883 742461.*
Green Rooms, *The Green, Godstone, RH9 8DZ* ☎ *01883 742288.*
La Bonne Auberge, *Tilburstow Hill Road, South Godstone, RH9 8JY* ☎ *01342 892318.*
Little Chef, *Halfway House, Water Lane, South Godstone, RH9 8JX* ☎ *01342 892316.*
White Hart(Beefeater), *71 High Street, Godstone, RH9 8DU* ☎ *01883 742521.*
Tea Room
Godstone Farm ☎ *01883 742546.*

Vineyard
  Godstone Vineyards, *Quarry Road, Godstone, RH9 8ZA* ☎ *01883 744590.*
  Open all year, daily, 10am - 5.30pm; vineyard trail, gift shop, morning coffees, light lunches, afternoon teas; signposted off A22, just north of M25.

See also Bletchingley, Blindley Heath, Caterham, Crowhurst, Nutfield, Oxted, Tandridge, Woldingham.

Gomshall

Tanning was once an important industry in Gomshall and known about throughout the world. The tanneries, which were rebuilt and enlarged after a fire in 1890, have only recently been closed down.

Gomshall Gallery. Exhibitions of contemporary arts and crafts, furniture, handmade pottery and paintings, combined with a fine wine cellar.

Gomshall Mill. A working water mill on the River Tillingbourne with origins going back to the 11th century. It has two water wheels which have both been carefully restored. The smaller wooden wheel is an exact reproduction of a clasp iron construction dating back to the 11th century and is capable of generating electricity. The larger 18ft wheel is the biggest water wheel in the south of England. Gomshall Mill became one of the most important mills in this industrial valley and operated commercially until 1952. The old mill pond has now been converted to gardens and the building to a restaurant and shop.

Antique Dealers
  Coach House Antiques, *The Coach House, Station Road, Gomshall, GU5 9NY* ☎ *01483 203838.*
  Nice Things, *Station Road, Gomshall, GU5 9NS* ☎ *01483 202963.*
Art Gallery
  Gomshall Gallery, *Station Road, Gomshall, GU5 9LB* ☎ *01483 203795.*
Pub
  ★Compasses, *Station Road, Gomshall, GU5 9LA* ☎ *01483 202506.*
Restaurants
  Gomshall Mill, *Station Road, Gomshall, GU5 9LB* ☎ *01483 202433.*
  Mulligan's, *Station Road, Gomshall, GU5 9NP* ☎ *01483 202242.*
Tea Room
  Gomshall Mill, *Station Road, Gomshall, GU5 9LB* ☎ *01483 202433.*
Water Mill
  Gomshall Mill, *Station Road, Gomshall, GU5 9LB* ☎ *01483 202433.*

See also Abinger Common, Albury, Blackheath, Clandon, Holmbury St Mary, Horsley, Merrow, Newlands Corner, Peaslake, Shere, Wotton.

NOTES

Grayswood

PARISH CHURCH. Designed and built in 1901 by a Swedish Naval architect, Axel Haig.

Antique Dealer
  JK Glover, *Grayswood Common, Grayswood, GU27 2EB* ☎ *01428 642184.*
Pub
  Wheatsheaf Inn, *Grayswood Road, Grayswood, GU27 2DE* ☎ *01428 644440.*

See also Brook, Chiddingfold, Haslemere, Hindhead, Thursley, Wormley. 2 miles from the Hampshire boundary & 2 miles from the Sussex boundary.

Guildford

For many centuries the ancient capital and county town of Surrey, Guildford stands where a ford crossed the River Wey in ancient times. It is tucked into a gap in the North Downs, and is surrounded by hills on all sides. Once an important stop on the Pilgrim's Way, the town's prosperity grew as a centre of dyeing and finishing cloth during the middle ages, when blue kersey material was produced exclusively in the town. Guildford now is one of the most impressive towns in the Home Counties and its steep and attractive cobbled High Street, lined with historic buildings, is one of the finest streets in southern England.

ANGEL HOTEL. This is the only survivor of the splendid coaching inns for which Guildford was once famous. There is an old wooden gallery, a coaching yard, and an undercroft with an internal staircase.

BELLERBY THEATRE & BELLAIRS PLAYHOUSE. Two theatres which belong to the Guildford School of Acting, and where a wide variety of plays are staged.

CASTLE ARCH. The medieval Castle Arch stands at the approach to the gardens which surround the castle keep.

CATHEDRAL OF THE HOLY SPIRIT. Built in the shape of a cross with pink bricks made from local clay, the Cathedral is a conspicuous landmark dominating the skyline on the top of Stag Hill west of the town. The simplified Gothic design by Sir Edward Maufe was accepted in 1932, and building began in 1936. The Second World War held up the building of the cathedral, which was finally consecrated in 1961. Surrey had no cathedral until this was built, and it is the only modern cathedral in the south of England.

CHURCH OF THE HOLY TRINITY. A large fine brick church at the top of the High Street rebuilt in the mid 18th century but having a late 19th century east end. Michael Rysbrack(1693-1770) is thought to be the sculptor of the monument to Arthur Onslow(1691-1768), speaker of the House of Commons for thirty three years.

CIVIC HALL. The home of the Guildford Philharmonic Orchestra, which gives a series of concerts here and at Guildford Cathedral. A wide programme of events is staged here including concerts from classical to pop.

GUILDFORD CASTLE. The Norman Castle built by Henry II during the 12th century has only one remaining part, the ruined shell of a mighty three-storeyed square castle keep, which is Guildford's oldest building. This is now surrounded by attractive public gardens, with a bandstand and an open air theatre. There is also a brass rubbing centre.

GUILDFORD HOUSE GALLERY. Built in 1660, Guildford House is a timber framed building with a carved staircase and finely decorated plaster ceilings. It is now Guildford Borough's art gallery showing changing exhibitions of painting, sculpture and craft work of regional and national interest and selections from the Borough's own art collection.

GUILDFORD MUSEUM & MUNIMENT ROOM. Adjoining Castle Arch is a 17th century brick building housing the town's museum. Exhibits cover the history and archaeology of Surrey, concentrating on the Guildford area and including items from the 6th century Saxon cemetery at

Guildown, medieval tiles from Chertsey Abbey, examples of Wealden ironwork, and needlework and needlework implements. In the Muniment Room are kept over 100,000 documents relating to Guildford and district.

GUILDHALL. The historic and decorative town hall houses many beautiful borough treasures and the mayoral insignia. It has a balcony and a bell tower, and features a great overhanging gilded clock made by John Aylward who, having been refused permission to work in Guildford in 1683, made this ornate clock, gave it to the Guildhall and was subsequently given the freedom to trade in the town.

The Guildhall Clock, Guildford

HOSPITAL OF THE BLESSED TRINITY. A group of almshouses better known as Abbot's Hospital after its founder, George Abbot, who was Archbishop of Canterbury in 1619. A magnificent arched gateway with four turrets leads to an enclosed courtyard in front of this Tudor brick building, which has been in continuous use as an almshouse for old people since it was built in 1619.

LEWIS CARROLL. The town's connection with the Reverend Charles Lutwidge Dodgson(1832-1898), better known as Lewis Carroll, is illustrated in the Museum, where his letters and other relics are preserved. He never married, living with his family in Castle Hill, and is buried in the Mount Cemetery.

RIVER WEY & GODALMING NAVIGATIONS. In 1653 the River Wey was dredged, the bends straightened and locks built so that heavy barges could come up from London as far as the town wharf by the bridge. In 1761 the navigation was extended to Godalming wharf, a total distance of 19 miles from the River Thames at Weybridge. The navigation is one of the earliest historic waterways and retains its old locks and weirs. The importance of the Wey declined when the railway arrived in 1845, but it is now popular once again. Boats can be hired along the river, which also supports many species of water birds, flora and fauna. Licenses are available from Thames Lock, Pyrford Marina, Stoke Lock, Guildford Boathouse or Farncombe Boat House. At Dapdune Wharf in Guildford there is an old horse-drawn Wey barge and the associated buildings for public viewing.

RIVERSIDE PARK. An informal parkland of 230 acres adjacent to the A3 north of the town. The park consists of four main habitats; meadow land, woodland, marshland, and open water, and special emphasis is on nature conservation and habitat creation.

ROYAL GRAMMAR SCHOOL. Founded from the provisions of the will of Robert Beckingham in 1509, the school acquired the right to style itself 'Royal Grammar School' from King Edward VI in 1552. The outstanding and unspoilt Tudor schoolhouse, containing a chained library dating from 1576, has stood at the top of the High Street for over 400 years.

ST MARY'S CHURCH. At the bottom of the High Street, the church has a saxon tower and some wall paintings.

SPECTRUM. Set in 26 acres, the Spectrum has a leisure pool; competition, teaching & diving pools; a 32 lane tenpin bowling centre; olympic sized ice arena; health & fitness suite; sports arena; squash courts, and athletics stadium.

THE FRIARY. The Friary Shopping Centre stands on the site of a Dominican friary founded in 1275, which in turn has also seen a house, some barracks and the Friary Meux brewery.

TUNSGATE ARCH. A somewhat formidable portico with four large columns, opposite the Guildhall, which until 1626 housed the corn market.

UNDERCROFT. This is a stone vaulted medieval basement at 72 High Street dating from the 13th century and described by English Heritage as the finest medieval building of its kind. Prior to November 1994, the Undercroft was the home of the Guildford Tourist Information Centre.

UNIVERSITY OF SURREY. The University of Surrey campus lies between the cathedral and the by-pass. The gallery shows various exhibitions, usually by contemporary artists. The theatre has a varied programme of events most days, including lunchtime and evening concerts, recitals, drama, dance and lectures. The Library Gallery houses exhibitions usually by contemporary artists.

YVONNE ARNAUD THEATRE. The theatre was opened in 1958 and is named after the actress. It is in a delightful setting overlooking the River Wey and its weeping willows, and is famous throughout the country for attracting major stars to its top quality productions, many of which later transfer to London's West End.

As from August 1995, all Guildford five figure telephone numbers will be changed to six figure numbers by adding a 5 in front of the existing five figure number.

Antique Dealers

Antique Centre, *22 Haydon Place, Guildford, GU1 4LL* ☎ *01483 67817.*
Back & Beyond, *64 Chertsey Street, Guildford, GU1 4HL* ☎ *01483 300434.*
David Nash Antiques, *81 Stoke Road, Guildford, GU1 4HT* ☎ *01483 38807.*
Denning Antiques, *1 Chapel Street, Guildford, GU1 3UH* ☎ *01483 39595.*
G Oliver & Sons, *St Catherines House, Portsmouth Road, Guildford, GU3 1LJ* ☎ *01483 575427.*
Gillinghams Antiques, *148 London Road, Guildford, GU1 1UF* ☎ *01483 61952.*
Peter Bradley, *9 Martyr Road, Guildford, GU1 4LF* ☎ *01483 505457.*
Peter Goodall, *Bull Head Gate, 12b Market Street, Guildford, GU1 4LB* ☎ *01483 36650.*
What-Not Antiques, *6 Woodbridge Road, Guildford, GU1 4PY* ☎ *01483 306358.*

Art Galleries - Public

Guildford House Gallery, *155 High Street, Guildford, GU1 3AJ* ☎ *01483 444740.*
University of Surrey Library Gallery, *Stag Hill, Guildford, GU2 5XH* ☎ *01483 300800 x2112.*

Art Gallery

Forest Gallery, *180 High Street, Guildford, GU1 3HW* ☎ *01483 66222.*

Art & Craft Equipment

Dome, *Pannells Court, Guildford, GU1 4EU* ☎ *01483 36000.*
Guildford Art Supplies, *59 Quarry Street, Guildford, GU1 3UA* ☎ *01483 572686.*

Boat Hire

Guildford Boat House, *Millbrook, Guildford, GU1 3XJ* ☎ *01483 504494.*

Book Shops

Avatar Comics, *5 The Quadrant, Bridge Street, Guildford, GU1 4SG* ☎ *01483 304781.*
Bookends, *1 Friary Street, Guildford, GU1 4EH* ☎ *01483 506484.*
Charles W Traylen, *49 Quarry Street, Guildford, GU1 3UA* ☎ *01483 572424.*
Penguin Bookshop, *27 White Lion Walk, Guildford, GU1 3DN* ☎ *01483 32971.*
Pilgrims' Bookshop, *60 Quarry Street, Guildford, GU1 3UA* ☎ *01483 573707.*
SPCK Bookshop, *St Marys Church, Quarry Street, Guildford, GU1 3UP* ☎ *01483 60316.*
Sherratt & Hughes, *20 Friary Shopping Centre, Guildford, GU1 4YN* ☎ *01483 502801.*
Thomas Thorp, *170 High Street, Guildford, GU1 3HW* ☎ *01483 62770.*
University Bookshop, *University of Surrey, Stag Hill, Guildford, GU2 5XH* ☎ *01483 259169.*
WH Smith, *56 High Street, Guildford, GU1 3ES* ☎ *01483 576217.*
Waterstone's, *35 North Street, Guildford, GU1 4TE* ☎ *01483 302919.*

Cathedral

Guildford Cathedral, *Stag Hill, Guildford, GU2 5UP* ☎ *01483 65287.*

Cinema

Odeon Cinema, *Epsom Road, Guildford, GU1 3JN* ☎ *01426 941049.*
ADVANCE BOOKING MASTERCARD & VISA; FRIDAY & SATURDAY 11AM, 7PM; SUNDAY TO THURSDAY 1PM, 7PM: 01483 578017.

Civic Hall

Guildford Civic Hall, *London Road, Guildford, GU1 2AA* ☎ *01483 444555.*

Crazy Golf

Guildford Lido, *Stoke Road, Guildford, GU1 1HB* ☎ *01483 444888.*

Garden Centres & Nurseries

Astolat Nurseries, *Old Portsmouth Road, Peasmarsh, Guildford, GU3 1NE* ☎ *01483 69790.*
B & Q, *Ladymead Retail Centre, Woodbridge Road, Guildford, GU1 1AJ* ☎ *01483 304881.*
Mayfields Nursery, *Whitmore Lane, Guildford, GU4 7QB* ☎ *01483 306622.*

Golf Course

Roker Park Golf Course, *Holly Lane, Aldershot Road, Guildford, GU3 3PB* ☎ *01483 236677.*

Guest Houses

Abeille House, *119 Stoke Road, Guildford, GU1 1ET* ☎ *01483 32200.*

Atkinsons, *129 Stoke Road, Guildford, GU1 1ET* ☎ *01483 38260.*

COMFORTABLE GUEST HOUSE NEAR TOWN CENTRE. COLOUR TV, TEA AND COFFEE IN ALL ROOMS; SOME EN-SUITE.

Bearstead, *16 Waterden Road, Guildford, GU1 2AW* ☎ *01483 575577.*

Bourne Weybrook House, *113 Stoke Road, Guildford, GU1 1ET* ☎ *01483 302394.*

QUIET FAMILY B&B NEAR TOWN, PARK, LEISURE CENTRE, STATIONS AND A3. FROM £14D/£18S INCLUDING DELICIOUS ENGLISH BREAKFAST.

Devon House, *11 Waterden Road, Guildford, GU1 2AN* ☎ *01483 67927.*

JS Youngs, *91 Portsmouth Road, Guildford, GU2 5BS* ☎ *01483 39308.*

Newman's, *24 Waterden Road, Guildford, GU1 2AY* ☎ *01483 60558.*

Guildford Institute

Guildford Institute, *Ward Street, Guildford, GU1 4LH* ☎ *01483 62142.*

FOUNDED 1834. PROVIDES A VARIETY OF ACTIVITIES FOR LOCAL PEOPLE; SOCIAL CLUB, RESTAURANT, LIBRARY, MEETING ROOMS, CENTRE FOR UNIVERSITY ADULT EDUCATION COURSES. FOR MEMBERSHIP DETAILS AND FURTHER INFORMATION CONTACT DURING OFFICE HOURS.

Historic Buildings

Guildford Castle, *Castle Street, Guildford (Enquiries* ☎ *01483 444702).*

Guildhall, *High Street, Guildford, GU1 3AA* ☎ *01483 444035.*

Hospital of the Blessed Trinity, *High Street, Guildford, GU1 3AJ (Enquiries* ☎ *01483 62670).*

Loseley Park - See under Loseley Park.

Hotels & Inns

★Angel Hotel, *91 High Street, Guildford, GU1 3DP* ☎ *01483 64555.*

Blanes Court Hotel, *4 Albury Road, Guildford, GU1 2BT* ☎ *01483 573171.*

Carlton Hotel, *36 London Road, Guildford, GU1 2AF* ☎ *01483 575158.*

Clavadel Hotel, *Epsom Road, Guildford, GU1 2JH* ☎ *01483 69066.*

Conference Office, *University of Surrey, Stag Hill, Guildford, GU2 5XH* ☎ *01483 259243.*

Crawford House Hotel, *73 Farnham Road, Guildford, GU2 5PF* ☎ *01483 579299.*

Days Inn, *2 The Billings, Walnut Tree Close, Guildford, GU1 4UL* ☎ *01483 440470.*

★Forte Crest, *Egerton Road, Guildford, GU2 5XZ* ☎ *01483 574444.*

Mary Rose, *3 Leapale Road, Guildford, GU1 4JX* ☎ *01483 572857.*

Rats Castle, *80 Sydenham Road, Guildford, GU1 3SA* ☎ *01483 572410.*

Royal Hotel, *132 Worplesdon Road, Guildford, GU2 6RT* ☎ *01483 575173.*

Quinns Hotel, *78 Epsom Road, Guildford, GU1 2BX* ☎ *01483 60422.*

★White Horse Hotel(Jarvis), *253 High Street, Guildford, GU1 3BZ* ☎ *01483 64511.*

Y Centre(YMCA), *Bridge Street, Guildford, GU1 4SB* ☎ *01483 32555.*

Ice Skating

Guildford Spectrum, *Parkway, Guildford, GU1 1UP* ☎ *01483 444777.*

Information Centre

County Information Centre, *Guildford Library* ☎ *01483 34120.*

Tourist Information Centre, *14 Tunsgate, Guildford, GU1 3QT* ☎ *01483 444007.*

Libraries

SCC Lending Library, *North Street, Guildford, GU1 4AL* ☎ *01483 68496.*

George Edwards Library, *University of Surrey, Stag Hill, Guildford, GU2 5XH* ☎ *01483 259287.*

Guildford Institute, *Ward Street, Guildford, GU1 4LH* ☎ *01483 62142.*

Guildford Muniment Room, *Castle Arch, Quarry Street, Guildford, GU1 3SX* ☎ *01483 573942.*

Surrey Archaeological Society Library, *Castle Arch, Quarry Street, Guildford, GU1 3SX* ☎ *01483 32454.*

Surrey Local Studies Library, *77 North Street, Guildford, GU1 4AW* ☎ *01483 34054.*

Model Shops

Antics, *89e Woodbridge Road, Guildford, GU1 4QD* ☎ *01483 39115.*

Model Aerodrome, *30 Friary Shopping Centre, Guildford, GU1 4YN* ☎ *01483 578682.*

GUILDFORD

Museum
Guildford Museum, *Castle Arch, Quarry Street, Guildford, GU1 3SX* ☎ *01483 503497.*
Nature Reserve
Riverside Park, *Riverside, Bellfields, Guildford (Enquiries* ☎ *01483 505050).*
Pubs
Astolat, *9 Old Palace Road, Onslow, Guildford, GU2 5TU* ☎ *01483 60708.*
Bell Inn, *2 Bellfields Road, Stoke, Guildford, GU1 1NH* ☎ *01483 61694.*
Britannia Inn, *9 Millmead, Guildford, GU2 5BE* ☎ *01483 572160.*
Cannon Inn, *3 Portsmouth Road, Guildford, GU2 5BL* ☎ *01483 575089.*
Cricketers, *Aldershot Road, Guildford, GU3 3AA* ☎ *01483 575901.*
Drummonds Arms, *55 Woodbridge Road, Guildford, GU1 4RF* ☎ *01483 578999.*
Elm Tree, *13 Stoke Fields, Guildford, GU1 4LS* ☎ *01483 62567.*
Greyhound, *11 High Street, Guildford, GU1 5AB* ☎ *Ex Dir.*
Hare & Hounds, *57 Broad Street, Park Barn, Guildford, GU3 3BG* ☎ *01483 63969.*
Holroyd Arms, *36 Aldershot Road, Guildford, GU2 6AF* ☎ *01483 60215.*
◆Jolly Farmer, *Millbrook, Guildford, GU1 3XJ* ☎ *01483 38779.*
Kings Head, *27 Kings Road, Guildford, GU1 4JW* ☎ *01483 68957.*
★Kings Head, *Quarry Street, Guildford, GU1 3TY* ☎ *01483 575004.*
Live & Let Live, *57 Haydon Place, Guildford, GU1 4NE* ☎ *01483 64372.*
Old Ship Inn, *St Catherines, Old Portsmouth Road, Guildford, GU2 5EB* ☎ *01483 575731.*
Parrot Inn, *Old Farm Road, Slyfield Green, Guildford, GU1 1QR* ☎ *01483 62705.*
Pig & Tater, *18 Cooper Road, Guildford, GU1 3LY* ☎ *01483 62297.*
Plough, *16 Park Street, Guildford, GU1 4XB* ☎ *01483 35610.*
Prince Albert, *85 Stoke Road, Guildford, GU1 4HT* ☎ *01483 36073.*
Robin Hood, *Sydenham Road, Guildford, GU1 3RH* ☎ *01483 576388.*
Rowbarge, *Riverside, Bellfields, Guildford, GU1 1LW* ☎ *01483 573358.*
Royal Oak, *15 Trinity Churchyard, Guildford, GU1 3RR* ☎ *01483 66637.*
Sanford Arms, *58 Epsom Road, Guildford, GU1 3PB* ☎ *01483 572551.*
Spread Eagle, *46 Chertsey Street, Guildford, GU1 4HD* ☎ *01483 35018.*
Star Inn, *2 Quarry Street, Guildford, GU1 3TY* ☎ *01483 32887.*
Stoke Hotel, *103 Stoke Road, Guildford, GU1 4JN* ☎ *01483 504296.*
Three Pigeons, *160 High Street, Guildford, GU1 3AJ* ☎ *01483 504227.*
Two Brewers, *29 Castle Street, Guildford, GU1 3UW* ☎ *01483 66152.*
Weavers Arms, *Southway, Park Barn, Guildford, GU2 6DT* ☎ *01483 573716.*
Wooden Bridge, *Woodbridge Hill, Guildford, GU2 6AA* ☎ *01483 572708.*
Putting Greens
Allen House, *Chertsey Street, Guildford.*
Stoke Park, *Nightingale Road, Guildford.*
Railway
Guildford Model Engineering Society, *Stoke Park, London Road, Guildford (Enquiries* ☎ *01252 629283).*
Restaurants
Alfred Leroy Cruising Restaurant, *Millbrook, Guildford, GU1 3XJ* ☎ *01483 36186.*
Amalfi Pizza House, *1 Swan Lane, Guildford, GU1 4EQ* ☎ *01483 506306.*
Blue Moon Cafe, *94 Woodbridge Road, Guildford, GU1 4PY* ☎ *01483 452253.*
Cafe De Paris, *35 Castle Street, Guildford, GU1 3UQ* ☎ *01483 34896.*
Cambio, *10 Chapel Street, Guildford, GU1 3UH* ☎ *01483 577702.*
Figaro's, *Yvonne Arnaud Theatre, Millbrook, Guildford, GU1 3UX* ☎ *01483 301969.*
Giovannis, *1 Sydenham Road, Guildford, GU1 3RT* ☎ *01483 577711.*
Gulshan Tandoori, *66 North Street, Guildford, GU1 4AH* ☎ *01483 575030.*
Harlequin, *Yvonne Arnaud Theatre, Millbrook, Guildford, GU1 3UX* ☎ *01483 69334.*
Kings Shade Coffee House, *20 Tunsgate, Guildford, GU1 3QS* ☎ *01483 576718.*
Kohinoor Tandoori, *24 Woodbridge Road, Guildford, GU1 1DY* ☎ *01483 306051.*
Little Chef, *Stag Hill, Guildford, GU2 5TW* ☎ *01483 574312.*
★Mandarin, *13 Epsom Road, Guildford, GU1 3JT* ☎ *01483 572293.*
Mississippi Exchange, *6 Ladymead Retail Park, Guildford, GU5 0RZ* ☎ *01483 302544.*
Olympic Grill, *4 The Quadrant, Bridge St, Guildford, GU1 4SG* ☎ *01483 577408.*

Pasta Connection, *8 Chapel Street, Guildford, GU1 3UH* ☎ *01483 300051.*

Peking Garden, *2 South Hill, Guildford, GU1 3SY* ☎ *01483 63729.*

Pizza Hut, *12 North Street, Guildford, GU1 4AF* ☎ *01483 300501.*

Pizzaland, *88 High Street, Guildford, GU1 3HE* ☎ *01483 60700.*

Poppins, *176 High Street, Guildford, GU1 3HW* ☎ *01483 63846.*

Roof Garden, *Friary Shopping Centre, Guildford, GU1 4YT* ☎ *01483 453313.*

Rum-Wong, *16 London Road, Guildford, GU1 2AF* ☎ *01483 36092.*

San Antonio, *11 Epsom Road, Guildford, GU1 3JT* ☎ *01483 34780.*

Shahee Mahal, *50 Chertsey Road, Guildford, GU1 4HD* ☎ *01483 572572.*

Shahin Tandoori, *29 Woodbridge Hill, Guildford, GU2 6AA* ☎ *01483 570137.*

Singapore Sam, *5 The Roof Garden, Friary Shopping Centre, Guildford, GU1 4YL* ☎ *01483 39776.*

Three Kingdoms Peking, *14 Park Street, Guildford, GU1 4XB* ☎ *01483 61458.*

Toby's, *1 The Shambles, High Street, Guildford, GU1 3EX* ☎ *01483 302190.*

Tong Kung, *22 Chertsey Street, Guildford, GU1 4HD* ☎ *01483 60485.*

Tudor Rose, *144 High Street, Guildford, GU1 3HJ* ☎ *01483 63887.*

River Wey & Godalming Navigations

Wey Navigations Office, *Dapdune Wharf, Guildford, GU1 4RR* ☎ *01483 61389.*

Special Pursuits

Bishop Reindorp Ski School, *Larch Avenue, Guildford, GU1 1JY* ☎ *01483 504988.*

Go Karting for Fun, *Midleton Industrial Estate, Midleton Road, Guildford, GU2 5XW* ☎ *01483 440524.*

Laser Quest, *The Friary Centre, Commercial Road, Guildford, GU1 4YP* ☎ *01483 456565.*

Sports & Leisure Centres

Guildford Spectrum, *Parkway, Guildford, GU1 1UP* ☎ *01483 444777.*

Surrey University Sports Hall, *Egerton Road, Guildford, GU2 5XH* ☎ *01483 444777.*

Swimming Pool

Guildford Lido (outdoor), *Stoke Road, Guildford, GU1 1HB* ☎ *01483 444888.*

Guildford Spectrum, *Parkway, Guildford, GU1 1UP* ☎ *01483 444777.*

Take-Aways

Bamboo Garden, *13 Guildford Park Road, Guildford, GU2 5NA* ☎ *01483 60361.*

Burger King, *24 North Street, Guildford, GU1 4TA* ☎ *01483 579311.*

Burger King, *5 Ladymead Retail Park, GU1 1BX* ☎ *01483 39822.*

Cathay House, *8 Guildford Park Road, Guildford, GU2 5ND* ☎ *01483 577044.*

Chips With Everything, *11 Madrid Road, Guildford, GU2 5NU* ☎ *01483 61764.*

Fish & Chips, *4 The Food Court, Friary Shopping Centre, Guildford, GU1 4YT* ☎ *01483 450683.*

Hampers, *1 New Cross Road, Guildford, GU2 6NS* ☎ *01483 573530.*

Ho Ho, *38 Barrack Road, Guildford, GU2 6RU* ☎ *01483 66405.*

Jo Clarks, *20 Market Street, Guildford, GU1 4LB* ☎ *01483 452503.*

Kabaday Ihsan, *15 Park Street, Guildford, GU1 4XB* ☎ *01483 570235.*

Kentucky Fried Chicken, *264 High Street, Guildford, GU1 3JL* ☎ *01483 32791.*

Le Bon Bouche, *14 Friary Shopping Centre, Guildford, GU1 4YL* ☎ *01483 304804.*

McDonald's, *219 High Street, Guildford, GU1 3BJ* ☎ *01483 38557.*

Riverside Fish Bar, *83 Stoughton Road, Guildford, GU1 1LH* ☎ *01483 66293.*

Seafare, *147 Worplesdon Road, Guildford, GU2 6XA* ☎ *01483 62547.*

Seafare, *206 London Road, Guildford, GU4 7JS* ☎ *01483 34253.*

Spago Sandwich Bar, *6 Chapel Street, Guildford, GU1 3UH* ☎ *01483 450658.*

Spud-u-Like, *1 The Roof Garden, Friary Shopping Centre, Guildford, GU1 4YL* ☎ *01483 35960.*

Tong, *1 Acacia Villas, Woodbridge Road, Guildford, GU1 1ED* ☎ *01483 62205.*

Tea Rooms & Cafes

Cathedral Refectory, *Stag Hill, Guildford, GU2 5UP* ☎ *01483 60421.*

Chicos Cafe, *Bus Station, The Friary, Guildford, GU1 4YP* ☎ *01483 306993.*

Continental Cafe, *6b Tunsgate Square, Guildford, GU1 3QZ* ☎ *01483 303619.*

Forum, *The Y Centre, Bridge Street, Guildford, GU1 4SB* ☎ *01483 32555.*

Guildford House Gallery, *155 High Street, Guildford, GU1 3AJ* ☎ *01483 444740.*

Hobbs Choice, *Guildford Lido, Stoke Road, Guildford, GU1 1HB* ☎ *01483 452502.*
Hobbs Choice, *Railway Station, Guildford, GU1 4UT* ☎ *01483 450160.*
Le Boulevard Cafe, *14 Friary Shopping Centre, Guildford, GU1 4YL* ☎ *01483 304804.*
Peppers Coffee House, *89a Woodbridge Road, Guildford, GU1 4QD* ☎ *01483 33638.*
Woodbridge Cafe, *Woodbridge Road, Guildford, GU1 4RN* ☎ *01483 31453.*

Ten Pin Bowling
Guildford Spectrum, *Parkway, Guildford, GU1 1UP* ☎ *01483 444777.*

Theatres
Bellairs Playhouse, *Millmead Terrace, Guildford, GU2 5AT* ☎ *01483 60701.*
Bellerby Theatre, *Leapale Lane, Guildford, GU1 4QG* ☎ *01483 60146.*
Guildford Civic Hall, *London Road, Guildford, GU1 2AA* ☎ *01483 444720.*
University of Surrey, *Stag Hill, Guildford, GU2 5XH* ☎ *01483 259905.*
Yvonne Arnaud Theatre, *Millbrook, Guildford, GU1 3UX* ☎ *01483 440000.*

Wine Bars & Cafe Bars
Bragg's, *222 High Street, Guildford, GU1 3JD* ☎ *01483 506585.*
Muswells, *16 North Street, Guildford, GU1 4AF* ☎ *01483 303218.*
Pews, *21 Chapel Street, Guildford, GU1 3UL* ☎ *01483 35012.*
Rogues, *10 Epsom Road, Guildford, GU1 3JN* ☎ *01483 579455.*
Rowley's, *124 High Street, Guildford, GU1 3HQ* ☎ *01483 63277.*

Water Sports
Waterside Centre, *Riverside, Guildford, GU1 1LW* ☎ *01483 36407.*

See also Bramley, Burpham, Chilworth, Compton, Farncombe, Hurtmore, Loseley, Merrow, Newlands Corner, Normandy, Puttenham, Send, Shalford, Sutton Green, Wanborough, Wood Street, Worplesdon.

Hale
(including Upper Hale)

Nursery
Brian Eavis Nursery, *13 Nutshell Lane, Upper Hale, GU9 0HG* ☎ *01252 724963.*

Pubs
Ball & Wicket, *104 Upper Hale Road, Hale, GU9 0PB* ☎ *01252 735278.*
Black Prince, *147 Upper Hale Road, Hale, GU9 0JF* ☎ *01252 714530.*
Castle Inn, *128 Upper Hale Road, Hale, GU9 0JH* ☎ *01252 716096.*
Cricketers, *40 Upper Hale Road, Hale, GU9 0NS* ☎ *01252 715892.*
Iron Duke Hotel, *Folly Hill, Hale, GU9 0BB* ☎ *01252 715549.*
Prince Alfred, *9 Bishops Road, Upper Hale GU9 0JA* ☎ *01252 712546.*

Restaurant
Shomraat, *133 Upper Hale Road, Upper Hale, GU9 0JF* ☎ *01252 714304.*

See also Badshot Lea, The Bourne, Farnham, Heath End, Runfold, The Sands, Seale, Tongham, Wrecclesham. On the Hampshire boundary.

Hambledon

Set in richly-wooded countryside with good views of the Hogs Back.

OAKHURST COTTAGE (National Trust). A very small timber-framed cottage dating from the 16th century, restored and furnished as a labourer's cottage in the 1800s, with a beautiful cottage garden. One of the gems of old Surrey, the cottage was painted by Helen Allingham(1848-1926). ST PETER'S CHURCH. The church was almost completely rebuilt in 1846, but three of the original

14th century nave arches and the chancel arch remain. Eric Parker, author of 'Highways and Byways of Surrey', is buried here.

Historic Building
  Oakhurst Cottage, *The Cricket Green, Hambledon (Enquiries ☎ 01428 684733).*
Pub
  Merry Harriers, *Rock Hill, Hambledon Road, Hambledon, GU8 4DR ☎ 01428 682883.*

See also Brook, Chiddingfold, Dunsfold, Godalming, Hascombe, Hydestile, Milford, Witley, Wormley.

Hascombe

A beautiful village with a pond and a number of fine old residences dating from the 16th century, surrounded by heavily-wooded hills.

HASCOMBE COURT. The house is surrounded by flower gardens, particularly beautiful in spring.
HASCOMBE HILL. On the summit of Hascombe Hill is the remains of an Iron Age hill fort, where pottery implements have been excavated. A semaphore tower was built here in 1822 as part of a chain which enabled messages to be sent between London and Portsmouth. (See Ockham).
ST PETER'S CHURCH. Originally Saxon and Norman, the church was rebuilt in 1864 and has a fine painted ceiling.
WINKWORTH ARBORETUM (National Trust). Winkworth Arboretum, is a 95 acre hill side planted with rare trees and shrubs around two lakes. From here there are fine views over the North Downs. Peak displays are in spring for bluebells and azaleas, and in autumn for colour.
WINKWORTH FARM. A 16th century building which was once the home of Dr Fox, who founded the Roads Beautifying Association between the wars, with the object of planting shrubs along many of the new roads being built at that time.

Park & Garden
  Winkworth Arboretum, *Hascombe (Enquiries ☎ 01483 208477).*
Pub
  ★◆White Horse, *The Street, Hascombe, GU8 4JA ☎ 01483 208258.*
    ATTRACTIVE SIXTEENTH CENTURY PUB AND RESTAURANT WITH BEAUTIFUL VIEWS ACROSS THE SURREY COUNTRYSIDE; EXCELLENT REPUTATION FOR HIGH QUALITY FOOD.
Tea Room
  Winkworth Tea Room, *Hascombe, GU8 4AD ☎ 01483 208265.*

See also Bramley, Dunsfold, Farncombe, Godalming, Hambledon, Hydestile, Milford, Shamley Green, Witley, Wonersh, Wormley.

Haslemere

Haslemere was for centuries a centre for the iron, glass, leather, paper and woodwork industries. It is also surrounded by dense woods and heathery valleys, through which smugglers once brought their pack trains of brandy from Sussex beaches to the outskirts of London. The town is now mainly residential, and there are several fine Georgian houses in the wide main street, together with some 17th century tiled houses behind the raised pavement. Haslemere has attracted many writers, including Alfred Lord Tennyson (1809-1892) who lived at Aldworth House, and a track known as Tennyson's Lane leads behind the town to Blackdown woods and the highest point in Sussex.

DOLMETSCH WORKSHOPS. Hand-crafted instruments are made in the Dolmetsch Workshop, including replicas of those that were popular in the 16th and 17th centuries. The family also arrange a music festival in the town every year.

GEORGIAN HOTEL. A fine 18th century house and now a hotel, with a great chestnut tree planted in 1792.

HASLEMERE MUSEUM. The Educational Museum was started in 1888 by a surgeon, Sir Jonathan Hutchinson(1828-1913), who saw the function of a museum to be not merely the display of random collections of rare or extraordinary objects, but a means of explaining the story of the earth and its life. The principal galleries are devoted to geology, zoology and history.

JESSES. This house contains the best collection of early English musical instruments in the country, but only the gardens are open to the public.

ST BARTHOLOMEW'S CHURCH. Heavily restored by the Victorians, it has a 13th century tower and a stained glass window in memory of Alfred, 1st Baron Tennyson(1809-1892) the poet who lived on Blackdown.

TOWN HOUSE. The home of Rev James Fielding, clergyman and magistrate, who in the 17th century by all accounts also operated as a highwayman to support his grand life-style.

Antique Dealers
   Bow Antiques, *6 Petworth Road, Haslemere, GU27 2HR* ☎ *01428 652886.*
   Grannies Attic, *Checkerboards, Hindhead Road, Haslemere, GU27 1LH* ☎ *01428 644572.*
   Haslemere Antique Market, *1a Causeway Side, High Street, Haslemere, GU27 2JZ*
   ☎ *01428 643959.*
   Surrey Antiques, *West Street, Haslemere, GU27 3AH* ☎ *01428 654014.*
   Woods Wharf Antiques, *56 High Street, Haslemere, GU27 2LA* ☎ *01428 642125.*
Art & Craft Equipment
   Goldhawk Framing, *75 Weyhill, Haslemere, GU27 1HN* ☎ *01428 642726.*
Book Shop
   Haslemere Bookshop, *2 Causeway Side, High Street, Haslemere, GU27 2JZ*
   ☎ *01428 652952.*
Cafe
   Seventy Fours Cafe, *74 Weyhill, Haslemere, GU27 1HN* ☎ *01428 652996.*
Cinema
   Haslemere Hall, *Bridge Road, Haslemere, GU27 2AS* ☎ *01428 642161.*
Craft Centre
   Dolmetsch Musical Industries, *107b Blackdown Rural Industries, Haste Hill, Haslemere, GU27 3AY* ☎ *01428 643235.*
Garden Centre & Nursery
   Fernhurst Growers, *Hurstfold Farm, Fernhurst, Haslemere, GU27 3JE* ☎ *01428 656116.*
Hotels & Inns
   Georgian Hotel, *High Street, Haslemere, GU27 2JY* ☎ *01428 651555.*
   Haslemere Hotel, *Lower Street, Haslemere, GU27 2PD* ☎ *01428 642006.*
   ★Lythe Hill Hotel, *Petworth Road, Haslemere, GU27 3BQ* ☎ *01428 651251.*
   White Horse Hotel, *22 High Street, Haslemere, GU27 2HJ* ☎ *01428 642103.*
Library
   SCC Lending Library, *91 Weyhill, Haslemere, GU27 1HP* ☎ *01428 642907.*
Museum
   Haslemere Museum, *78 High Street, Haslemere, GU27 2LA* ☎ *01428 642112.*
Pubs
   Crowns, *4 Wey Hill, Haslemere, GU27 1BX* ☎ *01428 653363.*
   Mill Tavern, *Liphook Road, Haslemere, GU27 3QE* ☎ *01428 643183.*
   Red Lion, *Lion Green, Haslemere, GU27 1JB* ☎ *01428 642816.*
   Royal Oak, *Critchmere Hill, Haslemere, GU27 1LS* ☎ *01428 642328.*
   Swan Inn, *13 High Street, Haslemere, GU27 2HG* ☎ *01428 644608.*
Restaurants
   Arco Felice, *off Lower Street, Haslemere, GU27 2WT* ☎ *01428 642681.*
   Auberge de France, *Lythe Hill Hotel* ☎ *01428 651251.*
   Choi, *59 Weyhill, Haslemere, GU27 1HN* ☎ *01428 641505.*
   Good Earth, *97 Weyhill, Haslemere, GU27 1HS* ☎ *01428 651240.*

★Morels, *25 Lower Street, Haslemere, GU27 2NY* ☎ *01428 651462.*
Tirol, *14 Petworth Road, Haslemere, GU27 2HR* ☎ *01428 652625.*
Shahanaz Tandoori, *17 Kings Road, Haslemere, GU27 2QA* ☎ *01428 651380.*
Simla Tandoori, *84 Weyhill, Haslemere, GU27 1HS* ☎ *01428 643885.*
Trishna, *64 Weyhill, Haslemere, GU27 1HN* ☎ *01428 643854.*

Sports & Leisure Centre
Haslemere Sports Centre, *Lion Green, Haslemere, GU27 1LB* ☎ *01428 642124.*

Swimming Pool
Haslemere Sports Centre ☎ *01428 642124.*

Take-Aways
Andy's Fish Bar, *72a Weyhill, Haslemere, GU27 1HN* ☎ *01428 651747.*
MJ's Sandwich Bar, *22 High Street, Haslemere, GU27 2HJ* ☎ *01428 652919.*
Tasty, *17 Junction Place, Haslemere, GU27 1LE* ☎ *01428 644666.*

Theatre
Haslemere Hall, *Bridge Road, Haslemere, GU27 2AS* ☎ *01428 642161.*

See also Brook, Grayswood, Hindhead. On the Hampshire & Sussex borders.

Haxted

HAXTED MILL. A working water mill on the River Eden, and a museum of related objects.
PUTTENDEN MANOR. A black and white house begun in 1477 and later enlarged. It is notable for
oak beams, open fireplaces, four-poster beds, copper and wood baths, and its fine gardens.

Restaurant
Haxted Mill ☎ *01732 862914.*

Water Mill Museum
Haxted Mill, *Haxted Road, Haxted, TN8 6PU* ☎ *01732 865720.*

See also Blindley Heath, Crowhurst, Dormansland, Lingfield, Newchapel, Oxted. 2 miles from
the Kent boundary.

Headley

CHURCH OF ST MARY THE VIRGIN. The church was built in 1859 to replace a 14th century
predecessor which was pulled down. G E Street(1824-1881), designer of the London Law
Courts, built the tower four years later. The oak panelling in the nave is reputed to have been
removed from Newgate Prison, when it was demolished in 1902.
HEADLEY COURT. Built in 1910 in a neo-Jacobean style, now a rehabilitation centre for the RAF.
HEADLEY GROVE. An 18th century house, once the home of Sir Malcolm Campbell.
HEADLEY HEATH. 500 acres owned by the National Trust.
PEBBLE COOMBE. The road through Pebble Coombe has the steepest incline of any along the
whole of the North Downs.

Pub
★Cock Inn, *Church Lane, Headley, KT18 6LE* ☎ *01372 377258.*

Special Pursuits
KEDA, *The Nower, Tilley Lane, Headley, KT18 6EE* ☎ *01372 361048.*

See also Ashtead, Betchworth, Box Hill, Brockham, Buckland, Burgh Heath, Kingswood,
Leatherhead, Mickleham, Tadworth, Walton on the Hill, Westhumble.

Heath End

Inn
  Elm Tree Hotel, *14 Weybourne Road, Heath End, GU9 9ES* ☎ *01252 23537.*
  Royal Arms, *172 Farnborough Road, Heath End, GU9 9AX* ☎ *01252 20149.*
Pubs
  Alma, *21 Alma Lane, Heath End, GU9 0LJ* ☎ *01252 20978.*
  Halfway House, *64 Farnborough Road, Heath End, GU9 9BE* ☎ *01252 24090.*
  Running Stream, *66 Weybourne Road, Heath End, GU9 9HE* ☎ *01252 23750.*

See also Ash, Badshot Lea, Farnham, Hale, Runfold, The Sands, Tongham, Wrecclesham.

Hersham

The present roads were laid down soon after the commons were enclosed in 1804, and by the 1820s Hersham was developing as a country retreat for wealthy Londoners. The arrival of the railway at Walton in 1838 accelerated this development, and by 1918 Hersham had ceased to be a small country village, but rather a suburb of Walton on Thames with a large network of roads and small industries.

ST PETER'S CHURCH. Built in 1887, the church replaced a chapel which had been built only 50 years earlier.

Cafe
  Archway Cafe, *311 Molesey Road, Hersham, KT12 4PZ* ☎ *01932 225165.*
Garden Centres & Nurseries
  Jacques Cann, *Hillview Nursery, Seven Hills Road, Hersham, KT12 4DD* ☎ *01932 844575.*
  Squire's Garden Centre, *151 Burwood Road, Hersham, KT12 4AR* ☎ *01932 247579.*
  Woodlark Nurseries, *Burhill Road, Hersham, KT12 4JD* ☎ *01932 229543.*
Inn
  Bricklayers Arms, *6 Queens Road, Hersham, KT12 5LS* ☎ *01932 220936.*
Library
  SCC Lending Library, *Hersham, Molesey Road, Hersham, KT12 4RF* ☎ *01932 226968.*
Pubs
  Old House at Home, *303 Molesey Road, Hersham, KT12 4SG* ☎ *01932 223284.*
  Royal George, *130 Hersham Road, Hersham, KT12 5QJ* ☎ *01932 220910.*
  Star, *39 Burwood Road, Hersham, KT12 4AD* ☎ *01932 244182.*
  Watermans Arms, *1 Queens Road, Hersham, KT12 5LT* ☎ *01932 220015.*
Restaurants
  Barley Mow(Chef & Brewer), *67 Molesey Road, Hersham, KT12 4RS* ☎ *01932 227293.*
  Curry Corner Tandoori, *90 Molesey Road, Hersham, KT12 4RG* ☎ *01932 241802.*
  Dining Room, *10 Queens Road, Hersham, KT12 5LS* ☎ *01932 231686.*
  Full Moon, *84 Molesey Road, Hersham, KT12 4RG* ☎ *01932 225531.*
  Panahar, *21 Molesey Road, Hersham, KT12 4RN* ☎ *01932 252683.*
Take-Away
  Winner, *109 Molesey Road, Hersham, KT12 4QN* ☎ *01932 241614.*
Wine Bar & Cafe Bar
  Jules, *7 The Hersham Centre, Hersham, KT12 1QG* ☎ *01932 242373.*

See also Claygate, Cobham, Esher, Hinchley Wood, Molesey, New Haw, Oxshott, Stoke D'Abernon, Thames Ditton, Walton on Thames, Weybridge, Whiteley Village.

Hinchley Wood

Originally part of Thames Ditton, the village came into existence when the Kingston by-pass was driven through the Surrey countryside in the 1920s and opened up land for residential development. This was accelerated when a railway station on the existing London to Guildford line was opened and named after nearby woodlands known locally as Hinchley Wood.

Pub
◆Hinchley Wood, *2 Manor Road North, Hinchley Wood, KT10 0SH* ☎ *0181-398 0223.*
Restaurant
  Thai Thani, *7 Station Approach, Hinchley Wood, KT10 0SP* ☎ *0181-398 9952.*

See also Chessington, Claygate, Esher, Hersham, Molesey, Oxshott, Thames Ditton, Walton on Thames, Weybridge. 2 miles from the Greater London boundary.

Hindhead

Hindhead was developed for its superb scenery and good air late in the 19th century. It is the highest village in Surrey, situated at 850ft above sea level on the edge of the Devil's Punchbowl, and is surrounded by National Trust land. Sir Arthur Conan Doyle(1859-1930) and George Bernard Shaw(1856-1950) both lived here.

DEVIL'S PUNCHBOWL. This is a huge natural wooded valley worn in the sandstone ridge, with nature trails and spectacular views.
GIBBET HILL. To the north east of Hindhead, is 45ft above the village. (see under Thursley)

Antique Dealers
  Albany Antiques, *8 London Road, Hindhead, GU26 6AF* ☎ *01428 605528.*
  Cooper Brothers, *The Golden Hind, London Road, Hindhead, GU26 6AB* ☎ *01428 606441.*
  MJ Bowdery, *12 London Road, Hindhead, GU26 6AF* ☎ *01428 606376.*
  Oriel Antiques, *3 Royal Parade, Tilford Road, Hindhead, GU26 6TD* ☎ *01428 606281.*
  Second Hand Rose, *Bramshott Chase, Portsmouth Road, Hindhead, GU26 6DB*
  ☎ *01428 604880.*
Book Shop
  Beacon Hill, *Brackendene, Beacon Hill Road, Hindhead, GU26 6QL* ☎ *01428 606783.*
Cafe
  Hillcrest Cafe, *NT Car Park, London Road, Hindhead, GU26 6AB* ☎ *01428 605225.*
Golf Course
  Hindhead Golf Club, *Churt Road, Hindhead, GU26 6HX* ☎ *01428 604614.*
Hotels & Inns
★Devils Punchbowl Hotel, *London Road, Hindhead, GU26 6AG* ☎ *01428 606565.*
  Springkell House Hotel, *Wood Road, Hindhead, GU26 6PT* ☎ *01428 605509.*
  Undershaw Hotel, *Portsmouth Road, Hindhead, GU26 6AH* ☎ *01428 604039.*
Pub
  Woodcock, *Churt Road, Beacon Hill, Hindhead, GU26 6PD* ☎ *01428 604079.*
Restaurants
  Happy Eater, *Portsmouth Road, Hindhead, GU26 6TF* ☎ *01428 604013.*
  Little Chef, *Bramshott Chase, Hindhead, GU26 6DG* ☎ *01428 604379.*
  Pepe's, *4 London Road, Hindhead, GU26 6AF* ☎ *01428 604333.*
★Xian, *9 London Road, Hindhead, GU26 6AB* ☎ *01428 604222.*
Take-Aways
  Great Wall, *Hartford House, Beacon Hill Road, Hindhead, GU26 6QL* ☎ *01428 606981.*
  Piggy's, *75 Tilford Road, Hindhead, GU26 6RH* ☎ *01428 606946.*

See also Churt, Frensham, Grayswood, Haslemere, Thursley. 1 mile from the Hampshire boundary & 2 miles from the Sussex boundary.

Holmbury St Mary

The village is largely a 19th century development and was known as Felday until 1879. Before that, the area was undoubtedly used as a refuge for smugglers and sheep stealers. The new name was taken from Holmbury Hill and the newly built village church of St Mary.

HOLMBURY HILL. At 857ft, Holmbury Hill is second only to Leith Hill in height on the sandstone ridge. At the summit are the earthworks of an iron age fort, and from here there are panoramic views of the North and South Downs.

ST MARY'S CHURCH. One of the best churches in the area, it was designed and built in 1879 at his own expense by George Edmund Street(1824-1881), designer of the London Law Courts, and given to the parish in memory of his second wife.

Guest House
Bulmer Farm, *Holmbury St Mary, RH5 6LG* ☎ *01306 730210.*
8 D/T ROOMS (5 ENSUITE). 2 SELF CATERING FLATS. SOME DISABLED FACILITIES.

Pubs
Kings Head, *Pitland Street, Holmbury St Mary, RH5 6NP* ☎ *01306 730282.*
Royal Oak, *Felday Glade, Holmbury St Mary, RH5 6PF* ☎ *01306 730120.*

See also Abinger Common, Ewhurst, Forest Green, Gomshall, Holmwood, Ockley, Peaslake, Shere, Westcott, Wotton.

Holmwood
(North, Mid & South)

Two villages with mid 19th century churches. North Holmwood has recently seen extensive residential development, but has still managed to keep its village character.

HOLMWOOD COMMON. 600 acres belonging to the National Trust.

REDLANDS WOOD. Here the Surrey Archaeological Society has preserved a section of Stane Street, the Roman road connecting London to Chichester.

Antique Dealer
Holmwood Antiques, *Norfolk House, Norfolk Road, South Holmwood, RH5 4LA*
☎ *01306 888468.*

Pubs
Plough, *Blackbrook Road, Holmwood, RH5 4DS* ☎ *01306 886603.*
Royal Oak, *Chart Lane South, Stonebridge, North Holmwood, RH5 4DJ* ☎ *01306 885420.*

Restaurants
★Gourmet Pizza Company, *Horsham Road, South Holmwood, RH5 4NG* ☎ *01306 889712.*
Happy Eater, *Horsham Road, Mid Holmwood, RH5 4EH* ☎ *01306 886934.*

See also Abinger Common, Beare Green, Betchworth, Box Hill, Brockham, Buckland, Capel, Coldharbour, Dorking, Holmbury St Mary, Leigh, Newdigate, Ockley, Westcott, Westhumble, Wotton.

NOTES

Hookwood

Pub
◆Black Horse, *Reigate Road, Hookwood, RH6 0HU* ☎ *01293 782303.*
Restaurant
  Little Chef, *Reigate Road, Hookwood, RH6 0HL* ☎ *01293 784787.*

See also Burstow, Charlwood, Copthorne, Horley, Norwood Hill, Salfords, Sidlow Bridge, Smallfield. On the Sussex boundary.

Hooley

Antique Dealer
  Sundial Antiques, *64 Brighton Road, Hooley, CR5 3EE* ☎ *01737 551991.*
Restaurant
  Happy Eater, *119 Brighton Road, Hooley, CR5 2NG* ☎ *01737 557459.*

See also Banstead, Burgh Heath, Chipstead, Kingswood, Merstham, Redhill, Tadworth. 1 mile from the Greater London boundary.

Horley

A small town developed firstly after the arrival of the London to Brighton railway and again more recently as Gatwick Airport expanded.

St Bartholomew's Church. Dating from the 14th century, it was almost wholly rebuilt in 1881 by Sir Arthur Blomfield(1829-1899). It has a tower and shingled spire.
Ye Olde Six Bells. Set beside the river, a 15th century tile hung building with thick timbers and a Horsham slab roof. Its foundations date back to AD827 and it is reputed to be the second oldest pub in Britain.

Antique Dealers
  C Lawrence, *7 Church Walk, Brighton Road, Horley, RH6 7EE* ☎ *01293 783243.*
  Gym Trading Company, *Bluebird House, Povey Cross Road, Horley, RH6 0AG* ☎ *01293 822469.*
  Surrey Antiques, *3 Central Parade, Massetts Road, Horley, RH6 7PP* ☎ *01293 775522.*
Book Shop
  New Horley Book Shop, *22 High Street, Horley, RH6 7BB* ☎ *01293 783558.*
Garden Centre
  Horley Garden Centre, *Station Approach, Horley, RH6 9HQ* ☎ *01293 782348.*
Guest Houses
  Acorns, *125 Balcombe Road, Horley, RH6 9BG* ☎ *01293 820423.*
  Belmont House, *46 Massetts Road, Horley, RH6 7DS* ☎ *01293 820500.*
  Berrens, *62 Massetts Road, Horley, RH6 7DS* ☎ *01293 786125.*
  Chalet, *77 Massetts Road, Horley, RH6 7EB* ☎ *01293 821666.*
  Copperwood, *3 Russells Crescent, Horley, RH6 7DJ* ☎ *01293 783388.*
  Corner House, *72 Massetts Road, Horley, RH6 7ED* ☎ *01293 784574.*
  Cumberland House, *39 Brighton Road, Horley, RH6 7HH* ☎ *01293 784379.*
  Felcourt, *79 Massetts Road, Horley, RH6 7EB* ☎ *01293 782651.*
  Furzedown, *11 Brighton Road, Horley, RH6 7HH* ☎ *01293 785074.*
  Gables, *50 Bonehurst Road, Horley, RH6 8QG* ☎ *01293 774553.*
  Gainsborough Lodge, *39 Massetts Road, Horley, RH6 7DT* ☎ *01293 783982.*
  Gatwick B&B, *30 Massetts Road, Horley, RH6 7DE* ☎ *01293 821803.*
  Gatwick Oak, *15 Church Road, Horley, RH6 7EY* ☎ *01293 775953.*

High Trees, *Oldfield Road, Horley, RH6 7EP* ☎ *01293 776397.*
Lar, *64 Massetts Road, Horley, RH6 7DS* ☎ *01293 773564.*
Lawns, *30 Massetts Road, Horley, RH6 7DE* ☎ *01293 775751.*
Logans, *93 Povey Cross Road, Horley, RH6 0AE* ☎ *01293 783363.*
Massetts Lodge, *28 Massetts Road, Horley, RH6 7DE* ☎ *01293 782738.*
Masslink House, *70 Massetts Road, Horley, RH6 7ED* ☎ *01293 785798.*
Melville Lodge, *15 Brighton Road, Horley, RH6 7HH* ☎ *01293 784951.*
Oakdene, *32 Massetts Road, Horley, RH6 7DS* ☎ *01293 772047.*
Prinsted, *Oldfield Road, Horley, RH6 7EP* ☎ *01293 785233.*
Rosemead, *19 Church Road, Horley, RH6 7EY* ☎ *01293 784965.*
Southbourne, *34 Massetts Road, Horley, RH6 7DS* ☎ *01293 771991.*
Springwood, *58 Massetts Road, Horley, RH6 7DS* ☎ *01293 775998.*
Vulcan Lodge, *27 Massetts Road, Horley, RH6 7DQ* ☎ *01293 771522.*
Whitehatch, *Oldfield Road, Horley, RH6 7EP* ☎ *01293 785391.*
Woodlands, *42 Massetts Road, Horley, RH6 7DS* ☎ *01293 776358.*
Yew Tree, *31 Massetts Road, Horley, RH6 7DQ* ☎ *01293 785855.*

Hotels & Inns
Cambridge Hotel, *Bonehurst Road, Horley, RH6 8PP* ☎ *01293 783990.*
★Chequers Hotel(Thistle), *Brighton Road, Horley, RH6 8PH* ☎ *01293 786992.*
★Forte Posthouse, *Povey Cross Road, Horley, RH6 0BA* ☎ *01293 771621.*
★Langshott Manor, *off Ladbroke Road, Horley, RH6 9LN* ☎ *01293 786680.*
★Moat House Hotel, *Longbridge Roundabout, Brighton Road, Horley, RH6 0AB* ☎ *01293 785599.*
★Ramada Hotel, *Povey Cross Road, Horley, RH6 0BE* ☎ *01293 820169.*
Skylane Hotel, *Bonehurst Road, Horley, RH6 8QG* ☎ *01293 786971.*

Library
SCC Lending Library, *Victoria Road, Horley, RH6 7AG* ☎ *01293 784141.*

Model Shop
Aviation Enterprises, *Horley Garden Centre* ☎ *01293 820066.*

Pubs
Bull Inn, *Horley Row, Horley, RH6 8DE* ☎ *01293 783701.*
Coppingham Arms, *263 Balcombe Road, Horley, RH6 9EF* ☎ *01293 782283.*
Farmhouse, *Ladbroke Road, Horley, RH6 9LJ* ☎ *01293 782146.*
Foresters Arms, *88 Victoria Road, Horley, RH6 7AB* ☎ *01293 782245.*
Game Bird, *60 Brighton Road, Horley, RH6 7HE* ☎ *01923 820188.*
Gatwick Arms, *42 High Street, Horley, RH6 7BB* ☎ *01293 783801.*
Kings Head, *63 Balcombe Road, Horley, RH6 9HY* ☎ *01293 820803.*
★Olde Six Bells, *Church Road, Horley, RH6 8AD* ☎ *01293 782209.*

Restaurants
Curry Inn, *5 Central Parade, Horley, RH6 7PP* ☎ *01293 784888.*
Khushboo, *69 Balcombe Road, Horley, RH6 9AB* ☎ *01293 821495.*
Pizzasta, *163 Victoria Road, Horley, RH6 7AR* ☎ *01293 820484.*
Shang, *13 Massetts Road, Horley, RH6 7PR* ☎ *01293 783545.*
Wings, *11 Station Road, Horley, RH6 9HW* ☎ *01293 775888.*

Special Pursuits
Kelly Karts, *Ellerton, Peeks Lane, Horley, RH6 9ST* ☎ *01293 822555.*

Sports & Leisure Centres
Horley Anderson Centre, *Thornton Close, Horley, RH6 8RJ* ☎ *01293 784075.*
Oakwood Sports Centre, *Balcombe Road, Horley, RH6 9AB* ☎ *01293 822238.*

Swimming Pool
Horley Anderson Centre, *Thornton Close, Horley, RH6 8RJ* ☎ *01293 784075.*

Take-Aways
Bhua Bhan Thai, *34 Victoria Road, Horley, RH6 7PZ* ☎ *01293 772026.*
Curry Bengal, *16 Station Road, Horley, RH6 9HL* ☎ *01293 784255.*
DW Dove, *78 Brighton Road, Horley, RH6 7JQ* ☎ *01293 782858.*
Dave Dove, *25a Station Road, Horley, RH6 9HW* ☎ *01293 782357.*
Far East House, *6 High Street, Horley, RH6 7AY* ☎ *01293 782767.*

Hon-ka-Lau, *35 Station Road, Horley, RH6 9HW* ☎ *01293 783119.*
Horley Charcoal Grill, *171 Victoria Road, Horley, RH6 7AR* ☎ *01293 821873.*
John's Fish Bars, *36 Victoria Road, Horley, RH6 7PZ* ☎ *01293 822176.*

Theatre
Archway Theatre, *The Drive, Horley, RH6 7NQ* ☎ *01293 784398.*

See also Burstow, Charlwood, Hookwood, Leigh, Norwood Hill, Outwood, Salfords, Shipley Bridge, Sidlow Bridge, Smallfield. 1 mile from the Sussex boundary.

Horne

A little village consisting of the church, the school and a few cottages.

CHURCH OF ST MARY THE VIRGIN. Originally dating from the 14th and 15th century, the building was extensively restored and altered in 1880. It is claimed that the oak of the carved organ case was brought from Reading Abbey.

Pub
Jolly Farmer, *Byers Lane, Horne, RH9 8JR* ☎ *01342 842867.*

See also Blindley Heath, Burstow, Copthorne, Felbridge, Lingfield, Newchapel, Outwood, Shipley Bridge, Smallfield.

Horsell

An ancient village, Horsell was still small until in the early 1900s the demand for housing grew as Woking developed.

CRICKETERS. A former jail and cart workshop.
HORSELL COMMON. Over 700 acres including the large sand pits that H G Wells(1866-1946) chose as the site for the martian landing scene in his 1898 novel 'The War of the Worlds'.
ST MARY'S CHURCH. A 14th century church, which is one of the oldest surviving buildings in the area.

Garden Centres & Nurseries
Charwood Nurseries, *95 High Street, Horsell, GU21 4SY* ☎ *01483 761474.*
Squire's Garden Centre, *Littlewick Road, Horsell, GU21 4XR* ☎ *01276 858446.*

Guest House
Elm Lodge, *Elm Road, Horsell, GU21 4DY* ☎ *01483 763323.*

Inn
★◆Wheatsheaf, *Chobham Road, Horsell, GU21 4AL* ☎ *01483 773047.*

Pubs
Cricketers, *Horsell Birch, Horsell, GU21 4XB* ☎ *01483 762363.*
Crown, *104 High Street, Horsell, GU21 4ST* ☎ *01483 771719.*
Plough, *Cheapside, South Road, Horsell, GU21 4JL* ☎ *01483 714105.*
Red Lion, *123 High Street, Horsell, GU21 4SS* ☎ *01483 768497.*

Restaurants
Binaka Tandoori, *97 High Street, Horsell, GU21 4SY* ☎ *01483 724430.*
Bridge Barn(Beefeater), *Bridge Barn Lane, Horsell, GU21 1NL* ☎ *01483 763642.*

Sports & Leisure Centre
Horsell Recreation Centre, *High School, Horsell Rise, Horsell, GU21 4BD (Enquiries* ☎ *01483 771122).*

See also Bisley, Brookwood, Byfleet, Chobham, Knaphill, Mayford, Ottershaw, Pyrford, Send, Sheerwater, Sutton Green, West End, Woking, Woodham.

Horsley
(East & West)

HORSLEY TOWERS, EAST HORSLEY. A mock-Tudor building in multi- coloured brickwork dating from the mid 1800s, when most of East Horsley was rebuilt in the same style under the direction of the Earl of Lovelace.

ST MARTIN'S CHURCH, EAST HORSLEY. Built in 1036, the church possesses four brasses, including a famous one of Bishop Bowthe, a former Bishop of Exeter.

ST MARY'S CHURCH, WEST HORSLEY. A largely 13th century church with a group of wall paintings on the west wall, including a 13ft high St Christopher. The head of Sir Walter Raleigh(1552-1618), courtier, navigator and author is buried here in the family burial place in the St Nicholas Chapel.

WEST HORSLEY PLACE. Built on a saxon site, the oldest part of the present building dates from the 14th century, and was formerly the seat of the lord of the manor. In 1643 the house was inherited by Carew Raleigh, third son of Sir Walter.

Antique Dealers
  AE Gould & Sons, *Old Rectory Cottage, Ockham Road South, East Horsley, KT24 6QJ* ☎ *01483 283747.*
  Old Curiosity Shop, *9 Bishopsmead Parade, East Horsley, KT24 6RT* ☎ *01483 284994.*
Farm Shop
  F Conisbee & Son, *Park Corner, East Horsley, KT24 6RZ* ☎ *01483 282073.*
  MEMBER OF 'A TASTE OF SURREY' - PRODUCERS OF TRADITIONALLY MATURED MEATS.
Garden Centres & Nurseries
  Crocknorth Nursery, *Crocknorth Road, East Horsley, KT24 5TG* ☎ *01483 285376.*
  West Horsley Garden Centre, *Epsom Road, West Horsley, KT24 6AR* ☎ *01483 284256.*
Golf Course
  Drift Golf Club, *The Drift, East Horsley, KT24 5HD* ☎ *01483 284641.*
Hotel
★Thatchers Hotel(Jarvis), *Epsom Road, East Horsley, KT24 6TB* ☎ *01483 284291.*
Library
  SCC Lending Library, *Station Parade, Ockham Road South, East Horsley, KT24 6QN* ☎ *01483 283870.*
Pubs
  Barley Mow, *The Street, West Horsley, KT24 6HR* ☎ *01483 282693.*
  Duke of Wellington, *Epsom Road, East Horsley, KT24 6BA* ☎ *01483 282164.*
◆King William IV, *The Street, West Horsley, KT24 6BG* ☎ *01483 282318.*
Restaurants
  Drift Fish Restaurant, Tapas & Oyster Bar, *The Drift Golf Club* ☎ *01483 282432.*
  Ganges, *15 Bishopsmead Parade, East Horsley, KT24 6RT* ☎ *01483 284484.*
  Grays, *8 Station Parade, East Horsley, KT24 6QN* ☎ *01483 282208.*
  La Meridiana, *Ockham Road South, East Horsley, KT24 6QU* ☎ *01483 284343.*
Theatre
  Nomad Theatre, *Bishopsmead Parade, East Horsley, KT24 6RT* ☎ *01483 284717.*

See also Bookham, Clandon, Downside, Effingham, Fetcham, Gomshall, Merrow, Newlands Corner, Ockham, Polesden Lacey, Pyrford, Ranmore Common, Ripley, Send.

Hurtmore

Golf Course
  Hurtmore Golf Club, *Hurtmore Road, Hurtmore, GU7 2RN* ☎ *01483 426492.*
  NO HANDICAP REQUIRED. RESTAURANT AND BAR. SOCIETIES WELCOME.

Inn

★Squirrels, *Hurtmore Road, Hurtmore, GU7 2RN* ☎ *01483 860223.*

See also Bramley, Compton, Eashing, Elstead, Farncombe, Godalming, Guildford, Hydestile, Loseley, Milford, Peper Harow, Puttenham, Shackleford, Shalford, Wanborough, Wood Street.

Hydestile

HYDON HEATH. Owned by the National Trust, the highest point is Hydon's Ball at 586ft.

Nursery

Hydon Nurseries, *Clock Barn Lane, Hydestile, GU8 4AZ* ☎ *01483 860252.*

See also Brook, Chiddingfold, Eashing, Farncombe, Godalming, Hambledon, Hascombe, Hurtmore, Milford, Peper Harow, Witley, Wormley.

Kingswood
(including Lower Kingswood)

CHURCH OF JESUS CHRIST THE WISDOM OF GOD, LOWER KINGSWOOD. Designed and built in 1892 by Sidney Barnsley and Dr Edwin Freshfield in Byzantine style. Standing apart from the church is a weather-boarded bell tower.

ST ANDREW'S CHURCH. Built in 1852, this church is an exact replica of the medieval church in Shottesbrooke in Berkshire.

Golf Course

Kingswood Golf Club, *Sandy Lane, Kingswood, KT20 6NE* ☎ *01737 832188.*

Inn

Fox Hotel, *Brighton Road, Lower Kingswood, KT20 6SU* ☎ *01737 832638.*

Pubs

★◆Kingswood Arms, *Waterhouse Lane, Kingswood, KT20 6EB* ☎ *01737 354053.*

◆Mint Arms, *83 Buckland Road, Mogador, Lower Kingswood, KT20 7EF* ☎ *01737 242957.*
FREE HOUSE. REAL ALES. OPEN ALL DAY. LARGE RESTAURANT. EXTENSIVE SAFE GARDEN.

★Sportsman, *Mogador Road, Mogador, Lower Kingswood, KT20 7ES* ☎ *01737 246655.*

Restaurant

Khyber Tandoori, *2a Waterhouse Lane, Kingswood, KT20 6EB* ☎ *01737 352813.*

Take-Aways

Chau's Garden, *3 Brighton Road, Lower Kingswood, KT20 6SY* ☎ *01737 833374.*

Circle C Stores, *Waterhouse Lane, Kingswood, KT20 6EB* ☎ *01737 373999 (home delivery only).*

See also Banstead, Buckland, Burgh Heath, Chipstead, Gatton, Headley, Hooley, Merstham, Reigate, Tadworth, Walton on the Hill. 3 miles from the Greater London boundary.

Knaphill

In the second half of the 19th century there were prisons in Knaphill for both men and women. These were later converted into Inkerman Barracks, which were closed in 1965 and have since been demolished.

Antique Dealer

Knaphill Antiques, *38 High Street, Knaphill, GU21 2PY* ☎ *01483 473179.*

Aquatic Centre
  Pentangle Water Gardens, *Knaphill Garden Centre* ☎ *01483 489757.*
Garden Centre
  Knaphill Garden Centre, *Barrs Lane, Knaphill, GU21 2JW* ☎ *01483 481212.*
Golf Course
  Chobham Golf Club, *Chobham Road, Knaphill, GU21 2TU* ☎ *01276 855584.*
Library
  SCC Lending Library, *High Street, Knaphill, GU21 2PE* ☎ *01483 473394.*
Pubs
  Anchor Hotel, *High Street, Knaphill, GU21 2PE* ☎ *01483 472677.*
  Crown Inn, *33 High Street, Knaphill, GU21 2PP* ☎ *01483 489755.*
  Garibaldi, *136 High Street, Knaphill, GU21 2QH* ☎ *01483 473374.*
  Hunters Lodge, *Bagshot Road, Knaphill, GU21 2RP* ☎ *01483 797240.*
  Nags Head, *Bagshot Road, Knaphill, GU21 2RP* ☎ *Ex Dir.*
  Queens Head, *75 Robin Hood Road, Knaphill, GU21 2LU* ☎ *Ex Dir.*
  Robin Hood, *88 Robin Hood Road, Knaphill, GU21 2LY* ☎ *01483 472173.*
  Royal Oak, *Anchor Hill, Knaphill, GU21 2JH* ☎ *01483 473330.*
  Surrey, *Hermitage Road, Knaphill, GU21 1TX* ☎ *01483 474312.*
Restaurants
  Chez Comus, *5 High Street, Knaphill, GU21 2PG* ☎ *01483 797800.*
  Khyber Pass, *12 Lower Guildford Road, Knaphill, GU21 2EG* ☎ *01483 797536.*
Sports Centre
  Winston Churchill Recreation Centre, *Winston Churchill School, Hermitage Road, Knaphill,
  GU21 1TL* ☎ *01483 797015.*
Take-Aways
  Anchor Hill Fish Bar, *1 Anchor Hill, Knaphill, GU21 2HL* ☎ *01483 473535.*
  Golden Coach, *14 Lower Guildford Road, Knaphill, GU21 2EG* ☎ *01483 472233.*
  Golden Curry, *8 Broadway, Knaphill* ☎ *01483 487878.*
  New Chop Suey House, *50 High Street, Knaphill, GU21 2PY* ☎ *01483 472497.*
  Woking Chop Suey House, *2 Creswell Corner, Knaphill, GU21 2JD* ☎ *01483 476475.*
Wine Bar & Cafe Bar
  Froggies, *42 High Street, Knaphill, GU21 2PY* ☎ *01483 480835.*

See also Bisley, Brookwood, Chobham, Deepcut, Horsell, Lightwater, Mayford, Pirbright, West
End, Windlesham, Woking, Worplesdon.

Laleham

CHURCH OF ALL SAINTS. A church with Norman arcades, a tower dated 1732 and otherwise largely
19th century. Matthew Arnold(1822-1888), the poet and critic who lived in Cobham, is buried
here.
LALEHAM PARK. 70 acres stretching along the river and formerly the grounds of Laleham Abbey,
built in 1806 for the Earl of Lucan and now divided into private housing.

Garden Centre
  Notcutts Garden Centre, *Bloomingdales, Staines Road, Laleham, TW18 2SF*
  ☎ *01784 460832.*
Park
  Laleham Park, *Ferry Road, Laleham.*
Pubs
★Feathers, *The Broadway, Laleham, TW18 1RZ* ☎ *01784 453561.*
  Lucan Arms, *Staines Road, Laleham, TW18 2RT* ☎ *01784 453386.*
★◆Three Horseshoes, *25 Shepperton Road, Laleham, TW18 1SE* ☎ *01784 452617.*
  Turks Head, *The Broadway, Laleham, TW18 1SB* ☎ *01784 469078.*

Restaurant
  El Meson, *99 Ashford Road, Laleham, TW18 1RX* ☎ *01784 453860.*

See also Ashford, Chertsey, Lyne, New Haw, Shepperton, Staines, Stanwell, Sunbury, Thorpe, Virginia Water, Walton on Thames, Weybridge. 3 miles from the Greater London boundary & 3 miles from the Berkshire boundary.

Leatherhead
(including Leatherhead Common)

Known to have existed in Saxon times, Leatherhead was once a small market town with narrow streets, and a number of old and historic buildings still remain. The coming of the railway in the 19th century led to the town's growth as a residential area.

CHURCH OF ST MARY & ST NICHOLAS. The church dates back nearly 1,000 years and has a very rare double dedication. The tower was added in the 15th century. Anthony Hope(1863-1933), the novelist and author of 'The Prisoner of Zenda', is buried here.
FIRE & IRON GALLERY. Displays of ornamental metalwork by leading artist-blacksmiths from around the world. Demonstrations show every aspect of metalwork from jewellery to large architectural pieces, including gilding, casting and forging.
LEATHERHEAD MUSEUM. Housed in Hampton Cottage, a 17th century timber framed cottage with a small garden, the museum tells the history of Leatherhead and the surrounding areas, and contains many items of local interest from Roman and Saxon artifacts to old photographs of the area. The most important permanent exhibit is a collection of art-deco tiles manufactured at Ashtead pottery between 1923 and 1935.
NOWER WOOD EDUCATIONAL NATURE RESERVE & FIELD CENTRE. 80 acres of mixed woodland owned by the Surrey Wildlife Trust and used for teaching children and adults about wildlife and the environment.
RUNNING HORSE. A 16th century inn beside the 18th century brick bridge over the River Mole.
THE MANSION. Built in 1730 on the site of a former manor house and now owned by Surrey County Council, it is the biggest house in the town.
THORNDIKE THEATRE. Named after the actress Dame Sybil Thorndike(1882-1976), the theatre opened in 1968 and offers a varied programme of plays, each running for three weeks, from new works to perennial favourites. Many of these high quality productions then tour nationally or transfer to London's West End. In summer there are visits from distinguished companies, drama workshops and events for young people. The Casson Room, named after Dame Sybil's husband Sir Lewis Casson(1875-1969) the actor manager and producer, provides a programme of experimental work and hosts Surrey Theatre Link productions.
WESLEY HOUSE. Formerly the old Leatherhead Urban District Council offices. John Wesley preached his last sermon here in 1791, in Kingston House which stood on this site and was demolished in 1933.

Antique Dealer
  Alan's Antiques, *63b High Street, Leatherhead, KT22 8AQ* ☎ *01372 360646.*
Book Shops
  Bookworm, *22 North Street, Leatherhead, KT22 7AT* ☎ *01372 377443.*
  John Menzies, *15 The Swan Centre, Leatherhead, KT22 8AH* ☎ *01372 378011.*
Craft Centre
  Fire & Iron Gallery, *Rowhurst Forge, Oxshott Road, Leatherhead, KT22 0EN*
  ☎ *01372 375148.*
Garden Centre
  B & Q, *Woodbridge Corner, Kingston Road, Leatherhead, KT22 7QB* ☎ *01372 373793.*
Golf Courses
  Leatherhead Golf Club, *Kingston Road, Leatherhead, KT22 0EE* ☎ *01372 843966.*
  Tyrells Wood Golf Club, *Tyrells Wood, Leatherhead, KT22 8QP* ☎ *01372 376025.*

Golf Course & Driving Range

Pachesham Park Golf Centre, *Oaklawn Road, Leatherhead, KT22 0BT* ☎ *01372 843453.*
GOLF COURSE EXTENSION NOW COMPLETED; DUE TO OPEN END MAY 1995. NEW LAYOUT WILL GIVE 2,750 YARDS IN LENGTH WITH A PAR OF 35. MEMBERSHIP CURRENTLY AVAILABLE.

Guest House

Swan, *39 Kingston Road, Leatherhead, KT22 7SL* ☎ *01372 376332.*

Hotel

Bull Hotel, *North Street, Leatherhead, KT22 7AX* ☎ *01372 372153.*

Library

SCC Lending Library, *The Mansion, Church Street, Leatherhead, KT22 8DP* ☎ *01372 373149.*

Museum

Local History Museum, *64 Church Street, Leatherhead, KT22 8DP* ☎ *01372 277611.*

Nature Reserve

Nower Wood *(Enquiries* ☎ *01372 379509).*

Pubs

Dukes Head Hotel, *57 High Street, Leatherhead, KT22 8AG* ☎ *01372 372076.*
Plough, *93 Kingston Road, Leatherhead, KT22 7SP* ☎ *01372 377608.*
Royal Oak, *265 Kingston Road, Leatherhead, KT22 7PJ* ☎ *Ex Dir.*
Running Horse, *38 Bridge Street, Leatherhead, KT22 8BZ* ☎ *01372 372081.*
★Star, *Kingston Road, Leatherhead, KT22 0DP* ☎ *01372 843683.*

Restaurants

Brennans, *23 Swan Courtyard, The Swan Centre, Leatherhead, KT22 8AH* ☎ *01372 363050.*
Caesars, *25 Church Street, Leatherhead, KT22 8DN* ☎ *01372 379915.*
Green Room, *Thorndike Theatre, Church Street, Leatherhead, KT22 8DF* ☎ *01372 374223.*
Lal Qillah Tandoori, *207a Kingston Road, Leatherhead, KT22 7PB* ☎ *01372 376715.*
Mario & Carlo Trattoria, *103 The Street, Leatherhead, KT22 9RD* ☎ *01372 372118.*
Pangs Villa, *1 Guildford Road, Leatherhead, KT22 9AL* ☎ *01372 373602.*
Piccolo-Paradiso, *14 Bridge Street, Leatherhead, KT22 8BZ* ☎ *01372 362262.*
Siam Crescent, *26 The Crescent, Leatherhead, KT22 8ED* ☎ *01372 360454.*

Sports & Leisure Centre

Leatherhead Leisure Centre, *Guildford Road, Leatherhead, KT22 9BL* ☎ *01372 377737.*

Swimming Pool

Leatherhead Leisure Centre, *Guildford Road, Leatherhead, KT22 9BL* ☎ *01372 377674.*

Take-Aways

Botan Kebabs, *13 Bridge Street, Leatherhead, KT22 8BL* ☎ *01372 379452.*
Chinese Take Away, *3 The Parade, Kingston Road, Leatherhead, KT22 7SR* ☎ *01372 373686.*
Dinner House, *28 The Crescent, Leatherhead, KT22 8ED* ☎ *01372 376952.*
Joy Garden, *209 Kingston Road, Leatherhead, KT22 7PB* ☎ *01372 377602.*
Lantern House, *39 Bridge Street, Leatherhead, KT22 8BN* ☎ *01372 372648.*
Lunchbox, *1 The Circus, Kingston Road, Leatherhead, KT22 7BZ* ☎ *01372 372601.*
Michaels Plaice, *66 Kingston Road, Leatherhead, KT22 7BW* ☎ *01372 372210.*
Red Apple Sandwich Bar, *7 North Street, Leatherhead, KT22 7AX* ☎ *01372 360500.*

Tea Rooms & Cafes

Mr Pickwick's, *37 High Street, Leatherhead, KT22 8AE* ☎ *01372 373399.*
Thorndike Theatre, *Church Street, Leatherhead, KT22 8DF* ☎ *01372 374223.*

Theatre

Thorndike Theatre, *Church Street, Leatherhead, KT22 8DF* ☎ *01372 377677.*

Wine Bar & Cafe Bar

Brahms & Liszt, *31 High Street, Leatherhead, KT22 8AB* ☎ *01372 375570.*

See also Ashtead, Bookham, Box Hill, Downside, Epsom, Fetcham, Headley, Mickleham, Oxshott, Polesden Lacey, Stoke D'Abernon, Westhumble. 2 miles from the Greater London Boundary.

Leigh

Often pronounced wrongly, the name of the village is pronounced 'Lie' after an old word for a forest clearing.

LEIGH PLACE. The house was rebuilt in the 19th century, but retains its original moat. It has a decorative clock tower and battlements over the front door.

PRIESTS HOUSE. A rambling medieval timbered house, originally built for the local priest by Newark Priory.

ST BARTHOLOMEW'S CHURCH. Much restored in the 19th century but some parts date back to 1200. There is an interesting east window by Kempe, dated 1890. The Lych gate is dated 1891.

SHELLWOOD COMMON. The scene of a pitched battle between Royalists and the old Commonwealth regime in the 17th century.

Pubs

★◆Plough, *Church Road, Leigh, RH2 8NJ* ☎ *01306 611348.*

★Seven Stars, *Bunce Common Road, Dawes Green, Leigh, RH2 8NP* ☎ *01306 611254.*

See also Betchworth, Brockham, Buckland, Dorking, Holmwood, Horley, Newdigate, Norwood Hill, Reigate, Salfords, Sidlow Bridge.

Lightwater

LIGHTWATER COUNTRY PARK. The 143 acre park is part of Bagshot Heath and consists mainly of heathland, pine and birch woods, and ponds. There are three waymarked walks and over 80 species of birds are to be found. The Heathland Visitor Centre provides displays and information on heathland and local natural history.

Country Park
  Heathland Visitor Centre, *Lightwater Country Park, The Avenue, Lightwater, GU18 5RG*
  ☎ *01276 479582.*

Pub
  Red Lion, *114 Guildford Road, Lightwater, GU18 5RP* ☎ *01276 472236.*

Take-Aways
  Goodwill, *56 Guildford Road, Lightwater, GU18 5SD* ☎ *01276 472206.*
  Lee Moon Che, *110 Guildford Road, Lightwater, GU18 5RP* ☎ *01276 474121.*

See also Bagshot, Bisley, Brookwood, Camberley, Chobham, Knaphill, West End, Windlesham. 2 miles from the Berkshire boundary.

Limpsfield
(including Limpsfield Chart)

Limpsfield is an attractive street village, set in wooded Wealden countryside, whilst Limpsfield Chart, on the Kent border, is an attractive area of heathland and mixed woodland owned mainly by the National Trust. To the north, the North Downs rise to one of their highest points at 876ft.

GRASSHOPPER INN, LIMPSFIELD CHART. An enormous mock-Tudor inn built in 1950 out of the dismantled timbers of various ancient properties.

OLD COURT COTTAGE. A 15th century building with an aisled hall.

ST JAMES'S CHURCH, TITSEY. Built in 1861 to replace an earlier church on the other side of the road, which was demolished in 1766 to make room for building at Titsey Place.

ST PETER'S CHURCH. A Norman church with 12th and 13th century additions. The tower is positioned unusually at the east end of the south wall. The lychgate is probably 14th century. Frederick Delius(1862-1934), the composer, is buried here.

TITSEY PLACE. Built in the 18th century and incorporating part of the Jacobean mansion which it replaced, Titsey Place is set in beautiful parkland with some very fine trees. A Roman villa was found in the grounds in 1847.

Art Gallery
  Limpsfield Watercolours, *High Street, Limpsfield, RH8 0DR* ☎ *01883 717010.*
Golf Course
  Limpsfield Chart Golf Club, *Limpsfield, RH8 0SL* ☎ *01883 723405.*
Pubs
  Bull Inn, *High Street, Limpsfield, RH8 0DR* ☎ *01883 713402.*
  Carpenters Arms, *12 Tally Road, Limpsfield Chart, RH8 0TG* ☎ *01883 722209.*
  Grasshopper Inn, *Westerham Road, Limpsfield Chart, TN16 2EU* ☎ *01959 563136.*
  Royal Oak, *Caterfield Lane, Limpsfield Chart, RH8 0RR* ☎ *01883 722207.*
Restaurant
  Old Lodge, *High Street, Limpsfield, RH8 0DR* ☎ *01883 714387.*
Tea Room & Cafe
  Joyces On The Chart, *Post Office Row, Limpsfield Chart, RH8 0TH* ☎ *01883 722195.*

See also Crowhurst, Oxted, Tandridge, Tatsfield, Woldingham. 2 miles from the Kent boundary.

Lingfield

A wealden village with buildings dating back to the 15th century and now best known for its racecourse.

CHURCH OF ST PETER AND ST PAUL. A 15th century church with slightly earlier work in the south west of the building. The font, screens, stalls with misericordes, and the lectern with its chained Bible are all contemporary. The church contains one of the finest collections of brasses in Surrey and there is a good series of monuments to the Cobham family. The area around the church is now a conservation area.

LINGFIELD PARK RACECOURSE. Opened in 1890, Lingfield is one of the South East's premier race courses and probably the most advanced racecourse in Europe, with both a traditional turf course and an all-weather track. Race meetings are held throughout the year except during April and there is Turf, National Hunt and all weather racing, and harness racing on the all weather track.

ST PETER'S CROSS AND CAGE. By the pond is St Peter's Cross, built in 1437 to mark the boundary between Puttenden and Billeshurst manors, and an unusual stone cage built in 1773 as the village lock-up and used until 1882.

STARBOROUGH CASTLE. Built in 1342 by the first Lord Cobham, who fought in the Battle of Crecy, it was garrisoned by Parliamentary forces during the Civil War, but was destroyed in 1649. Only the moat remains.

THE GUEST HOUSE. The only remaining part of The College founded by the third Lord Cobham, who fought in the Battle of Agincourt. It was restored and has been used as the public library since 1954.

Antique Dealers
   Jean Allens, *29 High Street, Lingfield, RH7 6AA* ☎ *01342 834995.*
   Lingfield Antiques, *4 East Grinstead Road, Lingfield, RH7 6EP* ☎ *01342 834501.*
Art Gallery
   Columbine Art, *4 Godstone Road, Lingfield, RH7 6BW* ☎ *01342 832103.*
Garden Centres & Nurseries
   Occasionally Yours, *Lingfield Common Road, Lingfield, RH7 6BZ* ☎ *01342 833937.*
   Scats, *High Street, Lingfield, RH7 6AA* ☎ *01342 833983.*
   Willow Tree Nursery, *Newchapel Road, Lingfield, RH7 6BL* ☎ *01342 834961.*
Golf Course & Driving Range
   Lingfield Park Golf Club, *Lingfield Park, Racecourse Road, Lingfield, RH7 6PQ*
   ☎ *01342 832659.*
Guest House
   Lingfield College, *College Close, Lingfield, RH7 6HG* ☎ *01342 834215.*
Inn
   Old Cage, *Plaistow Street, Lingfield, RH7 6AU* ☎ *01342 834271.*
Library
   Crawley Lending Library, *Guest House, Vicarage Lane, Lingfield, RH7 6HA* ☎ *01342 832058.*
Pubs
   Greyhound, *Plaistow Street, Lingfield, RH7 6AU* ☎ *01342 832147.*
   ★◆Hare & Hounds Inn, *Lingfield Common Road, Lingfield, RH7 6BZ* ☎ *01342 832351.*
   Star, *Church Road, Lingfield, RH7 6AH* ☎ *01342 832364.*
      MEXICAN/PASTA MENU, REAL ALES, LOG FIRES, LARGE GARDEN AND CAR PARK.
Race Course
   Lingfield Park, *Racecourse Road, Lingfield, RH7 6PQ* ☎ *01342 834800.*
Restaurants
   Curry Inn, *9 High Street, Lingfield, RH7 6AA* ☎ *01342 834117.*
   India Brasserie, *64 High Street, Lingfield, RH7 6AA* ☎ *01342 832277.*
Take-Aways
   Lingfield Fisheries, *1 The Mart, Newchapel Road, Lingfield, RH7 6BA* ☎ *01342 834776.*
   Mandarin, *4 New Building, Newchapel Road, Lingfield, RH7 6BA* ☎ *01342 834259.*
Tea Room
   Best Wishes Tea Room, *30 High Street, Lingfield, RH7 6AA* ☎ *01342 832428.*

See also Blindley Heath, Crowhurst, Dormansland, Felbridge, Haxted, Horne, Newchapel. 3 miles from the Kent boundary & 3 miles from the Sussex boundary.

Littleton

CHURCH OF ST MARY MAGDALENE. A 13th century church with a 16th century brick tower and additions right through to the 18th century. The pews are some of the oldest in England and the 15th century choir stalls are reputed to have been brought from Winchester Cathedral. Above the nave hang many former colours of the Grenadier Guards.

LITTLETON PARK. A 19th century mansion which is now part of Shepperton Studios. In the grounds are the remnants of the former ornamental garden.

See also Ashford, Chertsey, Laleham, Molesey, Shepperton, Sunbury, Thorpe, Walton on Thames, Weybridge. 2 miles from the Greater London boundary.

Loseley Park

LOSELEY PARK. An historic Elizabethan mansion built in 1562 by Sir William More, an ancestor of the present owner and occupier, from stone brought from the ruins of Waverley Abbey (Farnham). Inside are many fine works of art, including panelling from Henry VIII's Nonesuch Palace (Ewell), period furniture, paintings and magnificent ceilings and chimney pieces. Elizabeth I and James I are known to have stayed here. Set amid magnificent parkland scenery, the estate covers some 1,400 acres. Famous for its Jersey herd and dairy products, there are farm trailer rides to visit the dairy farm and rare breeds unit. The restaurant is in a 17th century tithe barn. The old walled garden is being restored, with a newly planted rose garden and a planned 'white garden' and vegetable garden.

Bakery
Loseley Park Farms, *Loseley Park, GU3 1HS* ☎ *01483 304440.*
MEMBER OF 'A TASTE OF SURREY' - FARM BAKED PRODUCE FROM ORGANIC WHEAT.
Historic Building
Loseley House, *Loseley Park, GU3 1HS* ☎ *01483 304440.*
Restaurant & Tea Room
Tithe Barn, *Loseley Park, GU3 1HS* ☎ *01483 304440.*

See also Blackheath, Bramley, Burpham, Chilworth, Compton, Eashing, Farncombe, Godalming, Guildford, Hurtmore, Merrow, Peper Harow, Puttenham, Shackleford, Shalford, Wanborough, Wonersh, Wood Street.

Lyne

ALMNERS PRIORY. A house dating partly from medieval times and partly from 1830. It was once the almoner's house at Chertsey Abbey and it has in its grounds a tall square brick dovecote.

GREAT COCKCROW RAILWAY. A 7 inch gauge miniature steam railway with a unique signalling system, started at a private address in Walton on Thames in 1946. It moved here in 1968 and has been growing continually ever since. Trains usually seat 12 passengers and each ride takes 15 to 20 minutes, travelling between three stations starting and finishing at Hardwick Central station.

Aquatic Centre
  World of Water, *Silverlands, Holloway Hill, Lyne, KT16 0AE* ☎ *01932 569690.*
Garden Centres & Nurseries
  Pantiles Nurseries, *Almners Road, Lyne, KT16 0BJ* ☎ *01932 872195.*
  Randall's Nursery, *The Brook, Lyne Lane, Lyne, KT16 0AW* ☎ *01932 565000.*
  Silverlands Stone Centre, *Holloway Hill, Lyne, KT16 0AE* ☎ *01932 563558.*
  Squire's Garden Centre, *Holloway Hill, Lyne, KT16 0AE* ☎ *01932 563727.*
Pub
  Royal Marine, *Lyne Lane, Lyne, KT16 0AN* ☎ *01932 873900.*
Railway
  Great Cockcrow Railway, *Hardwick Lane, Lyne (Enquiries* ☎ *01932 228950).*
Tea Room
  Great Cockcrow Railway ☎ *01932 228950.*

See also Addlestone, Chertsey, Egham, Englefield Green, Laleham, New Haw, Ottershaw, Shepperton, Sunningdale, Thorpe, Virginia Water, Weybridge. 3 miles from the Berkshire boundary.

Mayford

A village with a cluster of farms and cottages which have grown up around the green, and which has escaped large scale development.

Garden Centres & Nurseries
  Briarwood Nurseries, *Saunders Lane, Mayford, GU22 0NT* ☎ *01483 763216.*
  Jackmans, *The Garden Centre, Egley Road, Mayford, GU22 0NH* ☎ *01483 714861.*
Pubs
  ◆Bird in Hand, *Egley Road, Mayford, GU22 0NL* ☎ *01483 763261.*
  Mayford Arms, *Guildford Road, Mayford, GU22 9RQ* ☎ *01483 761018.*
Restaurant
  Il Nido, *The Bird in Hand* ☎ *01483 763261.*

See also Byfleet, Horsell, Knaphill, Merrow, Pyrford, Ripley, Send, Sheerwater, Sutton Green, Woking, Worplesdon.

Merrow

As is recalled by the name of the local inn, Merrow was originally the site of Guildford race-course, which was in regular use from 1701 until the mid 1800s, and which during this time was the most famous race course in England. Today, there are footpaths on the downs which still follow some parts of the old track.

ST JOHN'S CHURCH. Largely rebuilt in 1842, there are still some signs of the earlier building which stood here since the 12th century, including the north porch with its Norman arch and 14th century barge boards, and the pilgrim crosses cut into the 12th century chalk pillars in the south aisle.

Golf Course
  Guildford Golf Club, *High Path Road, Merrow, GU1 2HL* ☎ *01483 63941.*

Pub
◆Horse & Groom, *220 Epsom Road, Merrow, GU1 2RG* ☎ *01483 573161.*

See also Albury, Blackheath, Burpham, Chilworth, Clandon, Gomshall, Guildford, Horsley, Loseley, Mayford, Newlands Corner, Send, Shalford, Shere, Sutton Green, Wonersh.

Merstham

Since medieval times Merstham has been an important industrial centre, in particular for mining and quarrying firestone. In 1805 the horse drawn Surrey Iron Railway was extended to Merstham to convey the stone to London where it was used in many important buildings. The railway was also used to carry Fullers earth from Nutfield to the Thames in London for onward shipping. This was the first ever public railway and remains of the track are still visible near the A23 at Hooley. A section of track is also set into a paved area in the centre of the village.

QUALITY STREET. A delightful cul-de-sac with timbered and tile hung houses, where a fair is held each year.
ST KATHARINE'S CHURCH. Built just outside the village in the 13th century, the church is of local flint and soft sandstone. The lych-gate was made from parts of an old wind mill.

Antique Dealers
Merstham Antique Centre, *34 High Street, Merstham, RH1 3EA* ☎ *01737 646122.*
Old Smithy Antique Centre, *7 High Street, Merstham, RH1 4HH* ☎ *01737 642306.*
Cafe
Quality Cafe, *3 Station Road South, Merstham, RH1 3EF* ☎ *01737 644263.*
Hotels & Inns
Feathers Hotel, *36 High Street, Merstham, RH1 3EA* ☎ *01737 642498.*
Rookwood House Hotel, *13 London Road South, Merstham, RH1 3BN* ☎ *01737 643207.*
Library
SCC Lending Library, *Weldon Way, Merstham, RH1 3QB* ☎ *01737 642471.*
Pubs
Iron Horse, *27a Bletchingley Road, Merstham, RH1 3HU* ☎ *01737 642874.*
Limes, *Southcote Road, Merstham, RH1 3IJ* ☎ *01737 642085.*
Railway Arms, *London Road North, Merstham, RH1 3BG* ☎ *01737 645166.*
Shepherds Pen, *229 London Road North, Merstham, RH1 3BN* ☎ *01737 644116.*
Take-Aways
Chippy, *6 Portland Drive, Merstham, RH1 3HY* ☎ *01737 643166.*
Merstham Tandoori, *14 Portland Drive, Merstham, RH1 3HY* ☎ *01737 644670.*
Oriental, *52 Nutfield Road, Merstham, RH1 3EP* ☎ *01737 645515.*

See also Bletchingley, Caterham, Chipstead, Earlswood, Gatton, Hooley, Kingswood, Nutfield, Redhill, Reigate. 2 miles from the Greater London boundary.

Mickleham

The village is on the east bank of the River Mole and was bypassed in 1934 by one of the best examples of road landscaping in the country.

JUNIPER HALL FIELD CENTRE. An 18th century mansion virtually rebuilt in 1870 and now owned by the National Trust, it was a principal meeting place for aristocratic refugees from France during the revolution. Both the French statesman Talleyrand(1754-1838) and the greatest of French women writers Madam de Stael(1766-1817) lived here. The gardens contain some of the oldest and biggest cedar trees in the country. The Centre runs a wide range of environmental courses.

St Michael's Church. A distinctive church with a massive 12th century tower. It has early Flemish glass and several brasses, a 12th century font and a Belgian pulpit of about 1600.

Pubs
★King William IV, *4 Byttom Hill, Mickleham, RH5 6EL* ☎ *01372 372590.*
★◆The Running Horses, *Old London Road, Mickleham, RH5 6DU* ☎ *01372 372279.*
Restaurants
  Country Life, *The Priory, Norbury Park, Mickleham, RH5 6DN* ☎ *01372 378718.*
  Frascati, *London Road, Mickleham, RH5 6EH* ☎ *01372 373950.*
  St Michaels Cottage, *London Road, Mickleham, RH5 6EH* ☎ *01372 375224.*

See also Ashtead, Betchworth, Bookham, Box Hill, Brockham, Buckland, Dorking, Fetcham, Headley, Leatherhead, Polesden Lacey, Ranmore Common, Walton on the Hill, Westcott, Westhumble.

Milford

Antique Dealers
  E Bailey, *Portsmouth Road, Milford* ☎ *01483 422943.*
  Michael Andrews Antiques, *Portsmouth Road, Milford, GU8 5AU* ☎ *01483 420765.*
Art & Craft Centre
  Surrey Guild Craft Shop, *Mousehill Cottage, Mousbill Lane, Milford, GU8 5BH*
  ☎ *01483 424769.*
Farm Shop
  Secretts, *Old Portsmouth Road, Milford, GU8 5HL* ☎ *01483 426789.*
Garden Centre & Nursery
  Secretts, *Old Portsmouth Road, Milford, GU8 5HL* ☎ *01483 426633.*

Golf Course
   West Surrey Golf Club, *Enton Green, Milford, GU8 5AF* ☎ *01483 421275.*
Inn
◆Red Lion Hotel, *Old Portsmouth Road, Milford, GU8 5HJ* ☎ *01483 424342.*
Pick Your Own
   Secretts, *Hurst Farm, Chapel Lane, Milford, GU8 5HU* ☎ *01483 426543.*
Pub
   White Lion, *Portsmouth Road, Milford, GU8 5BB* ☎ *01483 421116.*
Restaurant
   Refectory Tavern(Chef & Brewer), *Old Portsmouth Road, Milford, GU8 5HJ*
   ☎ *01483 421234.*
Take-Away
   T & D Rogers, *2 New Road, Milford, GU8 5BE* ☎ *01483 416217.*

See also Brook, Compton, Eashing, Elstead, Farncombe, Godalming, Hambledon, Hascombe, Hurtmore, Hydestile, Peper Harow, Shackleford, Thursley, Witley, Wormley.

Molesey
(East & West)

Hampton Court, surrounded by its deer park and water meadows, dominated the area until the arrival of the railway in 1849. Most of the present roads were laid down at this time and thereafter the area was rapidly developed. The present bridge, built in 1933, is the fourth to have been built here, the first having been built of wood in 1753. The River Mole ends its 42 mile journey at East Molesey, where it joins the Thames. West Molesey now is a continuation of East Molesey and is almost surrounded by water.

BELL INN. A 16th century inn and one of the quaintest in Surrey.

HAMPTON COURT PALACE. Of Tudor origin with later Baroque additions, Hampton Court is one of the historic royal palaces. The Great Hall and Henry VIII's state apartments, Queen Mary II's state apartments and the Georgian rooms are all open to the public. The magnificent state and private rooms of King William III have been restored to their former glory after the fire of 1986, and many of the great renaissance paintings from the Royal Collection are displayed in the Wolsey Rooms and the Renaissance Picture Gallery. The Tudor kitchens have also been reinterpreted, and there is a real-tennis court. The palace gardens comprise acres of beautiful parkland, the Tudor, Baroque and Victorian gardens, the maze and the great vine. There is also an annual flower show and music festival.

ST MARY'S CHURCH. Built in 1865 to replace an older church damaged by fire, the church has retained a number of old memorials, the oldest being a brass dated 1611.

Antique Dealers
   Antique Arcade, *77 Bridge Road, East Molesey, KT8 9HH* ☎ *0181-979 7954.*
   Attic Antiques, *68 Bridge Road, East Molesey, KT8 9HF* ☎ *0181-941 9672.*
   Gooday Shop, *48 Bridge Road, East Molesey, KT8 9HA* ☎ *0181-979 9971.*
   Hampton Court Antiques, *75 Bridge Road, East Molesey, KT8 9HH* ☎ *0181-941 6398.*
   Howard Hope, *21 Bridge Road, East Molesey, KT8 9EU* ☎ *0181-941 2472.*
   John Lawrence, *30 Bridge Road, East Molesey, KT8 9HA* ☎ *0181-979 4317.*
   Nazare Antiques, *49 Bridge Road, East Molesey, KT8 9ER* ☎ *0181-941 4387.*
   Nicholas Antiques, *31 Bridge Road, East Molesey, KT8 9ER* ☎ *0181-979 0354.*
   Popletts, *12 Bridge Road, East Molesey, KT8 9HA* ☎ *0181-783 0371.*
   Sovereign Antique Centre, *53 Bridge Road, East Molesey, KT8 9ER* ☎ *0181-783 0595.*
Art Gallery
   Molesey Gallery, *46 Walton Road, East Molesey, KT8 0DQ* ☎ *0181-941 2706.*
Art & Craft Equipment
   EKA, *11 Hampton Court Parade, East Molesey, KT8 9HB* ☎ *0181-941 3047.*

Boat Hire
  TW Allen & Son, *Ash Island, East Molesey, KT8 9AN* ☎ *0181-979 1997.*
Cricket School
  Mickey Stewart Cricket School, *Orchard Lane, East Molesey, KT8 0BN* ☎ *0181-398 8177.*
Historic Building
  Hampton Court Palace, *East Molesey, KT8 9AU* ☎ *0181-781 9500.*
Hotel
  Mitre Hotel, *Hampton Court Road, East Molesey, KT8 9BN* ☎ *0181-979 9988.*
Library
  SCC Lending Library, *The Forum, Walton Road, West Molesey, KT8 2HZ* ☎ *0181-979 6348.*
Model Shop
  Thames Trains, *29 Walton Road, East Molesey, KT8 0DH* ☎ *0181-941 3303.*
Pubs
◆Albion, *34 Bridge Road, East Molesey, KT8 9HA* ☎ *0181-979 1035.*
  Bell Inn, *4 Bell Road, East Molesey, KT8 0SS* ☎ *0181-941 0400.*
  Cannon, *19 High Street, West Molesey, KT8 2NA* ☎ *0181-979 5160.*
  Europa, *171 Walton Road, East Molesey, KT8 0DX* ☎ *0181-979 8838.*
  Ferryboat Inn, *6 Bridge Road, East Molesey, KT8 9HA* ☎ *0181-941 7781.*
  Kings Arms, *152 Bridge Road, East Molesey, KT8 9HW* ☎ *0181-979 2855.*
  Lord Hotham, *360 Walton Road, West Molesey, KT8 2JE* ☎ *0181-224 7777.*
  New Inn, *50 Walton Road, East Molesey, KT8 0DQ* ☎ *0181-979 0909.*
  New Streets Of London, *1 Bridge Road, East Molesey, KT8 9EU* ☎ *0181-979 1244.*
  Paddock, *The Precinct, Hurst Road, East Molesey, KT8 9SE* ☎ *0181-979 5906.*
  Poyntz, *85 Walton Road, East Molesey, KT8 0DP* ☎ *0181-941 2323.*
  Prince of Wales, *23 Bridge Road, East Molesey, KT8 9EU* ☎ *0181-979 5561.*
  Royal Oak, *317 Walton Road, West Molesey, KT8 2QG* ☎ *0181-979 5452.*
  Surveyor, *Island Farm Road, West Molesey, KT8 2LQ* ☎ *0181-941 2075.*
Restaurants
  Chien Qui Fume, *107 Walton Road, East Molesey, KT8 0DR* ☎ *0181-979 7150.*
  Chu-Chin-Chow, *15 Hampton Court Parade, East Molesey, KT8 9HB* ☎ *0181-979 3870.*
  Etoile, *41 Bridge Road, East Molesey, KT8 9ER* ☎ *0181-979 2309.*
  Golden Curry, *19 Hampton Court Parade, East Molesey, KT8 9HB* ☎ *0181-979 4358.*
  Henry VIII, *19 Creek Road, East Molesey, KT8 9BE* ☎ *0181-979 0690.*
  Jenny's Burgers, *55 Walton Road, East Molesey, KT8 0DP* ☎ *0181-941 7814.*
  Louis, *17 Bridge Road, East Molesey, KT8 9EU* ☎ *0181-979 2376.*
  Molesey Tandoori, *508 Walton Road, West Molesey, KT8 2QF* ☎ *0181-783 0090.*
  New Anakarli, *160 Walton Road, East Molesey, KT8 0HP* ☎ *0181-979 5072.*
  Palace, *20 Bridge Road, East Molesey, KT8 9HA* ☎ *0181-979 1531.*
  Plummer's, *Old Park House, Hampton Court Road, East Molesey, KT8 9BY*
  ☎ *0181-943 2050.*
  San Marco (Osteria), *142 Walton Road, East Molesey, KT8 0HP* ☎ *0181-979 7449.*
  Shahee Mahal, *101 Walton Road, East Molesey, KT8 0DR* ☎ *0181-979 0011.*
  Tiltyard, *Hampton Court Palace* ☎ *0181-781 9500.*
  Vecchia Roma, *57 Bridge Street, East Molesey, KT8 9ER* ☎ *0181-979 5490.*
Take-Aways
  Golden River, *368 Walton Road, West Molesey, KT8 2JE* ☎ *0181-941 6039.*
  Mr Chips, *23 The Precinct, West Molesey, KT8 1SF* ☎ *0181-941 9559.*
  Pizza Rola, *288 Walton Road, West Molesey, KT8 2HT* ☎ *0181-941 2009.*
  Stocks Burgers, *121 Walton Road, East Molesey, KT8 0DT* ☎ *0181-979 8358.*
  Superfish, *90 Walton Road, East Molesey, KT8 0DL* ☎ *0181-979 2432.*
  Tai Lee, *146 Walton Road, East Molesey, KT8 0HP* ☎ *0181-979 3938.*
  Ying Wah, *100 Walton Road, East Molesey, KT8 0DL* ☎ *0181-979 2761.*
Tea Rooms & Cafes
  Central Cafe, *5a Central Parade, Central Avenue, West Molesey, KT8 2QY* ☎ *0181-979 9566.*
  Garden Cafe, *Hampton Court Palace* ☎ *0181-781 9500.*
  Green Leaf Snack Bar, *5 Creek Road, East Molesey, KT8 9BE* ☎ *0181-979 5960.*

Theatre
Hampton Court Theatre, *Hampton Court Green, East Molesey, KT8 9BS* ☎ *0181-977 7990.*
Wine Bars & Cafe Bars
Spooners Bar Cafe, *84 Walton Road, East Molesey, KT8 0DL* ☎ *0181-941 3703.*
Whistle Stop, *Park Cottage, Hampton Court Road, East Molesey, KT8 9DD*
☎ *0181-943 3111.*

See also Ashford, Claygate, Esher, Hersham, Hinchley Wood, Sunbury, Thames Ditton, Walton on Thames. On the Greater London boundary.

Mytchett

Between the Blackwater and Basingstoke canal.

BASINGSTOKE CANAL VISITOR CENTRE. Exhibitions and displays about canal history and life, and a bookshop. There are narrowboats, barges and locks, boat trips are available and the towpath can be explored.

Canal Centre & Boat Hire
Basingstoke Canal Visitor Centre, *Mytchett Place Road, Mytchett, GU16 6DD*
☎ *01252 370073.*
Guest House
Loganberry Lodge, *6 Mytchett Road, Mytchett, GU16 6EZ* ☎ *01252 544603.*
Inn
Miners Arms, *2 Mytchett Road, Mytchett, GU16 6EZ* ☎ *01252 544603.*
Pubs
Potters, *Mytchett Place Road, Mytchett, GU16 6DF* ☎ *01252 513934.*
Restaurant
Gourmet Cruises, *The Canal Centre, Mytchett Place Road, Mytchett, GU16 6DD*
☎ *01374 649540.*
Quays, *Coleford Bridge Road, Mytchett, GU16 6DS* ☎ *01252 372656.*
Satay, *57b Mytchett Road, Mytchett, GU16 6EG* ☎ *01252 541440.*
Water Sports
Quayside Water Sports & Leisure, *Coleford Bridge Road, Mytchett, GU16 6DS*
☎ *01252 524375.*

See also Ash, Brookwood, Camberley, Deepcut, Frimley, Normandy, Pirbright. On the Hampshire boundary.

New Haw

Antique Dealer
Advanced Antiques, *292 Woodham Lane, New Haw, KT15 3NT* ☎ *01932 343008.*
Library
SCC Lending Library, *The Broadway, New Haw, KT15 3HA* ☎ *01932 343091.*
Pubs
Black Horse, *New Haw Road, New Haw, KT15 2BX* ☎ *01932 842769.*
White Hart, *New Haw Road, New Haw, KT15 2DS* ☎ *01932 842927.*
FRIENDLY PUB WITH CANAL SIDE GARDEN. LUNCHES & BAR SNACKS. REAL ALES.
Woody's, *300 Woodham Lane, New Haw, KT15 3NT* ☎ *01932 341360.*
Putting Green
Heathervale Recreation Ground, *Parkside, New Haw.*
Restaurants
Ecluse, *10 Woodham Lane, New Haw, KT15 3NA* ☎ *01932 858709.*
Raj Cuisine, *31 The Broadway, New Haw, KT15 3EU* ☎ *01932 348400.*

Take-Away
  Fishermans Net, *11 The Broadway, New Haw, KT15 3EU* ☎ *01932 349791.*

See also Addlestone, Byfleet, Chertsey, Hersham, Laleham, Lyne, Ottershaw, Pyrford, Sheerwater, Shepperton, Walton on Thames, Weybridge, Whiteley Village, Wisley, Woodham.

Newchapel

THE MORMONS' LONDON TEMPLE and visitors centre is the main landmark.

Aquatic Centre
  Beaver Water Plant & Fish Farm, *Eastbourne Road, Newchapel, RH7 6HL* ☎ *01342 833144.*
Nursery
  Herons Bonsai, *Wire Mill Lane, Newchapel, RH7 6HJ* ☎ *01342 832657.*
Pubs
◆Blacksmiths Head, *Newchapel Road, Newchapel, RH7 6LE* ☎ *01342 833697.*
  Wiremill Inn, *Wiremill Lane, Newchapel, RH7 6HJ* ☎ *01342 832263.*
Restaurants
  Markeys, *Eastbourne Road, Newchapel, RH7 6HL* ☎ *01342 833918.*
  Peacock Lodge, *Eastbourne Road, Newchapel, RH7 6HL* ☎ *01342 832596.*

See also Blindley Heath, Burstow, Crowhurst, Dormansland, Felbridge, Haxted, Horne, Lingfield, Outwood, Shipley Bridge, Smallfield. 2 miles from the Sussex boundary.

Newdigate

Newdigate became relatively prosperous from about the 16th century when the oak forests here began to be felled for ship and house building. Newdigate was reputed to be the first village in the county to have an iron works at about this time, relying on the availability of two local materials, iron bearing sandstone and the ample supply of fuel. When these industries declined, the land was farmed and large estates were formed. Between the two World Wars a large area was converted to brick works, although these have since closed.

ST PETER'S CHURCH. Partly dating from the 12th century, the church was fully repaired and enlarged in 1876. The north aisle windows contain 14th century stained glass, and like St Bartholomew's church at Burstow, St Peter's has a tower built entirely of timber.
SIX BELLS. Reputed to have once been a smugglers' haunt with underground passages. The bell tower of St Peter's church opposite has six bells.

Golf Course
  Rusper Golf Club, *Rusper Road, Newdigate, RH5 5BX* ☎ *01293 871871.*
Pubs .
  Six Bells, *Village Street, Newdigate, RH5 5DH* ☎ *01306 631276.*
★◆Surrey Oaks, *Parkgate Road, Newdigate, RH5 5DZ* ☎ *01306 631200.*
    SIXTEENTH CENTURY PUB WITH OAK BEAMS, INGLENOOK FIREPLACE AND STONE FLAGGED BAR. REAL ALES.
    RESTAURANT MEALS AND BAR SNACKS. LARGE GARDEN.
Tea Room
  Lisa's Bakery, *Village Street, Newdigate, RH5 5DN* ☎ *01306 631287.*

See also Beare Green, Capel, Charlwood, Coldharbour, Holmwood, Leigh, Norwood Hill, Ockley. 3 miles from the Sussex boundary.

Newlands Corner

From the grassy slopes here on the North Downs(567ft), amongst ancient yews and overlooking the Weald and the Greensand Ridge, there is one of the finest viewpoints in the south of England. On a clear day it is possible to see Windsor Castle and the South Downs. Newlands Corner is a favourite picnicking spot and there are good footpaths through the woodland and across the chalky grassland.

Cafe
  Barn Cafe, *Newlands Corner, GU4 8SE* ☎ *01483 222820.*
Hotel
  Manor Hotel, *Newlands Corner, GU4 8SE* ☎ *01483 222624.*
Nature Reserve
  Countryside Centre, *Shere Road, Newlands Corner (Enquiries* ☎ *0181-541 9339).*
Restaurant
  Carlos Trattoria, *Shere Road, Newlands Corner, GU4 8SE* ☎ *01483 224180.*

See also Albury, Blackheath, Bramley, Burpham, Chilworth, Clandon, Gomshall, Guildford, Horsley, Merrow, Send, Shalford, Shere, Wonersh.

Normandy

William Cobbett, the politician and writer who was born and buried in Farnham, lived at Henley Park and died here in 1835.

Antique Dealer
  LCM Staniford, *Verdure, Westwood Lane, Normandy, GU3 2JJ* ☎ *01483 811203.*
Pubs
  Anchor, *Guildford Road, Normandy, GU3 2AR* ☎ *01483 235195.*
  Duke of Normandy, *Guildford Road, Normandy, GU3 2AU* ☎ *01483 235157.*

See also Ash, Brookwood, Compton, Guildford, Mytchett, Pirbright, Puttenham, Seale, Tongham, Wanborough, Wood Street, Worplesdon. 3 miles from the Hampshire boundary.

Norwood Hill

Pub
★The Fox Revived, *Norwood Hill, RH6 0ET* ☎ *01293 862362.*

See also Charlwood, Hookwood, Horley, Leigh, Newdigate, Salfords, Sidlow Bridge. 2 miles from the Sussex boundary.

Nutfield
(including South Nutfield)

Although predominantly a farming area, fullers earth has been gathered here since Roman times, and extraction has only recently stopped. The railway station is at South Nutfield, one mile south of Nutfield.

CHURCH OF ST PETER & ST PAUL. Originally 13th century, it was enlarged in the 14th century and extensively restored in 1882. Most notable are the Burne-Jones window and the 15th century font.
REDHILL AERODROME. Established in 1934 and used by the RAF during the second World War. Since then it has been used by flying clubs and charter companies. It is also the headquarters of the largest private helicopter operator in the world.

Farm Shop
  Priory Farm, *Sandy Lane, South Nutfield, RH1 4EJ* ☎ *01737 822603.*
    <u>MEMBER OF 'A TASTE OF SURREY' - COUNTRY AND GOURMET FOODS.</u>
Garden Centre & Nursery
  Priory Farm, *Sandy Lane, South Nutfield, RH1 4EJ* ☎ *01737 822484.*
Hotel
  ★Nutfield Priory, *Nutfield Road, Nutfield, RH1 4EN* ☎ *01737 822066.*
Indoor Tennis Centre
  Eugene Bann Tennis School, *Crab Hill Lane, South Nutfield, RH1 5PG* ☎ *01737 822526.*
Pick Your Own
  Priory Farm, *Sandy Lane, South Nutfield, RH1 4EJ* ☎ *01737 822484.*
Pubs
  Crown, *1 High Street, Nutfield, RH1 4HH* ☎ *01737 823240.*
  ★Inn On The Pond, *Nutfield Marsh Road, Nutfield, RH1 4EU* ☎ *01737 643000.*
  Queens Head, *High Street, Nutfield, RH1 4HH* ☎ *01737 822252.*
  Station Hotel, *South Station Approach, South Nutfield, RH1 5RU* ☎ *01737 823223.*
Tea Room
  Priory Farm, *Sandy Lane, South Nutfield, RH1 4EJ* ☎ *01737 822484.*
Water Sports
  Aqua Sports, *Mercers Park, Nutfield Marsh Road, Nutfield, RH1 5DG* ☎ *01737 644288.*

See also Bletchingley, Caterham, Earlswood, Gatton, Godstone, Merstham, Outwood, Redhill, Reigate, Salfords. 3 miles from the Greater London boundary.

Oakwood Hill

CHURCH OF ST JOHN THE BAPTIST. Built in a wood far from the village, this church is the most isolated church in Surrey.

Pubs

★Punchbowl Inn, *Oakwood Hill Lane, Oakwood Hill, RH5 5PU* ☎ *01306 627249.*

★Scarlett Arms, *Walliswood Green Road, Oakwood Hill, RH5 5RD* ☎ *01306 627243.*

See also Capel, Ellen's Green, Ewhurst, Forest Green, Ockley. 1 mile from the Sussex boundary.

St. John the Baptist

Ockham

A largely unspoilt village, and until recently almost entirely in the ownership of one family, the Lovelaces. The village centre was built by the first Lord Lovelace and the distinctive Victorian buildings, many of which bear family crests, were constructed of locally made red bricks.

CHATLEY HEATH SEMAPHORE TOWER. Situated twenty minutes walk from the car park, the 61ft tower was built at the end of the Napoleonic Wars and was one of a chain which enabled messages to be sent to and from the Admiralty in London and Portsmouth Dockyard in just 15 minutes. The exhibition and models at the tower illustrate the method used. There are also magnificent views from the roof top platform.

CHURCH OF ALL SAINTS. A medieval church, with a fine seven-lancet east window and a 15th century tower. There is a carved monument by Michael Rysbrack to Lord King, formerly Lord Chancellor and ancestor of the Earls of Lovelace, who died in 1734. There is also a brick mausoleum to the King family, which may have been designed by Nicholas Hawksmoor(1661-1736).

OCKHAM PARK. The Lovelaces' family home which was built in the 17th century and almost completely destroyed by fire in 1948.

Historic Building

Chatley Heath Semaphore Tower, *from Old Lane Car Park, Ockham Common* ☎ *01932 862762.*

Pub

★◆Black Swan, *Old Lane, Martyrs Green, Ockham, KT11 1NG* ☎ *01932 862364.*

Restaurant

Hautboy Inn, *Ockham Lane, Ockham, GU23 6NP* ☎ *01483 225355.*

Water Sports

Boldermere, *Ockham Common, Ockham (Enquiries* ☎ *01483 740242).*

See also Byfleet, Clandon, Cobham, Downside, Effingham, Horsley, Pyrford, Ripley, Send, Stoke D'Abernon, Woodham.

NOTES

Ockley

A village standing along 'Stane Street', the old Roman road between London and Chichester. It has a long green and many brick and tile hung cottages, some of which date back to the 16th century.

HANNAH PESCHAR GALLERY. A exhibition of contemporary sculpture and ceramics in an exotic and romantic water garden.
ST MARGARET'S CHURCH. Extensively rebuilt in 1873, the west tower survives unaltered as does the 15th century wooden porch.

Antique Dealer
  Ockley Antiques, *The Green, Ockley, RH5 5SS* ☎ *01306 712266.*
Farm Shop
  Ockley Court Farm, *Coles Lane, Ockley, RH5 5LS* ☎ *01306 711365.*
  MEMBER OF 'A TASTE OF SURREY' - FRESH FARM PRODUCE.
Garden
  Hannah Peschar Gallery, *Black & White Cottage, Standon Lane, Ockley, RH5 5QR*
  ☎ *01306 627269.*
Golf Course
  Gatton Manor Golf & Country Club, *Standon Lane, Ockley, RH5 5PG* ☎ *01306 627557.*
Hotels & Inns
  ★Gatton Manor Hotel, *Standon Lane, Ockley, RH5 5PQ* ☎ *01306 627555.*
  ◆Kings Arms Inn, *Stane Street, Ockley, RH5 5SZ* ☎ *01306 711224.*
Pick Your Own
  Ockley Court Farm, *Coles Lane, Ockley, RH5 5LS* ☎ *01306 711365.*
Pubs
  ★◆Cricketers Arms, *Stane Street, Ockley, RH5 5TP* ☎ *01306 627205.*
  ◆Old School House, *Stane Street, Ockley, RH5 5TH* ☎ *01306 627430.*
  ◆Red Lion, *Stane Street, Ockley, RH5 5TD* ☎ *01306 711032.*

See also Beare Green, Capel, Coldharbour, Ewhurst, Forest Green, Holmbury St Mary, Holmwood, Newdigate, Oakwood Hill. 2 miles from the Sussex boundary.

Ottershaw

A widespread village built on the heath between Woking and Chertsey, and close to Fairoaks Airport.

CHRIST CHURCH. Built in patterned brickwork by George Gilbert Scott(1811-1878) in 1864.

Art & Craft Equipment
  Bolden Fraser, *9 Brox Road, Ottershaw, KT16 0HG* ☎ *01932 874376.*
  Craft Accessories, *KT16 0LR (Telephone enquiries only* ☎ *01932 874790).*
Book Shop
  Lane Educational & Business, *24 Brox Road, Ottershaw, KT16 0HL* ☎ *01932 872332.*
Golf Course & Driving Range
  Foxhills Golf Club, *Stonehill Road, Ottershaw, KT16 0EL* ☎ *01932 872050.*
Hotel
  Foxhills, *Stonehill Road, Ottershaw, KT16 0EL* ☎ *01932 872050.*
Nursery
  Otter Nursery, *Murray Road, Ottershaw, KT16 0HT* ☎ *01932 874875.*
Park
  Memorial Fields, *Foxhills Road, Ottershaw (Enquiries* ☎ *01932 873646).*
Pub
  Castle, *222 Brox Road, Ottershaw, KT16 0LW* ☎ *01932 872373.*

Putting Green
 Memorial Fields, *Foxhills Road, Ottershaw (Enquiries ☎ 01932 873646).*
Restaurants
 Manor, *Foxhills Hotel ☎ 01932 872050.*
 Otter(Harvester), *Guildford Road, Ottershaw, KT16 0PQ ☎ 01932 873217.*
 Otters Spicy Cottage, *13 Brox Road, Ottershaw, KT16 0HG ☎ 01932 872022.*

See also Addlestone, Byfleet, Chertsey, Horsell, Lyne, New Haw, Pyrford, Ripley, Sheerwater, Shepperton, Weybridge, Whiteley Village, Woking, Woodham.

Outwood

CHURCH OF ST JOHN THE BAPTIST. A Victorian church designed by William Burges, with a large West tower. An unusual tombstone commemorates various members of the Hoare family.

OUTWOOD COMMON. Owned by the National Trust, who own some 2,000 acres of land around Outwood.

POST MILL. On the east side of the village stands one of the country's best preserved post mills which dates from 1665, and is the oldest working mill in England. The entire wooden body carrying the sails revolves around a central upright oak post, and is turned by hand to face the wind. Visitors can watch the millstones at work, and buy the flour. A second windmill, which was built in 1790 and stood alongside, was blown down in a storm in 1960. There is also a small agricultural museum and farm animals.

The Post Mill

Pubs
★◆Bell Inn, *Outwood Lane, Outwood, RH1 5PN*
 ☎ 01342 842989.
 Castle Inn, *Millers Lane, Outwood, RH1 5QB ☎ 01342 842754.*
★◆Dog & Duck, *Prince of Wales Road, Outwood, RH1 5QU ☎ 01342 842964.*
Windmill
 Post Mill, *Outwood Common, Outwood, RH1 5PW ☎ 01342 843458.*

See also Bletchingley, Blindley Heath, Burstow, Earlswood, Horley, Horne, Newchapel, Nutfield, Salfords, Shipley Bridge, Smallfield.

Oxshott

Until the arrival of the railway in the 1880s Oxshott was a small hamlet set in the heather and woodlands and, although the village had two pubs, the church was not built until 1912.

Nursery
 Willoughby's Nurseries, *Leatherhead Road, Oxshott, KT22 0HG ☎ 01372 842434.*
Pubs
◆Bear, *Leatherhead Road, Oxshott, KT22 0JE ☎ 01372 842747.*
◆Victoria Hotel, *High Street, Oxshott, KT22 0JR ☎ 01372 843562.*

Restaurant
  Oxshott Tandoori, *4 High Street, Oxshott, KT22 0JN* ☎ *01372 844327.*

See also Ashtead, Chessington, Claygate, Cobham, Downside, Esher, Fetcham, Hersham, Hinchley Wood, Leatherhead, Stoke D'Abernon. 2 miles from the Greater London boundary.

Oxted
(including Old Oxted)

A village recorded in the Domesday Book, Old Oxted is still a charming place but inevitably there has been a lot of development centred on the new town since the railway arrived. Of interest is the Pound in Sandy Lane and the Old Lock-Up in the High Street.

ST MARY'S CHURCH. A restored medieval church in stone, brick and flint with a solid 12th century tower. The 14th century stained glass east window depicts the four evangelists.

Antique Dealers
  Antique Centre, *80 Station Road East, Oxted, RH8 0PG* ☎ *01883 712806.*
  Francis Antiques, *27 Station Road West, Oxted, RH8 9EE* ☎ *01883 730316.*
  Treasures, *151 Station Road East, Oxted, RH8 0QE* ☎ *01883 713301.*
Cinema
  Plaza Cinema, *Station Road West, Oxted, RH8 9EE* ☎ *01883 712567.*
Golf Course
  Tandridge Golf Club, *Godstone Road, Oxted, RH8 9NQ* ☎ *01883 712274.*
Leisure Centre
  Tandridge Leisure Centre, *Hoskins Road, Oxted, RH8 9HP* ☎ *01883 716717.*
Library
  SCC Lending Library, *12 Gresham Road, Oxted, RH8 0BQ* ☎ *01883 714225.*
Pubs
★◆Crown, *53 High Street, Old Oxted, RH8 9LN* ☎ *01883 717853.*
  Diamond, *Holland Road, Hurst Green, Oxted, RH8 9BQ* ☎ *01883 716040.*
★◆George Inn, *52 High Street, Old Oxted, RH8 9LP* ☎ *01883 713453.*
★◆Haycutter, *69 Tanhouse Road, Old Oxted, RH8 9PE* ☎ *01883 712550.*
  Wheatsheaf, *9 High Street, Old Oxted, RH8 9LN* ☎ *01883 713154.*
Restaurants
  Coltsford Mill, *Mill Lane, Hurst Green, Oxted, RH8 9DG* ☎ *01883 713962.*
  Costalotti's, *113 Station Road East, Oxted, RH8 0AX* ☎ *01883 716167.*
  Golden Bengal Tandoori, *51 Station Road East, Oxted, RH8 0AX* ☎ *01883 717373.*
  Golden Palace, *40 Station Road West, Oxted, RH8 9EU* ☎ *01883 715323.*
  Mahatma Cote, *111 Station Road East, Oxted, RH8 0AX* ☎ *01883 722621.*
  Old Bell(Chef & Brewer), *68 High Street, Old Oxted, RH8 9LP* ☎ *01883 712181.*
  Rainbow, *30 Station Road East, Oxted, RH8 0PT* ☎ *01883 713988.*
Swimming Pool
  Tandridge Leisure Centre, *Hoskins Road, Oxted, RH8 9HP* ☎ *01883 716717.*
Take-Aways
  Fishers, *17 Station Road East, Oxted, RH8 0BD* ☎ *01883 712689.*
  Jade Garden, *94 Station Road East, Oxted, RH8 0QA* ☎ *01883 730754.*
Theatre
  Barn Theatre, *25 Blue House Lane, Oxted, RH8 0AA* ☎ *01883 713669.*

See also Caterham, Crowhurst, Godstone, Haxted, Limpsfield, Tandridge, Tatsfield, Woldingham. 2 miles from the Kent boundary.

Peaslake

One of the county's most out of the way villages, on the slopes of Hurtwood Common which rises over 100 feet behind the village.

Hotel
★Hurtwood Inn Hotel, *Walking Bottom, Peaslake, GU5 9RR* ☎ *01306 730851.*
Turkey Farm
  Hazelbrow Farm, *Rad Lane, Peaslake, GU5 9PB* ☎ *01306 730313.*
  MEMBER OF 'A TASTE OF SURREY' - TRADITIONAL TURKEY PRODUCERS.

See also Abinger Common, Albury, Ewhurst, Forest Green, Gomshall, Holmbury St Mary, Shamley Green, Shere, Wotton.

Peper Harow

A completely self contained medieval manorial estate which encompasses the hamlet of Peper Harow, including the church.

PEPER HAROW HOUSE. The present mansion was built in 1763 of brick and stone, and from about 1700 was the seat of the Lords Middleton of Cork. It is now a remedial school and stands in a spacious park which is famed for its splendid cedars.
ST NICHOLAS'S CHURCH. Although it still retains its Norman chancel arch, the church was enriched by Augustus Pugin(1812-1852) who restored the church in 1843. In the churchyard stands a double yew believed to be over 600 years old and planted on an old Saxon worshipping place. There is also a hawthorn tree nearby, believed to be over 800 years old and the oldest of its kind in Surrey.

See also Compton, Eashing, Elstead, Farncombe, Godalming, Hurtmore, Hydestile, Loseley, Milford, Puttenham, The Sands, Seale, Shackleford, Wanborough, Witley, Wormley.

Pirbright

The village has one of the most attractive and best kept greens in the district, complete with a duck pond. Pirbright is also synonymous with the Guards' Depot, and the neighbouring ranges of the National Rifle Association at Bisley.

ST MICHAEL'S CHURCH. With foundations dating back to about 1100, the church was rebuilt in 1784, and the organ was given to the church in 1903 by Lord Pirbright. Sir Henry Stanley(1841-1904), the explorer and journalist (and finder of Dr Livingstone), lived in Pirbright and is buried here.

Garden Centre & Nursery
  Barralet's Nursery, *Guildford Road, Pirbright, GU24 0LW* ☎ *01483 476154.*
Golf Course
  Goal Farm Par Three, *Gole Road, Pirbright, GU24 0PZ* ☎ *01483 473183.*
Pubs
  Cricketers Inn, *The Green, Pirbright, GU24 0JT* ☎ *01483 473198.*
★Royal Oak, *Aldershot Road, Pirbright, GU24 0DQ* ☎ *01483 232466.*
◆White Hart, *The Green, Pirbright, GU24 0LP* ☎ *01483 472366.*

See also Bisley, Brookwood, Deepcut, Knaphill, Mytchett, Normandy, West End, Wood Street, Worplesdon.

Polesden Lacey

POLESDEN LACEY (National Trust). Originally an 1820s' Regency villa, remodelled after 1906 by the Hon. Mrs Ronald Greville, a well-known Edwardian hostess. The house contains fine paintings, furniture, porcelain and silver, and photographs from Mrs Greville's albums. The 1200 acre park was planted with some 20,000 trees many of which have grown into fine specimens and which complement the more formal flower gardens, walled rose garden, and lawn. King George VI and Queen Elizabeth (now the Queen Mother) spent part of their honeymoon here. The open air theatre is used for a theatre season in mid July.

Polesden Lacey

Historic Building
   Polesden Lacey, *Dorking,*
   RH5 6BD ☎ *01372 458203.*
Open Air Theatre
   Polesden Lacey, *Dorking, RH5 6BD* ☎ *01372 457223.*

See also Bookham, Box Hill, Dorking, Effingham, Fetcham, Horsley, Leatherhead, Mickleham, Ranmore Common, Westcott. Westhumble, Wotton

Poyle

Pubs
   Golden Cross, *Poyle Road, Poyle, SL3 0BN* ☎ *01753 682231.*
   Punch Bowl, *Old Bath Road, Poyle, SL3 0PH* ☎ *Ex Dir.*
   Star & Garter, *Park Street, Poyle, SL3 0JF* ☎ *01753 682157.*

See also Staines, Stanwell. On the Berkshire, Buckinghamshire & Greater London boundaries.

Puttenham

Situated on the southern slopes of the Hogs Back, Puttenham has been inhabited for thousands of years, as evidenced by finds of stone age flints in the locality. The older buildings have been well preserved and some put to modern uses while still retaining much of their original character.

CHURCH OF ST JOHN THE BAPTIST. A large Norman church that was well restored in 1861. Also restored is the village well which is in the churchyard.
PUTTENHAM PRIORY. A fine Palladian mansion dating from 1762.

Golf Course
   Puttenham Golf Club, *Heath End, Puttenham, GU3 1AL* ☎ *01483 810498.*
Pub
   Good Intent, *62 The Street, Puttenham, GU3 1AR* ☎ *01483 810387.*
Restaurant
   Jolly Farmer(Harvester), *Puttenham Heath Road, Puttenham, GU3 1AP* ☎ *01483 810374.*

See also Ash, Compton, Eashing, Elstead, Farncombe, Guildford, Hurtmore, Loseley, Normandy, Peper Harow, The Sands, Shackleford, Tongham, Wanborough, Wood Street

Pyrford

An ancient village without a traditional village centre, but now a residential area with pleasant tree lined roads.

NEWARK PRIORY. In private grounds south of Pyrford are the ruins of the 12th century Augustinian Newark Priory which was abandoned after its dissolution in 1536.

ST NICHOLAS'S CHURCH. On a hill top above the ruined Newark Priory stands the virtually unaltered Norman church. It is set in a circular churchyard near a prehistoric standing stone. The church is famous for the crosses carved by pilgrims and for the wall paintings. A fresco painted in 1140 and depicting fighting men on horseback was recently discovered under wall drawings of the Passion dating from 1200, which themselves were not discovered until 1869.

Golf Course
  Pyrford Golf Club, *Warren Lane, Pyrford, GU22 8XR* ☎ *01483 723555.*
Pub
★Anchor, *Pyrford Lock, Lock Lane, Pyrford, GU23 6QW* ☎ *01932 342507.*

See also Byfleet, Horsell, Horsley, Mayford, New Haw, Ockham, Ottershaw, Ripley, Send, Sheerwater, Sutton Green, Weybridge, Wisley, Woking, Woodham.

Ranmore Common

The village is still a remote place with just a few houses set around a long green.

RANMORE COMMON. The National Trust owns nearly 500 acres of land on the Common and there are superb views overlooking Dorking and surrounding countryside.

ST BARTHOLOMEW'S CHURCH. Designed by Sir George Gilbert Scott(1811-1878) and built in 1859, the church is cruciform in plan and has an octagonal central tower.

Inn
★Ranmore Arms, *Ranmore Common Road, Ranmore Common, RH5 6SX* ☎ *01483 283783.*
Nursery
  Foliage Scented and Herb Plants, *Crocknorth Road, Ranmore Common, RH5 6SX*
  ☎ *01483 282273.*
  MEMBER OF 'A TASTE OF SURREY' - HERB GARDENS OPEN 10AM - 5PM, WEDNESDAY - SUNDAY, APRIL - SEPTEMBER. COOKERY DEMONSTRATIONS AND TALKS ON THE CULTIVATION AND USE OF HERBS.
Tea Room
  Old Cartlodge, *Dunley Hill Farm, Ranmore Common Road, Ranmore Common, RH5 6SX*
  ☎ *01483 282222.*
  MEMBER OF 'A TASTE OF SURREY' - COFFEES, LUNCHES AND TEAS. HOME BAKED FOOD. OPEN TUESDAY TO SUNDAY 10AM TO 5PM (WINTER 4.30PM). AVAILABLE FOR PRIVATE SUPPERS AND WEDDINGS.

See also Abinger, Bookham, Box Hill, Dorking, Effingham, Fetcham, Horsley, Mickleham, Polesden Lacey, Westcott, Westhumble, Wotton.

Redhill

Redhill came into existence with the arrival of the railway in 1841, after the residents of Reigate objected to the prospect of having the line go through their town. With a large station and goods yard, the railway attracted much of the area's industry and commerce, which is still centred in Redhill, a town which has been modernised only recently.

HARLEQUIN THEATRE. This impressive theatre/concert hall complex offers an exciting and mixed programme of arts and entertainment. There are regular professional touring shows and screenings of popular feature films.

St John's Church. Originally early 19th century, but reconstructed in 1889 by J L Pearson, who added the spire.

Aquatic Centre
Pond Construction & Management, *12 Cronks Hill Road, Redhill, RH1 6LZ*
☎ *01737 226066.*
Art & Craft Shop
Indigo West Gemstones, *The Arcade, Station Road, Redhill, RH1 1PA* ☎ *01737 763777.*
Book Shops
Claude Gill Bargains, *46 The Belfry, Station Road, Redhill, RH1 1SA* ☎ *01737 771848.*
Hammicks, *12 The Belfry Centre, Redhill, RH1 1SA* ☎ *01737 770334.*
WH Smith, *The Belfry, Station Road, Redhill, RH1 1SA* ☎ *01737 770096.*
Cafe
Cafe Belfry, *38 Station Road, Redhill, RH1 1PH* ☎ *01737 763781.*
Cinema
Harlequin Theatre, *Warwick Quadrant, London Road, Redhill, RH1 1NN* ☎ *01737 765547.*
Golf Course
Redhill & Reigate Golf Club, *Pendleton Road, Redhill, RH1 6LB* ☎ *01737 240777*
Guest Houses
Arun Lodge, *37 Redstone Hill, Redhill, RH1 4AW* ☎ *01737 761933.*
Brompton, *6 Crossland Road, Redhill, RH1 4AN* ☎ *01737 765613.*
Fengates Lodge, *1 Fengates Road, Redhill, RH1 6AQ* ☎ *01737 764462.*
Lynwood, *50 London Road, Redhill, RH1 1LN* ☎ *01737 766894.*
Hotels & Inns
Ashleigh House Hotel, *39 Redstone Hill, Redhill, RH1 4BG* ☎ *01737 764763.*
★Hunters Lodge Hotel, *Nutfield Road, Redhill, RH1 4ED* ☎ *01737 773139.*
Lakers Hotel(Toby), *2 Redstone Hill, Redhill, RH1 4BL* ☎ *01737 768434.*
Information Centre
County Information Centre, *Redhill Library* ☎ *01737 773204.*
Library
SCC Lending Library, *18 Warwick Quadrant, Redhill, RH1 1NN* ☎ *01737 763332.*
Pubs
Elmshades, *26 Pendleton Road, Redhill, RH1 6QF* ☎ *01737 766052.*
Garibaldi, *29 Mill Street, Redhill, RH1 6PA* ☎ *01737 761239.*
Garland, *5 Brighton Road, Redhill, RH1 6PP* ☎ *01737 760377.*
Gatton Point, *171 London Road, Redhill, RH1 2JH* ☎ *01737 765180.*
Greyhound, *82 Brighton Road, Redhill, RH1 6QP* ☎ *01737 767147.*
Hatch, *44 Hatchlands Road, Redhill, RH1 6AT* ☎ *01737 764593.*
◆Home Cottage, *3 Redstone Hill, Redhill, RH1 4AW* ☎ *01737 762771.*
Jolly Brickmakers, *60 Frenches Road, Redhill, RH1 2JE* ☎ *01737 763915.*
◆Marquis of Granby, *6 Hooley Lane, Redhill, RH1 6ET* ☎ *01737 761959.*
Old Oak, *40 Somerset Road, Redhill, RH1 6LT* ☎ *Ex Dir.*
★◆Plough, *11 Church Road, Redhill, RH1 6QE* ☎ *01737 766686.*
Red Lion, *48 Linkfield Lane, Redhill, RH1 1JF* ☎ *01737 768215.*
Ship, *23 Copse Road, Redhill, RH1 6NW* ☎ *01737 244589.*
Wheatsheaf, *1 High Street, Redhill, RH1 1RD* ☎ *Ex Dir.*
White Lion, *40 Linkfield Street, Redhill, RH1 6BY* ☎ *01737 764045.*
Restaurants
Balcony, *The Belfry, Station Road, Redhill, RH1 1SA* ☎ *01737 773929.*
Curry Garden, *79 Brighton Road, Redhill, RH1 6PS* ☎ *01737 772083.*
Exotica Tandoori, *18 Cromwell Road, Redhill, RH1 1RT* ☎ *01737 778624.*
I Paparazzi, *37 High Street, Redhill, RH1 1RX* ☎ *01737 770383.*
Maxwells, *20 Station Road, Redhill, RH1 1PD* ☎ *01737 766872.*
Peach Blossom, *11 Hatchlands Road, Redhill, RH1 6AA* ☎ *01737 760289.*
Pizza Piazza, *3 Linkfield Street, Redhill, RH1 1HQ* ☎ *01737 766154.*
Plough Inn, *11 Church Road, Redhill, RH1 6QE* ☎ *01737 766686.*
Redstone Room, *East Surrey College, Claremont Road, Redhill, RH1 2JX* ☎ *01737 766023.*

Tang's, *28 High Street, Redhill, RH1 1RH* ☎ *01737 769405*.
Tong Fung, *19 Brighton Road, Redhill, RH1 5BT* ☎ *01737 762330*.

Sports & Leisure Centre
  Donyngs Recreation Centre, *Linkfield Lane, Redhill,
  RH1 1DP* ☎ *01737 764732*.

Swimming Pool
  Donyngs Recreation Centre, *Linkfield Lane, Redhill,
  RH1 1DP* ☎ *01737 764732*.

Take-Aways
  Burger King, *22 The Belfry, High Street, Redhill,
  RH1 1SA* ☎ *01737 767336*.
  Cater Express, *Redhill Station, Redhill, RH1 1RB*
  ☎ *01737 767428*.
  Chiu's Chicken, *11 Brighton Road, Redhill, RH1 6PP*
  ☎ *01737 765928*.
  Lotus House, *10 Linkfield Corner, Redhill, RH1 1BB*
  ☎ *01737 762590*.
  Master Fryer, *2 Linkfield Corner, Redhill, RH1 1BB*
  ☎ *01737 766091*.
  McDonald's, *12 The Quadrant, Redhill, RH1 1NT* ☎ *01737 760930*.
  Redhill Kebab House, *15 Brighton Road, Redhill, RH1 6PP* ☎ *01737 778045*.
  Ron Tozer's Fish Bar, *20 Station Road, Redhill, RH1 1PD* ☎ *01737 766872*.

Theatre
  Harlequin, *Warwick Quadrant, London Road, Redhill, RH1 1NN* ☎ *01737 765547*.

Wine Bar & Cafe Bar
  Oliver's, *8 Cromwell Road, Redhill, RH1 1RT* ☎ *01737 767040*.

The Warwick Quadrant

See also Bletchingley, Earlswood, Gatton, Hooley, Merstham, Nutfield, Reigate, Salfords, Sidlow
Bridge.

Reigate and Banstead Borough Council Leisure Link unit is responsible for:

Event Organisation
Livetime
Youth in Action
Playschemes
Arts & Entertainment
Cycling Development

Tourism Promotion
Leisure Development
Music in the Parks
Heritage Trails
Playgrounds

for more information on any of the above, write to:
Leisure Link
Town Hall, Castlefield
Reigate Surrey
RH2 0SH
or call the Leisure Link Hotline on

01737 242477

Reigate
(including Reigate Heath)

An ancient and historic market town with some fine old buildings, although little has survived from early times. The original settlement was centred around St Mary's church, whilst the castle and priory were developed to the west. Remarkable in its time is the old road tunnel driven under the castle mound in 1824 to ease the route for coaches on the London to Brighton road.

BARON'S CAVE. An extraordinary passage with a vaulted roof, hewn with great labour out of the soft stone underneath the castle, and one of several tunnels. It is not known when the cave was built or for what purpose. William de Warrenne was present with King John at the signing of the Magna Carta and legend has it that the barons who drew up the document met here before it was signed by the King. The tunnels can be visited by appointment.

CASTLE GROUNDS. The original castle was built around 1090 by William de Warenne, a hero of the Battle of Hastings and subsequently Earl of Surrey. Although later enlarged and strengthened, the castle fell into disrepair in the 17th century after the Civil War. By the late 18th century only the earthworks of the castle remained, the Castle grounds were tidied up, and in 1777 a mock gateway was erected in the architectural style of the old castle using original stones from the site. The Grounds are now public gardens.

CHURCH OF ST MARY MAGDALENE. The church dates back to the 11th century, and the vestry contains Britain's earliest public lending library founded in 1701. In the church is a large monument to Truth and Justice with their emblems, dating from about 1730 by an almost unknown sculptor Joseph Rose. Admiral Lord Charles Howard of Effingham is buried here.

COLLEY HILL. An area of great natural beauty with magnificent views, both Colley Hill and Reigate Hill are owned by the National Trust.

HOLMESDALE NATURAL HISTORY MUSEUM. The museum houses local maps and photographs and finds from archaeological digs in Reigate.

MARGOT FONTEYN. Dame Margot Fonteyn de Arias(1919-1991), prima ballerina assoluta of the Royal Ballet, was born in a house over the old post office in London Road. The statue, opposite where the house stood, depicts her in her favourite ballet as Ondine the water sprite dancing with her shadow. The sculpture is by Nathan David FRBS, and was unveiled by Dame Margot.

OLD TOWN HALL. Built in 1728 in Georgian red brick with a rounded end, it has an open arcaded ground floor and a court room above. The cupola and clock were added in the early 19th century.

PRIORY PARK. 65 acres of parkland around the Priory, which includes a large lake. Immediately adjoining is Reigate Park, a further 90 acres of woodland including Park Hill, given to the people of Reigate in 1921.

REIGATE HEATH. Lying to the west of the town and once reputed to have been the haunt of smugglers and highwaymen, Reigate Heath comprises about 130 acres of heath and woodland, and is a site of special scientific interest. Part of it is used for a private golf course, and the windmill stands on the highest point.

REIGATE PRIORY. Founded in the early 13th century by the Warrennes as an Augustinian monastery and dissolved by Henry VIII in 1536. The estate was granted to Lord William Howard of Effingham who converted the Priory into a magnificent residence, and admiral Lord Charles Howard of Effingham(1536-1624) who commanded the fleet that defeated the Spanish armada lived at the Priory for most of his life. More recently the house was owned by admiral Earl Beatty(1871-1936). The original buildings have been altered and the house now has a stuccoed Georgian front, but inside is a superb Tudor fireplace and an early Georgian staircase. The building now houses Reigate Priory Middle School.

REIGATE PRIORY MUSEUM. A children's history museum in part of the school, with changing exhibitions.

WINDMILL CHURCH. On Reigate Heath stands a post mill which dates from 1765. It is in excellent condition, the roundhouse having been converted to a chapel at the end of the 19th century. Church services are held once a month.

Antique Dealers
Bertram Noller, *14a London Road, Reigate, RH2 9HY* ☎ *01737 242548.*
Dorset Antiques, *61a High Street, Reigate, RH2 9AE* ☎ *01737 765065.*
Penny Black, *16 High Street, Reigate, RH2 9AY* ☎ *01737 244222.*
Reigate Antiques, *10 London Road, Reigate, RH2 9HY* ☎ *01737 226308.*

Art Galleries
Bourne Gallery, *31 Lesbourne Road, Reigate, RH2 7JS* ☎ *01737 241614.*
Nutley Galleries, *82 High Street, Reigate, RH2 9AP* ☎ *01737 222424.*

Book Shops
Ancient House Bookshop, *51 Bell Street, Reigate, RH2 7AQ* ☎ *01737 242806.*
Pilgrims, *90 High Street, Reigate, RH2 9AP* ☎ *01737 247534.*
Reigate Galleries, *45a Bell Street, Reigate, RH2 7AQ* ☎ *01737 246055.*

Business Information Centre
Surrey Business Network, *77 Bell Street, Reigate, RH2 7AN* ☎ *01737 222663.*

Cafe
Corner Cafe, *4 Dovers Green Road, Reigate, RH2 8BS* ☎ *01737 249186.*

Cinema
The Screen, *Bancroft Road, Reigate, RH2 7RP* ☎ *01737 223213.*

Garden Centres & Nurseries
Hartswood Nurseries, *146 Dovers Green Road, Reigate, RH2 8BY* ☎ *01737 242296.*
Heathfield Nurseries, *Flanchford Road, Reigate, RH2 8AA* ☎ *01737 247641.*
Reigate Garden Centre, *143 Sandcross Lane, Reigate, RH2 8HH* ☎ *01737 248188.*
Sunnyside Nurseries, *Chart Lane, Reigate, RH2 7BW* ☎ *01737 242857.*

Golf Course
Reigate Heath Golf Course, *Reigate Heath, Reigate, RH2 8QR* ☎ *01737 242610.*

Hotels & Inns
★Bridge House Hotel, *Reigate Hill, Reigate, RH2 9RP* ☎ *01737 244821.*
★Cranleigh Hotel, *41 West Street, Reigate, RH2 9BL* ☎ *01737 223417.*
Prince of Wales, *2 Holmesdale Road, Reigate, RH2 0BD* ☎ *01737 243112.*
★Reigate Manor Hotel, *Reigate Hill, Reigate, RH2 9PF* ☎ *01737 240125.*
White Hart, *12 Church Street, Reigate, RH2 0AN* ☎ *01737 242184.*

Library
SCC Lending Library, *Bancroft House, Bancroft Road, Reigate, RH2 7RP* ☎ *01737 244272.*

Model Shop
Reigate Toys & Models, *7 Prices Lane, Reigate, RH2 8BB* ☎ *01737 244155.*

Museums
Homesdale Natural History Museum, *14 Croydon Road, Reigate, RH2 0PG (Enquiries* ☎ *01737 247296)*
Reigate Priory Museum, *Reigate Priory School, Bell Street, Reigate, RH2 7RL* ☎ *01737 245065.*
Surrey Fire Brigade Museum, *Croydon Road, Reigate, RH2 0EJ* ☎ *01737 221759.*

Pubs
Admiral, *109a Nutley Lane, Reigate, RH2 9EF* ☎ *01737 240117.*
Angel, *1a Woodhatch Road, Reigate, RH2 7LG* ☎ *01737 241800.*
Barley Mow, *3 Eastnor Road, Reigate, RH2 8NE* ☎ *01737 241891.*

Beehive, *90 Doversgreen Road, Reigate, RH2 8PN* ☎ *01737 244634.*
Bell, *21 Bell Street, Reigate, RH2 7AD* ☎ *01737 244438.*
Black Horse, *93 West Street, Reigate, RH2 9JZ* ☎ *01737 245694.*
Blue Anchor, *27 West Street, Reigate, RH2 9BL* ☎ *01737 222823.*
Bulls Head, *55 High Street, Reigate, RH2 9AE* ☎ *Ex Dir.*
Castle, *85 Bell Street, Reigate, RH2 7AN* ☎ *Ex Dir.*
◆Desert Rat, *11 Lesbourne Road, Reigate, RH2 7JP* ☎ *01737 243524.*
Market Hotel, *2 High Street, Reigate, RH2 9AY* ☎ *01737 240492.*
Nutley Hall, *8 Nutley Lane, Reigate, RH2 9HP* ☎ *01737 241741.*
Panther, *50 Croydon Road, Reigate, RH2 0NH* ☎ *01737 244545.*
Red Cross Hotel, *96 High Street, Reigate, RH2 9AP* ☎ *01737 243955.*
★Skimmington Castle, *Bonnys Road, Reigate Heath, RH2 8RL* ☎ *01737 243100.*
Yew Tree, *99 Reigate Hill, Reigate, RH2 9PJ* ☎ *01737 244944.*

Restaurants
Curry Kutir, *2 London Road, Reigate, RH2 9AN* ☎ *01737 243934.*
Dining Room, *59a High Street, Reigate, RH2 9AE* ☎ *01737 226650.*
Red Rickshaw, *7 Holmesdale Road, Reigate, RH2 0BA* ☎ *01737 221567.*
Friendly Villa, *2 Western Parade, Reigate, RH2 8AU* ☎ *01737 241809.*
Golden Curry Tandoori, *57 Bell Street, Reigate, RH2 7AQ* ☎ *01737 244260.*
★La Barbe, *71 Bell Street, Reigate, RH2 7AN* ☎ *01737 241966.*
La Lanterna, *73 Bell Street, Reigate, RH2 7AN* ☎ *01737 245113.*
Mandarin, *27 Bell Street, Reigate, RH2 7AD* ☎ *01737 243374.*
Pizza Pavilion, *75 High Street, Reigate, RH2 9AE* ☎ *01737 222059.*
Raj, *10 West Street, Reigate, RH2 9BS* ☎ *01737 245695.*
Reigate Tandoori, *10 West Street, Reigate, RH2 9BS* ☎ *01737 245695.*
River Kwai, *94 High Street, Reigate, RH2 9AP* ☎ *01737 246528.*
Tortellini, *59 High Street, Reigate, RH2 9AE* ☎ *01737 242525.*

Take-Aways
Dove Fish, *19a Church Street, Reigate, RH2 0AA* ☎ *01737 226394.*
Dovers Green Fish Bar, *6 Dovers Green Road, Reigate, RH2 8BS* ☎ *01737 244288.*
Perfect Pizza, *10 Church Street, Reigate, RH2 0AN* ☎ *01737 223580.*
Priory Fish Bar, *54 Priory Road, Reigate, RH2 8JB* ☎ *01737 243214.*
Reigate Fish Bar, *41 Lesbourne Road, Reigate, RH2 7JS* ☎ *01737 245072.*
Tai Loy, *88 High Street, Reigate, RH2 9AP* ☎ *01737 243915.*
Wimpy, *11 Bell Street, Reigate, RH2 7AD* ☎ *01737 225574.*

Tea Room
Pantry, *65 High Street, Reigate, RH2 9AE* ☎ *01737 242762.*

Windmill
Windmill Church, *Reigate Heath, Reigate, RH2 8QR* ☎ *01737 221100.*

Wine Bars & Cafe Bars
Cage 1811, *Cage Yard, Reigate, RH2 9AB* ☎ *01737 221811.*
Red River Cafe, *1 Church Street, Reigate, RH2 0AA* ☎ *01737 243989.*

See also Betchworth, Buckland, Earlswood, Gatton, Kingswood, Leigh, Merstham, Nutfield, Redhill, Salfords, Sidlow Bridge, Walton on the Hill.

Ripley

An old coaching village on the route between London and Portsmouth, with half timbered houses and inns. Admiral Lord Nelson often stopped at the Talbot Hotel. During the latter part of the 19th century it became a popular location for cyclists, with as many as 7,000 a year signing the visitors's book at the Anchor Hotel.

ST MARY'S CHURCH. Rebuilt in 1864, the church still retains its Norman chancel dating from about 1160.

Antique Dealers
Anthony Welling, *Broadway Barn, High Street, Ripley, GU23 6AQ* ☎ *01483 225384.*

J Hartley Antiques, *186 High Street, Ripley, GU23 6BB* ☎ *01483 224318.*
Manor House Antiques, *High Street, Ripley, GU23 6AF* ☎ *01483 225350.*
Ripley Antiques, *67 High Street, Ripley, GU23 6AN* ☎ *01483 224981.*

Art Gallery
  CEDAR HOUSE GALLERY, *HIGH STREET, RIPLEY, GU23 6AE* ☎ *01483 211221.*
  OPEN 7 DAYS (RESIDENT ON PREMISES). RING BELL. SPECIALISE: C19TH OILS AND WATERCOLOURS OF FINE
  QUALITY; SURREY VIEWS; C19TH SURREY ARTISTS.

Golf Course
  Wisley Golf Club, *Ripley, GU23 6QU* ☎ *01483 211022.*

Hotels & Inns
  Half Moon, *High Street, Ripley, GU23 6AN* ☎ *01483 224380.*
  Talbot Hotel, *High Street, Ripley, GU23 6BB* ☎ *01483 225188.*

Nurseries
  Bentinck Nursery, *Portsmouth Road, Ripley, GU23 6JA* ☎ *01483 225132.*
  DC Jarman, *Wayside, Polesden Lane, Ripley, GU23 6DX* ☎ *01483 225114.*
  Ripley Nursery, *Portsmouth Road, Ripley, GU23 6EY* ☎ *01483 225090.*

Pick Your Own
  Nutberry Fruit Farm, *Portsmouth Road, Ripley* ☎ *01483 224842.*

Pubs
  Anchor Hotel, *High Street, Ripley, GU23 6AE* ☎ *01483 224120.*
  Seven Stars, *Newark Lane, Ripley, GU23 6DL* ☎ *01483 225128.*
★Ship, *High Street, Ripley, GU23 6AZ* ☎ *01483 225371.*

Restaurants
  Curry Garden Tandoori, *High Street, Ripley, GU23 6AY* ☎ *01483 224153.*
  Happy Eater, *Ripley Bypass Northbound, Ripley, GU23 6PT* ☎ *01483 225115.*
  Happy Eater, *Ripley Bypass Southbound, Ripley, GU23 6PU* ☎ *01483 225138.*
  Michels, *Clock House, High Street, Ripley, GU23 6AQ* ☎ *01483 224777.*
  Toby Cottage, *High Street, Ripley, GU23 6AF* ☎ *01483 224225.*

Tea Rooms & Cafes
  4 Coffee, *Amberley Cottage, High Street, Ripley, GU23 6AF* ☎ *01483 224040.*
  Rio Cafe, *Bridge End, High Street, Ripley, GU23 6AX* ☎ *01483 225003.*

See also Byfleet, Clandon, Horsley, Mayford, Ockham, Ottershaw, Pyrford, Send, Sheerwater,
Sutton Green, Wisley, Woking, Woodham.

Rowledge

Rowledge is on the border with Hampshire, and on the edge of Alice Holt Forest,
which is a relic of what was once a huge medieval hunting forest.

Farm Attraction
  Borderfield Farm Centre, *Boundary Road, Rowledge, GU10 4EP* ☎ *01252 793985.*

Pubs
  Cherry Tree, *Cherry Tree Road, Rowledge, GU10 4AB* ☎ *01252 792105.*
  Hare & Hounds, *2 The Square, Rowledge, GU10 4AA* ☎ *01252 792287.*

See also The Bourne, Churt, Farnham, Frensham, Tilford, Wrecclesham. On the Hampshire
boundary.

Runfold

At the foot of the Hog's Back, Runfold was once a centre of the hop growing
industry.

Pubs
  Jolly Farmer, *Guildford Road, Runfold, GU10 1PG* ☎ *01252 782074.*
  Princess Royal, *Guildford Road, Runfold, GU10 1NX* ☎ *01252 782243.*

See also Ash, Badshot Lea, The Bourne, Elstead, Farnham, Hale, Heath End, The Sands, Seale,
Tilford, Tongham, Wanborough, Wrecclesham. 1 mile from the Hampshire boundary.

Salfords

Guest House
  Mill Lodge, *25 Brighton Road, Salfords, RH1 5DA* ☎ *01293 771170.*
Inns
  Mill House(Beefeater), *Brighton Road, Salfords, RH1 5BT* ☎ *01737 767277.*
Pub
  General Napier, *54 Brighton Road, Salfords, RH1 5BZ* ☎ *01293 820298.*
Restaurant
  Viceroy of India, *22 Brighton Road, Salfords, RH1 5BX* ☎ *01293 783609.*
Take-Away
  Bright House, *52 Brighton Road, Salfords, RH1 5BX* ☎ *01293 782354.*

See also Earlswood, Hookwood, Horley, Leigh, Norwood Hill, Nutfield, Outwood, Redhill, Reigate, Sidlow Bridge, Smallfield. 3 miles from the Sussex boundary.

The Sands

CROOKSBURY COMMON. There are excellent views of the Wey Valley from the nearby Crooksbury Hill.

Golf Course
  Farnham Golf Club, *The Sands, GU10 1PX* ☎ *01252 783163.*
Pub
  Barley Mow, *Littleworth Road, The Sands, GU10 1NE* ☎ *01252 782200.*

See also Ash, Badshot Lea, The Bourne, Compton, Elstead, Farnham, Hale, Heath End, Peper Harow, Puttenham, Runfold, Seale, Shackleford, Tilford, Tongham, Wanborough, Wrecclesham. 3 miles from the Hampshire boundary.

Seale

Situated on the Pilgrims Way, there has been evidence of human occupation here dating back to the stone age.

HOG'S BACK HOTEL. The hotel was built on the site of the old semaphore tower built in 1822 as part of a chain which enabled messages to be sent between London and Portsmouth. (See Ockham).
MANOR FARM CRAFT CENTRE. Housed in picturesque old farm buildings in the centre of the village are craft shops producing pottery, interior furnishings, knitwear, jewellery, dried flowers and calligraphy. There is also a restaurant, and a health and beauty clinic.

Art & Craft Centre
  Manor Farm Craft Centre, *Wood Lane, Seale, GU10 1HR* ☎ *01252 783661.*
Hotel
  ★Hog's Back Hotel(Jarvis), *Hog's Back, Seale, GU10 1EX* ☎ *01252 782345.*
Nursery
  Oak Lodge Nursery, *Seale Lane, Seale, GU10 1LD* ☎ *01252 782410.*
Restaurants
  Happy Eater, *Hog's Back, Seale, GU10 1EU* ☎ *01252 783186.*
  Manor Restaurant, *Manor Farm Craft Centre* ☎ *01252 783333.*
  Squires Holt, *Hog's Back, Seale, GU10 1HE* ☎ *01483 810272.*

See also Ash, Badshot Lea, Compton, Elstead, Farnham, Hale, Normandy, Peper Harow, Runfold,

The Sands, Shackleford, Tilford, Tongham, Wanborough.

Send
(including Send Marsh)

Pick Your Own
  Nuthill Farm, *London Road, Send, GU23 7LW* ☎ *01483 458458.*
Pubs
  Jovial Sailor, *Portsmouth Road, Send Marsh, GU23 6EZ* ☎ *01483 224360.*
  New Inn, *Send Road, Send, GU23 7EN* ☎ *01483 762736.*
  Saddlers Arms, *Send Marsh Road, Send Marsh, GU23 6JQ* ☎ *01483 224209.*
Take-Away
  Ocean Fish Bar, *149 Send Road, Send, GU23 7EZ* ☎ *01483 223749.*

See also Burpham, Clandon, Guildford, Horsell, Horsley, Mayford, Merrow, Newlands Corner, Ockham, Pyrford, Ripley, Sheerwater, Sutton Green, Wisley, Woking, Worplesdon.

Shackleford

Restaurant
  Cyder House Inn, *Peperharow Lane, Shackleford, GU8 6AN* ☎ *01483 810360.*

See also Compton, Eashing, Elstead, Farncombe, Godalming, Hurtmore, Loseley, Milford, Peper Harow, Puttenham, The Sands, Seale, Tongham, Wanborough, Witley.

Shalford

Shalford is the point at which the River Tillingbourne joins the River Wey. In the village, near St Mary's church, are the old village stocks and a whipping post. John Bunyan(1628-1688) is reputed to have lived here for a time, and Shalford Fair, once held regularly on the water meadows, is said to have been the model for Vanity Fair in his Pilgrims Progress.

BROADFORD. Once a tiny port on the River Wey Navigation, from where gunpowder from Chilworth was shipped to London.
SHALFORD MILL (National Trust). An attractive 18th century water mill on the River Tillingbourne, which was donated to the National Trust in 1932 by an anonymous group of preservationists known as Ferguson's gang. The old storage area of the mill has been converted into a house which is tenanted, but the working part of the mill, where all the principal machinery remains intact, is open to the public.

Pubs
  Parrot Inn, *Broadford Road, Shalford, GU4 8DW* ☎ *01483 61400.*
  Queen Victoria, *Station Row, Shalford, GU4 8BY* ☎ *01483 61733.*
  Seahorse, *54 The Street, Shalford, GU4 8BU* ☎ *01483 61917.*
Restaurant
  Royal Garden, *2 Kings Road, Shalford, GU4 8JU* ☎ *01483 452550.*
Watermill
  Shalford Mill, *The Street, Shalford, GU4 8BS.*

See also Albury, Blackheath, Bramley, Burpham, Chilworth, Compton, Farncombe, Godalming, Guildford, Hurtmore, Loseley, Merrow, Newlands Corner, Shamley Green, Wonersh.

Shamley Green

A picturesque hamlet which was granted a charter by Oliver Cromwell to hold an annual fair.

FARLEY HEATH. The site of a Roman settlement where in 1939 the footings of a Romano-Celtic temple(c100AD) were found.

Inn
  Red Lion Inn, *Guildford Road, Shamley Green, GU5 0UB* ☎ *01483 892202.*
Pick Your Own
  Hullbrook Farm, *Long Common, Shamley Green, GU5 0TF* ☎ *01483 898460.*
Pub
  Bricklayers Arms, *Guildford Road, Shamley Green, GU5 0UA* ☎ *01483 898377.*

See also Albury, Blackheath, Bramley, Chilworth, Hascombe, Peaslake, Shalford, Shere, Wonersh.

Sheerwater

The Sheerwater Valley had been a lake until the 1820s, and was still waterlogged when it was purchased by the London County Council in 1948 to provide overspill housing for the capital. By the mid 1950s this 230 acres of land between the railway and the canal had been transformed into a complete village.

Cafe
  Oasis Cafe, *39 Dartmouth Avenue, Sheerwater, GU21 5PE* ☎ *01932 346325.*
Pub
  Birch & Pines, *22 Dartmouth Avenue, Sheerwater, GU21 5PJ* ☎ *Ex Dir.*
Take-Aways
  Harvey Burger & Pizza, *53 Dartmouth Avenue, Sheerwater, GU21 5PE* ☎ *01932 346687.*
  Jade House, *59 Dartmouth Avenue, Sheerwater, GU21 5PE* ☎ *01932 343105.*

See also Addlestone, Byfleet, Chobham, Horsell, Mayford, New Haw, Ottershaw, Pyrford, Ripley, Send, Wisley, Woking.

Shepperton

Shepperton was a quiet riverside village in private ownership until the early 19th century. The charm of Church Square owes much to its proximity to the river and the 16th, 17th and 18th century buildings, which are now mainly hotels and restaurants.

ST NICHOLAS'S CHURCH. An unusual church in that the transepts are so wide that the building is almost square. The church was rebuilt in 1614 after the river had undermined the foundations of the earlier building, and the battlemented tower was added in 1710.
THE RECTORY. A 16th century building clad with 'mathematical-tiles'. Richard III is said to have stayed here before Bosworth Field(1485), and Erasmus(1466-1536) often stayed here as the protegee of William Grocyn(1446-1519) the scholar and humanist and for some years rector of Shepperton. In later years the novelist George Eliot(1819-1880) was also often a guest.

Antique Dealers
  Crown Antiques, *Russell Road, Shepperton, TW17 9WF* ☎ *01932 247709.*
  Rickett & Co, *Church Square, Shepperton, TW17 9JY* ☎ *01932 243571.*
  Shepperton Antiques, *130 High Street, Shepperton, TW17 9BG* ☎ *01932 223723.*
Art & Craft Equipment
  Redburn Crafts, *Squire's Garden Centre* ☎ *01932 788052.*
Garden Centres & Nurseries
  Hidden Garden, *Nutty Lane, Shepperton, TW17 0RQ* ☎ *01932 781474.*
  Laleham Nurseries, *Laleham Road, Shepperton, TW17 0JP* ☎ *01932 563322.*
  Squire's Garden Centre, *Halliford Road, Shepperton, TW17 8RU* ☎ *01932 784121.*
Golf Course & Driving Range
  Sunbury Golf Club, *Charlton Lane, Shepperton, TW17 8QA* ☎ *01932 772898.*
Guest House
  Willow House, *Russell Road, Shepperton, TW17 9HS* ☎ *01932 246594.*
Hotels & Inns
  ★Anchor Hotel, *Church Square, Shepperton, TW17 9JY* ☎ *01932 221618.*
  Barley Mow, *67 Watersplash Road, Shepperton, TW17 0EE* ☎ *01932 225580.*
  ★Bull Inn, *152 Laleham Road, Shepperton, TW17 0DB* ☎ *01932 221667.*
  ★Moat House Hotel, *Felix Lane, Shepperton, TW17 8NP* ☎ *01932 241404.*
  Ship Hotel, *Russell Road, Shepperton, TW17 9HX* ☎ *01932 227320.*
  ★Warren Lodge Hotel, *Church Square, Shepperton, TW17 9JZ* ☎ *01932 242972.*
Library
  SCC Lending Library, *High Street, Shepperton, TW17 9AU* ☎ *01932 225047.*
Pubs
  Bell, *Old Charlton Road, Shepperton, TW17 8BT* ☎ *Ex Dir.*
  Bugle, *Upper Halliford Road, Shepperton, TW17 8SN* ☎ *01932 782405.*
  Crossroads, *Laleham Road, Shepperton, TW17 8EQ* ☎ *01932 220319.*
  ★Harrow Inn, *142 Charlton Road, Shepperton, TW17 0RJ* ☎ *01932 783122.*
  Kings Head, *Church Square, Shepperton, TW17 9JY* ☎ *01932 221910.*
  ★Red Lion, *Russell Road, Shepperton, TW17 9HX* ☎ *01932 220042.*
  Three Horseshoes, *131 High Street, Shepperton, TW17 9BL* ☎ *01932 225726.*
Restaurants
  Barn on the Green, *Sunbury Golf Club* ☎ *01932 770298.*
  Blubeckers, *Church Street, Shepperton, TW17 9JY* ☎ *01932 243377.*
  Edwinns, *Church Square, Shepperton, TW17 9JY* ☎ *01932 223543.*
  Forum, *23 High Street, Shepperton, TW17 9AJ* ☎ *01932 229124.*
  Goat Inn(Chef & Brewer), *47 Upper Halliford Road, Shepperton, TW17 8RX* ☎ *01932 782415.*
  Heaven, *2 Station Approach, Shepperton, TW17 8AR* ☎ *01932 229400.*
  Ivory Tusk, *78 High Street, Shepperton, TW17 9AU* ☎ *01932 246899.*
  Rumbles, *1 High Street, Shepperton, TW17 9AJ* ☎ *01932 227475.*
  Thames Court Hotel, *Towpath, Shepperton Lock, Shepperton, TW17 9LJ* ☎ *01932 221957.*
Take-Aways
  Golden Pan, *150 Laleham Road, Shepperton, TW17 0AX* ☎ *01932 223110.*
  Number 88, *88 High Street, Shepperton, TW17 9AU* ☎ *01932 232800.*
  Sun Hing, *90 High Street, Shepperton, TW17 9AU* ☎ *01932 223416.*
  Wing Wah House, *205 Laleham Road, Shepperton, TW17 0AH* ☎ *01932 244111.*
Tea Room
  Orangery Tea Rooms, *Squire's Garden Centre* ☎ *01932 789823.*
Water Sports
  Twickenham & Whitewater Canoe Centre, *Shepperton Marina, Felix Lane, Shepperton, TW17 8NJ* ☎ *01932 247978.*

See also Addlestone, Ashford, Chertsey, Laleham, Lyne, New Haw, Ottershaw, Sunbury, Thorpe, Virginia Water, Walton on Thames, Weybridge, Whiteley Village, Woodham.

Shere

Probably of Saxon origin and recorded in the Domesday Book, Shere has many charming cottages of the 16th, 17th, and 18th centuries, a small 17th century prison and an ancient church. Situated on the Tillingbourne River, between the greensand hills and the North Downs, the village is one of the prettiest and most popular in Surrey. Sir Edwin Lutyens(1869-1944) built the gate lodge to the manor house, some cottages nearby and designed the lych-gate to St James's Church. J M Barrie(1860-1937) lived for a while at Anchor Cottage where he wrote The Professor's Love Story.

OLD FARM. There are tours and demonstrations showing the production of flour from corn, chips from potatoes, linen from flax, and barns from trees. In spring there are baby lambs, and there are demonstrations of shearing, spinning and weaving. The entrance to the farm is behind the Church.

ST JAMES'S CHURCH. A fine early Norman church built on the site of an earlier Saxon church. In the 14th century, a woman hermit was walled up in a cell outside the church where a squint, an oblique opening through the wall, gave her a view of the altar. The font is 13th century.

SHERE MUSEUM. Exhibitions of local history with an interesting and wide range of mainly Victorian and later bygones.

SILENT POOL. One mile west of Shere is the romantic 'Silent Pool'. Legend has it that a peasant girl bathing there was frightened by King John and drowned, and that a stone thrown in the pool causes no ripple.

Antique Dealers
  Asters Antiques, *Middle Street, Shere, GU5 9HF* ☎ *01483 202846.*
  Yesterdays Pine, *Gomshall Lane, Shere, GU5 9HE* ☎ *01483 203198.*
Art Gallery
  Forge Gallery, *Middle Street, Shere, GU5 9HF* ☎ *01483 202388.*
Farm Attraction
  Old Farm, *behind Shere Church (Enquiries* ☎ *01483 203034).*
Farm Shop
  Old Scotland Farmhouse, *off Staple Lane, Shere* ☎ *01483 222526.*
    MEMBER OF 'A TASTE OF SURREY' - ENGLISH FARMHOUSE CHEESE PRODUCERS.
Museum
  Shere Museum, *The Malt House, Shere Lane, Shere, GU5 9HS* ☎ *01483 203245.*
Pubs
  Prince of Wales, *Shere Lane, Shere, GU5 9HS* ☎ *01483 202313.*
★White Horse, *Shere Lane, Shere, GU5 9HS* ☎ *01483 202518.*
Restaurant
  Kinghams, *Gomshall Lane, Shere, GU5 9HB* ☎ *01483 202168.*
Tea Room
  Asters Tea Shop, *Middle Street, Shere, GU5 9HF* ☎ *01483 202445.*

See also Abinger, Albury, Blackheath, Chilworth, Clandon, Gomshall, Holmbury St Mary, Merrow, Newlands Corner, Peaslake, Shamley Green, Wonersh, Wotton.

Shipley Bridge

Golf Course
  Burstow Park Golf Club, *Antlands Lane, Shipley Bridge, RH6 9TF* ☎ *01293 820303.*
Guest House
  Park House, *Green Lane, Shipley Bridge, RH6 9TJ* ☎ *01293 786806.*
Nursery
  Burstow Nurseries, *Antlands Lane, Shipley Bridge, RH6 9TE* ☎ *01293 771942.*

Restaurant
Shipley Bridge Inn, *Antlands Lane, Shipley Bridge, RH6 9TE* ☎ *01293 771878.*

See also Burstow, Copthorne, Felbridge, Horley, Horne, Newchapel, Outwood, Smallfield. On the Sussex boundary.

Sidlow Bridge

Inn
Three Horseshoes Inn, *Ironsbottom, Sidlow Bridge, RH2 8PT* ☎ *01293 862315.*

See also Betchworth, Buckland, Earlswood, Hookwood, Horley, Leigh, Norwood Hill, Redhill, Reigate, Salfords.

Smallfield

The origins of this small village go back to the reign of Edward III, when the estate of Smallfield Place was given to John de Burstow and the village was named accordingly.

SMALLFIELD PLACE. One of the most important examples of domestic building in the country. Built in the early 1600s of local sandstone and roofed with Horsham slab, it contains fine panelling and a great fireplace in the hall. The estate was given to John de Burstow by Lord Burghersh in the 14th century in recognition of personal service during the French Wars.

Book Shop
Burnetts, *Smallfield Post Office, Wheelers Lane, Smallfield, RH6 6PT* ☎ *01342 842001.*
Pub
◆Plough, *Plough Road, Smallfield, RH6 9JN* ☎ *01342 842212.*

See also Blindley Heath, Burstow, Copthorne, Felbridge, Hookwood, Horley, Horne, Newchapel, Outwood, Salfords, Shipley Bridge. 2 miles from the Sussex boundary.

Staines

Occupation of the Staines area goes back to neolithic times, a causewayed enclosure being found by aerial photography. Since Roman times, when the town was called Pontes, it has been important as a crossing point of the River Thames. Staines was also a flourishing fair and market town until the end of the 19th century. With the coming of the railway in 1848 the district started to develop into a major residential and light industrial area. The world's first linoleum was made here in 1862.

The Old Town Hall

BLUE ANCHOR. Built in red and black brick, the pub has five windows which were bricked up with the imposition of the 18th century Window Tax.
CHURCH STREET. An interesting street with buildings from the 17th and 18th centuries, many of which have been well restored.
OLD TOWN HALL ARTS CENTRE. Formerly the Town Hall, built in 1880 to replace the old market hall, the Centre presents a diverse programme of professional events including theatre, dance, classical music, light music and world music, mime comedy, jazz, exhibitions, children's shows, workshops and classes.

ST MARY'S CHURCH. Built on a site used for worship by ancient druids, the present church dates from only 1828. It contains some fine stained glass windows given by Kaiser Wilhelm.

SPELTHORNE MUSEUM. Currently closed.

STAINES BRIDGE. Many bridges have been built here and either collapsed or were demolished. The present bridge, built of granite, was designed by John and George Rennie, sons of John Rennie who built London's original Waterloo, London and Southwark bridges, and opened by King William IV in 1832.

STAINES MOOR. Designated a site of special scientific interest, along with the King George VI and Staines Reservoirs, Shortwood Common and Poyle Meadows, Staines Moor is situated to the north of the town on the flood plain of the lower Colne Valley, and has a recorded history dating back to 1065.

Antique Dealers
KW Dunster, *23 Church Street, Staines, TW18 4EN* ☎ *01784 453297.*
Staines Antiques, *145 Kingston Road, Staines, TW18 1PD* ☎ *01784 461306.*
Arts Centre
Old Town Hall Arts Centre, *Market Square, Staines, TW18 4RH* ☎ *01784 461617.*
Boat Hire
Aquamarine Pleasure Boats, *The Causeway, Staines, TW18 3BA* ☎ *01784 456310.*
J Tims & Sons, *Boat House, Timsway, Staines, TW18 3JY* ☎ *01784 452093.*
Book Shops
Canaan Christian Bookshop, *121 High Street, Staines, TW18 4PD* ☎ *01784 457194.*
John Menzies, *42 Elmsleigh Centre, Staines, TW18 4QB* ☎ *01784 461107.*
WH Smith, *49 High Street, Staines, TW18 4QH* ☎ *01784 452700.*
Cafe
Grand Cafe, *169 High Street, Staines, TW18 4PA* ☎ *01784 453924.*
Cinema
MGM Cinema, *Clarence Street, Staines, TW18 4SP* ☎ *01784 464748.*
Crazy Golf
Staines Park *(Enquiries: The Pavilion* ☎ *01784 455387).*
Garden Centre
Rosemead Garden Centre, *44 Wraysbury Road, Staines, TW19 6HA* ☎ *01784 482146.*
Guest House
Albany House, *2 Glebe Road, Staines, TW18 1BX* ☎ *01784 441223.*
Hotels & Inns
Angel Hotel(Galleon), *High Street, Staines, TW18 4EE* ☎ *01784 452509.*
Anne Boleyn Hotel, *The Hythe, Staines, TW18 3JD* ☎ *01784 455930.*
Blue Anchor Inn, *13 High Street, Staines, TW19 7JR* ☎ *01784 452622.*
◆Swan Hotel, *The Hythe, Staines, TW18 3JB* ☎ *01784 452494.*
★Thames Lodge(Forte), *Thames Street, Staines, TW18 4SF* ☎ *01784 464433.*
Information Centre
Staines Information Centre, *Staines Library* ☎ *01784 463071.*
Library
SCC Lending Library, *Friends Walk, Staines, TW18 4PG* ☎ *01784 454430.*
Museum
Spelthorne Museum, *Market Square, Staines, TW18 4RH* ☎ *01784 461804.*
Park
Staines Park, *Knowle Green, Staines (Enquiries* ☎ *01784 455387).*
Pubs
Beehive, *35 Edgell Road, Staines, TW18 2EP* ☎ *01784 452663.*
★Bells, *124 Church Street, Staines, TW18 4YA* ☎ *01784 454240.*
Cock Inn, *46 Church Street, Staines, TW18 4XR* ☎ *01784 462467.*
Dog & Partridge, *Edinburgh Drive, Staines, TW18 1PX* ☎ *01784 255482.*
Garibaldi, *116 High Street, Staines, TW18 4BY* ☎ *01784 452510.*
Halfway House, *The Causeway, Staines, TW18 3AX* ☎ *01784 453717.*
Hobgoblin, *14 Church Street, Staines, TW18 4EP* ☎ *01784 452012.*
Jolly Butcher, *174 Kingston Road, Staines, TW18 1PE* ☎ *01784 453281.*

Jolly Farmer, *The Hythe, Staines, TW18 3JA* ☎ *01784 452807.*
Old Red Lion, *Leacroft, Staines, TW18 4NN* ☎ *01784 453355.*
Phoenix, *43 Church Street, Staines, TW18 4EN* ☎ *01784 452384.*
Swan, *Moor Lane, Staines, TW19 6EB* ☎ *01784 465106.*
Three Tuns, *63 London Road, Staines, TW18 4BN* ☎ *01784 453743.*
◆Wheatsheaf & Pigeon, *Penton Road, Staines, TW18 2LL* ☎ *01784 452922.*
Putting Green
Ashby Lammas Recreation Ground, *Wraysbury Road, Staines.*
Restaurants
Ancient Raj, *157 High Street, Staines, TW18 4PA* ☎ *01784 456987.*
Cavalier, *Kingston Road, Staines, TW18 4LN* ☎ *01784 454548.*
Crooked Billet(Beefeater), *163 London Road, Staines, TW18 4HR* ☎ *01784 452247.*
Mamma Mia, *21b Clarence Street, Staines, TW18 4SU* ☎ *01784 454911.*
Pizza Express, *14 Clarence Street, Staines, TW18 4SP* ☎ *01784 456522.*
Riverside Carvery(Chef & Brewer), *1 Clarence Street, Staines, TW18 4SU* ☎ *01784 457546.*
San Remo, *11 Church Street, Staines, TW18 4EN* ☎ *01784 450706.*
Shahee Mahal, *151 High Street, Staines, TW18 4PA* ☎ *01784 454728.*
Staines Steak House, *130 High Street, Staines, TW18 4BY* ☎ *01784 451181.*
Staines Tandoori, *11 London Road, Staines, TW18 4AJ* ☎ *01784 452142.*
Szechuan, *139 High Street, Staines, TW18 4PA* ☎ *01784 452613.*
Ting, *20 Bridge Street, Staines, TW18 4TW* ☎ *01784 451577.*
Sports & Leisure Centres
Spelthorne Leisure Centre, *Knowle Green, Staines, TW18 1AJ* ☎ *01784 469729.*
Staines Youth Sports Centre, *Leacroft, Staines, TW18 4NN* ☎ *01784 453220.*
Swimming Pool
Spelthorne Leisure Centre ☎ *01784 464873.*
Take-Aways
Hungry Haven, *18 Central Trading Estate, Staines, TW18 4UX* ☎ *01784 440792.*
Kebab Elite, *19 Clarence Street, Staines, TW18 4SU* ☎ *01784 456262.*
Kentucky Fried Chicken, *159 High Street, Staines, TW18 4PA* ☎ *01784 455032.*
Kings, *6 Stainash Parade, Kingston Road, Staines, TW18 1BB* ☎ *01784 451094.*
McDonald's, *62 High Street, Staines, TW18 4DY* ☎ *01784 454184.*
Mr Chips, *12 Clarence Street, Staines, TW18 4SP* ☎ *01784 455724.*
Pizza Hut, *152 High Street, Staines, TW18 4AH* ☎ *01784 449977.*
Rasa Number Wan, *29 Church Street, Staines, TW18 4EN* ☎ *01784 456840.*
Slices, *10 Church Street, Staines, TW18 4EP* ☎ *01784 456544.*
Wan Ying House, *143 Kingston Road, Staines, TW18 1PD* ☎ *01784 453946.*
Theatre
Old Town Hall Arts Centre, *Market Square, Staines, TW18 4RH* ☎ *01784 446396.*

See also Ashford, Egham, Englefield Green, Laleham, Poyle, Stanwell, Thorpe, Virginia Water. 1 mile from the Berkshire boundary & 2 miles from the Greater London boundary.

Stanwell
(including Stanwell Moor)

Stanwell is famous among rose growers for the discovery in 1838 of a previously unknown variety which was duly named Stanwell Perpetual.

LORD KNYVETT'S SCHOOL. A school built in 1624 by Sir Thomas Knyvett, the man who arrested Guy Fawkes, and now an adult education centre.

ST MARY'S CHURCH. A church of 13th century origin with work of the 14th and 15th centuries. There is an elegant monument of about 1622 by Nicholas Stone(1586-1647) of Lord and Lady Knyvett. Stone was master-mason to Charles I during most of the period that Inigo Jones was Surveyor-General, but he also worked as a sculptor, introducing the use of black and white marble into England. He is particularly noted for his monument to John Donne in St Pauls Cathedral.

Garden Centre & Nursery
   Vermeulen's Garden Centre, *Horton Road, Stanwell Moor, TW19 6AE* ☎ *01784 451737.*
Pubs
   Anchor, *Horton Road, Stanwell Moor, TW19 6AQ* ☎ *Ex Dir.*
   Five Bells, *54 High Street, Stanwell, TW19 7JS* ☎ *01784 244822.*
   Happy Landing, *Clare Road, Stanwell, TW19 7QT* ☎ *Ex Dir.*
   Hope, *53 Hithermoor Road, Stanwell Moor, TW19 6AR* ☎ *Ex Dir.*
   Rising Sun, *110 Oaks Road, Stanwell, TW19 7LB* ☎ *01784 244080.*
   Stanwell Hall Hotel, *171 Town Lane, Stanwell, TW19 7PN* ☎ *01784 252292.*
   Swan, *16 High Street, Stanwell, TW19 7JS* ☎ *Ex Dir.*
   Three Crowns, *Long Lane, Stanwell, TW19 7AU* ☎ *01784 252713.*
   Wheatsheaf, *Park Road, Stanwell, TW19 7PB* ☎ *01784 253372.*
Putting Greens
   Recreation Ground, *Long Lane, Stanwell.*
   Recreation Ground, *Oaks Road, Stanwell.*

See also Ashford, Laleham, Poyle, Staines, Sunbury. 2 miles from the Berkshire boundary & 1 mile from the Greater London boundary.

Stoke D'Abernon

The Romans settled here and later the Saxons erected the church. Roger d'Abernon came to England with William the Conqueror and was rewarded with land at Molesey. A century later his descendants were securely settled in Stoke.

CHURCH OF ST MARY THE VIRGIN. Said to be anglo-saxon, this is the oldest church in the county, although the south wall, with an original doorway, is the only part to survive from that time. The church contains the monumental brasses to the D'Abernon knights. That to Sir John, who died in 1277, is the oldest brass in England. The 15th century Norbury Chapel contains 17th century monuments.
SIR YEHUDI MENUHIN SCHOOL. A boarding school for training young musicians, named after the American violinist.
SLYFIELD HOUSE. One of the best groups of domestic Jacobean buildings in England.

Garden Centre
   Peters Garden Centre, *Stoke Road, Stoke D'Abernon, KT11 3PU* ☎ *01932 862530.*
Hotel
   ★Woodlands Park Hotel, *Woodlands Lane, Stoke D'Abernon, KT11 3QB* ☎ *01372 843933.*
Pub
   ★Plough, *3 Station Road, Stoke D'Abernon, KT11 3BN* ☎ *01932 862244.*

See also Bookham, Claygate, Cobham, Downside, Fetcham, Hersham, Leatherhead, Ockham, Oxshott, Whiteley Village. 3 miles from the Greater London boundary.

Sunbury-on-Thames

Sunbury became a fashionable place of residence for wealthy Londoners moving out of town, after the restoration of Charles II. The town as we know it today came into being between 1690 and 1800, extensive estates being laid out and houses being built on the banks of the Thames.

KEMPTON PARK RACECOURSE. Kempton was used as a royal residence until the late 1400s, the park having been enclosed in 1246 and stocked with deer until 1835. The racecourse was laid out on part of the grounds in 1878, and today Kempton Park offers some of the finest facilities to be found at any racecourse in the country. There are also seven evening race meetings, that in June being combined with a musical programme and spectacular fireworks display. The highlight of the year is the traditional two-day Christmas festival.

ST MARY'S CHURCH. A church dating from 1752 on the site of a 14th century building, but renovated in 1856 with multi-coloured brickwork and other decorative features.

SUNBURY COURT. A fine 18th century building with Ionic pilasters and a pediment. In the Saloon are Arcadian wall paintings by the Swedish painter Elias Martin. It is the only surviving large mansion in Sunbury and now a Salvation Army youth centre.

SUNBURY PARK WALLED GARDEN. Designed on formal lines, the garden includes various styles of garden types from past centuries, including knot gardens, parterres and a Victorian rose garden. There are also four large areas of island beds in which are displayed collections of plants from all parts of the world. The garden offers quiet seclusion, and is also the venue for regular Sunday afternoon band concerts throughout the summer.

Arts Centre
Riverside Arts Centre, *59 Thames Street, Sunbury, TW16 5QF* ☎ *01932 789249.*
Boat Hire
George Wilson & Sons, *Ferry House, Thames Street, Sunbury, TW16 6AQ* ☎ *01932 782067.*
Garden
Sunbury Park Walled Garden, *Thames Street, Sunbury.*
Garden Centres & Nurseries
GH Roote & Sons, *Watersplash Farm, Fordbridge Road, Sunbury, TW16 6AU*
☎ *01932 783057.*
Jungle Gardens, *Fordbridge Road, Sunbury, TW16 6AX* ☎ *01932 772136.*
Golf Course and Driving Range
Hazelwood Golf Centre, *Croysdale Avenue, Green Street, Sunbury, TW16 6QU*
☎ *01932 770932.*
Hotels & Inns
Flower Pot Hotel, *Thames Street, Lower Sunbury, TW16 6AA* ☎ *01932 780741.*
Magpie Hotel, *64 Thames Street, Sunbury, TW16 6AF* ☎ *01932 782024.*
Library
SCC Lending Library, *The Parade, Staines Road West, Sunbury, TW16 7AB* ☎ *01932 783131.*
Pubs
Admiral Hawke, *81 Green Street, Sunbury, TW16 6RD* ☎ *01932 781326.*
George, *244 Staines Road East, Sunbury, TW16 5AX* ☎ *01932 785383.*
Grey Horse, *63 Staines Road East, Sunbury, TW16 5AA* ☎ *01932 782981.*
  REAL ALES; LARGE BEER GARDEN; HOT AND COLD LUNCHES (WEEKDAYS ONLY).
Hare & Hounds, *132 Vicarage Road, Sunbury, TW16 7QX* ☎ *01932 782242.*
Jockey, *French Street, Sunbury, TW16 5JH* ☎ *01932 783352.*
Jolly Gardeners, *101 Nursery Road, Sunbury, TW16 6LU* ☎ *01932 782251.*
Jubilee, *144 Staines Road East, Sunbury, TW16 5AY* ☎ *01932 782053.*
Phoenix, *26 Thames Street, Sunbury, TW16 6AF* ☎ *01932 785358.*
Prince Albert, *165 Staines Road West, Sunbury, TW16 7BQ* ☎ *01932 787229.*
◆Rosie's & Robbie's, *30 Sunbury Cross Centre, Sunbury, TW16 7AZ* ☎ *01932 766183.*
Shears, *192 Staines Road West, Sunbury, TW16 7BP* ☎ *Ex Dir.*
Three Fishes, *35 Green Street, Sunbury, TW16 6RE* ☎ *01932 782133.*
White Horse, *69 Thames Street, Sunbury, TW16 5QF* ☎ *Ex Dir.*
Race Course
Kempton Park, *Staines Road East, Sunbury, TW16 5AQ* ☎ *01932 782292.*
Restaurants
Castle, *21 Thames Street, Sunbury, TW16 5QF* ☎ *01932 783647.*
Shahin Tandoori, *67 Thames Street, Sunbury, TW16 5QF* ☎ *01932 785001.*
Sunbury Tandoori, *98 Windmill Road, Sunbury, TW16 7HB* ☎ *01932 780327.*
Yum Yum Tree, *9 Staines Road West, Sunbury, TW16 7AB* ☎ *01932 780973.*

Sports & Leisure Centre
Sunbury Leisure Centre, *Nursery Road, Sunbury, TW16 6LG* ☎ *01932 772287.*
Swimming Pool
Sunbury Leisure Centre, *Nursery Road, Sunbury, TW16 6LG* ☎ *01932 772287.*
Take-Aways
D James & Son, *189 Vicarage Road, Sunbury, TW16 7TP* ☎ *01932 783258.*
Po-On, *123 Groveley Road, Sunbury, TW16 7JZ* ☎ *0181-890 2985.*
Red Herring Fish Bar, *37a Green Street, Sunbury, TW16 6RE* ☎ *01932 787757.*
Shappi Tandoori, *135 Vicarage Road, Sunbury, TW16 7QB* ☎ *01932 771433.*
Starburger, *11 Sunbury Cross Centre, Sunbury, TW16 7BB* ☎ *01932 788051.*
Sunbury Chinese, *52 Nursery Road, Sunbury, TW16 6LG* ☎ *01932 770538.*
Theatres
Riverside Arts Centre, *59 Thames Street, Sunbury, TW16 5QF* ☎ *01932 789249.*

See also Ashford, Laleham, Molesey, Shepperton, Stanwell, Walton on Thames. On the Greater
London boundary.

Sunningdale

Sunningdale is mainly in Berkshire, but the eastern edges are in Surrey.

Pubs
Chequers, *London Road, Sunningdale, SL5 0DQ* ☎ *01344 22397.*
Red Lion, *London Road, Sunningdale, SL5 0LE* ☎ *01344 22038.*

See also Egham, Englefield Green, Lyne, Thorpe, Virginia Water. On the Berkshire
boundary.

Sutton Green

A village with a cluster of farms and cottages which have grown up around the
green, and which has so far escaped large scale development.

SUTTON PLACE. An impressive brick mansion, built between 1520 and 1530 by Sir Richard
Weston. It was one of the first non-fortified mansions built in Britain during Elizabethan times,
and has been described as the best Tudor house in the South of England. The American oil
magnate, John Paul Getty, used it for a time as his English home. Since his death, the house has
been restored under the direction of Sir Hugh Casson, and the garden has been totally recreated
by Sir Geoffrey Jellicoe in what is said to be the greatest garden scheme of the 20th century. The
gardens are open to the public on a limited basis.

Historic Building
Sutton Place, *Sutton Park, Sutton Green, GU4 7QN* ☎ *01483 504455.*
Nursery
Sutton Green Nursery, *Guildford Road, Sutton Green, GU4 7QA* ☎ *01483 232366.*
Pub
Fox & Hounds, *Sutton Green Road, Sutton Green, GU4 7QD* ☎ *01483 772289.*

See also Burpham, Clandon, Guildford, Horsell, Mayford, Merrow, Pyrford, Ripley, Send,
Woking.

Tadworth

The site of a settlement since pre-Saxon times. The present Red House used to be the 'Red Lion' coaching inn, frequented by Regency travellers on their way to Brighton. The splendid mansion of Tadworth Court, built in about 1700, is now a children's hospital.

Antique Dealer
Ian Caldwell, *9a The Green, Dorking Road, Tadworth, KT20 5SQ* ☎ *01737 813969.*
Nursery
Meare Close Nurseries, *Tadworth Street, Tadworth, KT20 5RF* ☎ *01737 812449.*
Pubs
Blue Anchor, *Dorking Road, Tadworth, KT20 5SL* ☎ *01737 812376.*
Dukes Head, *Dorking Road, Tadworth, KT20 5SL* ☎ *01737 812173.*
Tumble Beacon, *Dorking Road, Tadworth, KT20 5RX* ☎ *Ex Dir.*
Restaurants
Gemini, *28 Station Approach Road, Tadworth, KT20 5AH* ☎ *01737 812179.*
Gourmet 38, *1 Boxhill Road, Tadworth, KT20 7PR* ☎ *01737 842848.*
Tadworth Cottage, *17 High Street, Tadworth, KT20 5QU* ☎ *01737 812319.*
Sports & Leisure Centre
Banstead Sports Centre, *Merland Rise, Tadworth, KT20 5JG* ☎ *01737 361933.*
Swimming Pool
Banstead Sports Centre, *Merland Rise, Tadworth, KT20 5JG* ☎ *01737 361933.*
Take-Aways
Chinatown, *3 Brighton Road, Tadworth, KT20 6SY* ☎ *01737 833374.*
Master Chippy, *65 Marbles Way, Tadworth, KT20 5JP* ☎ *01737 360286.*

See also Ashtead, Banstead, Buckland, Burgh Heath, Epsom, Gatton, Headley, Hooley, Kingswood, Walton on the Hill. 3 miles from the Greater London boundary.

Tandridge

Sir George Gilbert Scott(1811-1878), the Victorian architect who restored so many Surrey churches, lived here at Rook's Nest.

Sᴛ Pᴇᴛᴇʀ's Cʜᴜʀᴄʜ. A Norman church restored by Sir George Gilbert Scott(1811-1878). The 13th century tower is one of the oldest of its type in Surrey with spectacular timber work, the tower and spire being supported by four massive oak corner posts. In the churchyard stands one of the largest yew trees in the country, at the foot of which is buried Lady Gilbert Scott, who died in 1872.

Pub
◆Barley Mow, *Tandridge Lane, Tandridge, RH8 9NJ* ☎ *01883 716171.*

See also Bletchingley, Blindley Heath, Caterham, Crowhurst, Godstone, Limpsfield, Oxted, Woldingham.

Tatsfield

The land here was owned by Edward the Confessor before the Norman conquest and by the Bishop of Bayeux at the time of the Domesday Book. High on the North Downs at 788ft above sea level the village overlooks Biggin Hill and has views far into Surrey, Kent and Sussex.

BEAVER WATERWORLD & REPTILE ZOO. Set in attractive grounds, the zoo houses alligators, giant pythons, lizards and many other reptiles. There are tropical and cold water fish, birds and a pet section.

ST MARY'S CHURCH. Dating back to 1075, there is a 15th century font and a beautiful 13th century chancel window.

Pubs
Old Bakery, *Westmore Green, Tatsfield, TN16 2AG* ☎ *01959 577605.*
Old Ship, *Ship Hill, Tatsfield, TN16 2AG* ☎ *01959 577315.*

Wildlife Park
Beaver Waterworld & Reptile Zoo, *Waylands Farm, Approach Road, Tatsfield, TN16 2JT* ☎ *01959 577707.*

See also Limpsfield, Oxted, Warlingham, Woldingham. On the Kent & Greater London boundary.

Thames Ditton
(including Long Ditton)

Thames Ditton still retains some of its village origins around the area of the church.

IMBER COURT. The house was built in about 1640 to the design of Inigo Jones(1573-1652) and later surrounded by a park by Arthur Onslow(1691-1768), speaker of the House of Commons for thirty three years. During the Great War the near derelict mansion was taken over by the Ministry of Munitions.

ST NICHOLAS'S CHURCH. Built of flint and stone, the church shows work of every century from the 12th to the 20th. The font is decorated with mysterious motifs that have given rise to much learned argument. In the churchyard is the gravestone of Lady Pamela Fitzgerald, brought from the cemetery of Montmartre in Paris.

THAMES DITTON MINIATURE RAILWAY. A raised and ground level passenger carrying miniature railway.

Antique Dealers
Acorn Antiques, *2 Station Road, Thames Ditton, KT7 0NR* ☎ *0181-398 3406.*
C&R Dade, *Boldre House, Hampton Court Way, Thames Ditton, KT7 0JP* ☎ *0181-398 6293.*
Crocus Antiques, *34 High Street, Thames Ditton, KT7 0RY* ☎ *0181-398 9432.*
Fern Cottage Antique Centre, *28 High Street, Thames Ditton, KT7 0RY* ☎ *0181-398 2281.*
Michael Moule Antiques, *26 Basing Way, Thames Ditton, KT7 0NX* ☎ *0181-398 8072.*

Art Gallery
David Curzon Gallery, *1 High Street, Thames Ditton, KT7 0SD* ☎ *0181-398 7860.*

Boat Hire
Ferryline Cruisers, *Ferry House, Ferry Road, Thames Ditton, KT7 0XZ* ☎ *0181-398 0271.*

Book Shop
Elizabeth Gant, *52 High Street, Thames Ditton, KT7 0SA* ☎ *0181-398 0962.*

Garden Centre
Woodstock Garden Centre, *3 Woodstock Lane North, Long Ditton, KT6 5HN* ☎ *0181-398 6040.*

Hotel
Dittons Hotel, *47 Lovelace Road, Long Ditton, KT6 6NA* ☎ *0181-399 7482.*
COUNTRY SETTING NEAR HAMPTON COURT, WIMBLEDON, SANDOWN PARK AND LONDON CENTRE.

Library
SCC Lending Library, *Mercer Close, Watts Road, Thames Ditton, KT7 0BS* ☎ *0181-398 2521.*

Pubs
Albany Hotel, *Queens Road, Thames Ditton, KT7 0QY* ☎ *0181-398 7031.*
◆Angel, *Portsmouth Road, Thames Ditton, KT7 0SY* ☎ *0181-398 4511.*

◆Cricketers, *Hampton Court Way, Thames Ditton, KT7 0JX* ☎ *0181-398 3982.*
Crown, *Summer Road, Thames Ditton, KT7 0QQ* ☎ *0181-398 2376.*
Ferry Tavern, *Ferry Road, Thames Ditton, KT7 0XY* ☎ *0181-398 1749.*
George & Dragon, *High Street, Thames Ditton, KT7 0RY* ☎ *0181-398 2206.*
◆Greyhound, *Hampton Court Way, Thames Ditton, KT7 0JP* ☎ *0181-398 1155.*
Lamb & Star, *Hampton Court Way, Thames Ditton, KT7 0JW* ☎ *0181-398 0834.*
Masons Arms, *Portsmouth Road, Thames Ditton, KT7 0XR* ☎ *0181-398 3394.*
New Inn, *15 Rushett Road, Thames Ditton, KT7 0UX* ☎ *0181-398 1893.*
◆Old Harrow Inn, *Weston Green Road, Thames Ditton, KT7 0JZ* ☎ *0181-398 1688.*
Old Swan, *Summer Road, Thames Ditton, KT7 0QQ* ☎ *0181-398 1814.*
◆Plough & Harrow, *64 Ditton Hill Road, Long Ditton, KT6 5JD* ☎ *0181-398 0923.*
◆Red Lion, *85 High Street, Thames Ditton, KT7 0SF* ☎ *0181-398 8662.*

Railway
Thames Ditton Miniature Railway, *Claygate Lane, Thames Ditton, KT7 0DL*
☎ *0181-398 3985.*

Restaurants
Bengal Lancer, *1 Portsmouth Road, Thames Ditton, KT7 0SY* ☎ *0181-398 7576.*
Ditton Brasserie, *35 High Street, Thames Ditton, KT7 0SD* ☎ *0181-398 3390.*

Take-Away
Annie's Sandwich Bar, *6 Station Road, Thames Ditton, KT7 0NR* ☎ *0181-398 8118.*

See also Chessington, Claygate, Esher, Hersham, Hinchley Wood, Molesey, Worcester Park.
1 mile from the Greater London boundary.

Thorpe

An interesting village with many listed buildings, and mentioned in the Domesday Book.

Sᴛ Mᴀʀʏ's Cʜᴜʀᴄʜ. A stone church with a brick tower, partly dating from the 12th century. There is a brass to William Denham and his family, and also two squints, or oblique openings, which afford a view of the altar from the aisles.

Tʜᴏʀᴘᴇ Pᴀʀᴋ. Created from disused gravel pits, Thorpe Park is Britain's first, and one of Europe's leading, theme parks. There are over 100 rides and attractions, including such favourites as Loggers Leap, Thunder River, the Flying Fish, Carousel Kingdom, the Depth Charge and the Family Tea Cup Ride.

Tʜᴏʀᴘᴇ Fᴀʀᴍ. Part of Thorpe Park and an opportunity to experience life on a 1930s working farm, with rare breeds of sheep, goats and cattle. Old skills are demonstrated in the 17th century buildings and craft centre. There is also a nature trail.

Tʀᴜss's Isʟᴀɴᴅ. An extensive riverside park with facilities for the disabled.

Farm Attraction
Thorpe Farm, *Thorpe Park, Staines Lane, Thorpe, KT16 8PN* ☎ *01932 569393.*

Pubs
Red Lion, *Village Road, Thorpe, TW20 8UE* ☎ *01932 563350.*
Rose & Crown, *Green Road, Thorpe, TW20 8QL* ☎ *01344 842338.*

Theme Park
Thorpe Park, *Staines Lane, Thorpe, KT16 8PN* ☎ *01932 562633.*

Water Sports
Ski Training, *Thorpe Park, Staines Lane, Thorpe, KT16 8PN* ☎ *01932 561171*

See also Addlestone, Ashford, Chertsey, Egham, Englefield Green, Laleham, Lyne, Shepperton, Staines, Sunningdale, Virginia Water. 2 miles from the Berkshire boundary.

Thursley

This pretty village was once a centre of the Surrey iron industry, and an important staging post on the coach route from London to the coast. The extensive common to the north is a national nature reserve. Sir Edwin Lutyens(1869-1944) the architect lived in Thursley.

Sᴛ Mɪᴄʜᴀᴇʟ's Cʜᴜʀᴄʜ. The chancel dates from Saxon times and retains two original windows that were rediscovered in 1927. The font is probably Saxon and the great timber frame, which supports the tower and dates from the time of Henry VIII, is said to be the best example of its type in Surrey. In the churchyard is a well maintained memorial to an unknown sailor who in 1786 was murdered near the Devil's Punchbowl. The murderers were hanged on Gibbet Hill, where an inscribed stone recalls the event, and the chains used to hang the murderers were made at Thursley Forge.

Sᴛʀᴇᴇᴛ Hᴏᴜsᴇ. The birthplace of Sir Edwin Lutyens(1869-1944), the architect.

Pub
★Three Horseshoes, *Dye House Road, Thursley, GU8 6QD* ☎ *01252 703268.*

See also Brook, Churt, Elstead, Grayswood, Hindhead, Milford, Tilford, Witley, Wormley.

Tilford

The focal point of this village is the attractive triangular green, well known as a cricket ground. On the green stands the historic King's Oak believed to be at least 800 years old and one of the finest in Surrey. Tilford bridge is believed to have been constructed at the time the village was founded. The bridge is one of three medieval bridges, with Eashing and Elstead, which crosses the Wey.

Oʟᴅ Kɪʟɴ Mᴜsᴇᴜᴍ. One of the largest private collections relating to village and rural life, featuring many aspects of skilled crafts and industries associated with farming at the turn of the century.

On show are farm implements and machines, carts, waggons, ploughs and dairy equipment. There is also a working smithy and wheelwright's shop. Set in ten acres of fields and woodlands, there is also a narrow gauge railway and an arboretum with over 100 varieties of young trees from all parts of the world, showing colour throughout the year.

Tilford Bridge

Golf Course
Hankley Common Golf Club, *Tilford Road, Tilford, GU10 2DD*
☎ *01252 792493.*

Museum
Old Kiln Museum, *Rural Life Centre, Reeds Road, Tilford, GU10 2DL* ☎ *01252 795571.*

Pubs
★Barley Mow, *The Green, Tilford, GU10 2BU* ☎ *01252 792205.*

★Donkey, *Charleshill, Farnham-Milford Road, Tilford, GU10 2AU* ☎ *01252 702124.*

Duke of Cambridge, *Tilford Road, Tilford, GU10 2DD* ☎ *01252 792236.*

Tea Room
Old Kiln Museum ☎ *01252 792300.*

See also Badshot Lea, The Bourne, Elstead, Farnham, Frensham, Rowledge, Runfold, The Sands, Seale, Tongham, Thursley, Wrecclesham. 3 miles from the Hampshire boundary.

Tongham

Once a major hop growing area, the village still has its own brewery.

HOG'S BACK BREWERY. Surrey's largest brewery where real ale is brewed in the 18th century barn. There is a viewing gallery from which visitors can observe the brewery.

Brewery
  Hog's Back Brewery, *Manor Farm, The Street, Tongham, GU10 1DE* ☎ *01252 783000.*
Pick Your Own
  Manor Farm, *The Street, Tongham, GU10 1DG* ☎ *01252 782680.*
Pubs
  Cricketers, *12 Oxenden Road, Tongham, GU10 1AF* ☎ *01252 331340.*
  White Hart, *76 The Street, Tongham, GU10 1DH* ☎ *01252 782419.*

See also Ash, Badshot Lea, The Bourne, Elstead, Farnham, Hale, Heath End, Normandy, Puttenham, Runfold, The Sands, Seale, Shackleford, Tilford, Wanborough. On the Hampshire boundary.

Virginia Water

CHRIST CHURCH. Built in 1838 and now modernised inside and out with the addition of a glass roofed church hall which can be used as an extension to the main church.

COLONNADE. The colonnade was taken from Leptis Magna in Tripoli and stands on the south bank of the lake.

TOTEM POLE. The 100ft totem pole commemorates the centenary of British Columbia and was set up in 1958.

VALLEY GARDENS. The gardens cover some 400 acres on the north bank of Virginia Water Lake. Begun in 1949, the area is today one of the finest woodland gardens in the world and contains an unrivalled collection of rhododendrons, azaleas, camellias, magnolias and countless other spring flowering trees and shrubs. There is also a ten acre heather garden which provides colour and interest during winter and summer, the two seasons of the year when the woodland garden is less colourful.

VIRGINIA WATER LAKE. The enormous artificial woodland lake on the south eastern corner of Windsor Great Park was constructed by landscape gardeners Paul Sandby(1725-1809) and Thomas Sandby(1721-1798) for the Duke of Cumberland in 1746. It is 1$\frac{1}{2}$ miles long and was created out of marshland. The water is alive with wildfowl and coarse fish.

WENTWORTH ESTATE. The golf courses and housing estate were created in the 1920s from land which originally belonged to Lady Ann Fitzroy, sister of the Duke of Wellington. Her husband Charles Culling-Smith built the original mansion, which is now owned by the Wentworth Club.

Golf Course
  Wentworth Club, *Virginia Water, GU25 4LS* ☎ *01344 842201.*
Parks & Gardens
  Valley Gardens, *London Road, Virginia Water (Enquiries* ☎ *01753 860222).*
  Virginia Water Lake, *London Road, Virginia Water.*
Pubs
  Crown, *Trumpsgreen Road, Virginia Water, GU25 4HN* ☎ *01344 843283.*
  Dog & Fireside, *Christchurch Road, Virginia Water* ☎ *Ex Dir.*
  Rose & Olive Branch, *Callow Hill, Virginia Water, GU25 4LH* ☎ *01344 843713.*
  Royal Standard, *Stroude Road, Virginia Water, GU25 4BU* ☎ *01344 843146.*
  Stag & Hounds, *Wellington Avenue, Virginia Water, GU25 4HU* ☎ *Ex Dir.*
Restaurant
  Wheatsheaf(Chef & Brewer), *London Road, Virginia Water, GU25 4QF* ☎ *01344 842057.*

See also Addlestone, Chertsey, Egham, Englefield Green, Laleham, Lyne, Shepperton, Staines, Sunningdale, Thorpe. 2 miles from the Berkshire boundary.

Walton on Thames

Until 1800 Walton was a tiny village which survived mainly on agriculture but its rich history is derived from the several large surrounding country estates. After the railway arrived in 1838 and Oatlands Park (Weybridge) was sold in the 1840s, residential expansion began and has continued to this day.

OLD MANOR HOUSE. A long timber framed and brick building dating back to the middle ages. It is the oldest building in the area and John Bradshaw, president of the court which sentenced Charles I to death, is reputed to have lived here.

RIVERHOUSE BARN. Recently restored and offering regular programmes of professional music, dance and drama.

ST MARY'S CHURCH. Of Saxon origin, parts date from the 12th to 15th centuries. The church has a monument by Louis Roubiliac(1702-1762), the greatest of English mid 18th century sculptors, to Field Marshal Viscount Shannon, who died in 1740.

WALTON BRIDGE. There has in succession been a wooden bridge, a brick bridge and an iron bridge over the Thames at Walton. All of these were toll bridges and the toll house can still be seen on the Shepperton side. The iron bridge was damaged during the last war and in 1955 it was declared unsafe for traffic. A temporary bailey bridge has been in use ever since.

Antique Dealer
Harpers Jewellers, *4a Bridge Street, Walton on Thames, KT12 1AA* ☎ *01932 225942.*
SPECIALIZING IN GOOD QUALITY ANTIQUE, SECOND HAND AND NEW JEWELLERY AND SILVER, WITH A RESIDENT JEWELLER IN OUR WORKSHOP FOR REPAIRS, COMMISSIONS AND VALUATIONS.

Art Gallery
Bernard E Clark, *The Towpath, Manor Road, Walton on Thames, KT12 2PG* ☎ *01932 242718.*

Art & Craft Equipment
Bernard E Clark, *The Towpath, Manor Road, Walton on Thames, KT12 2PG* ☎ *01932 242718.*

Arts Centre
Riverhouse Barn, *Manor Road, Walton on Thames, KT12 2NZ* ☎ *01932 254198.*

Boat Hire
DBH Marine, *Anglers Wharf, Thameside, Walton on Thames, KT12 2PG* ☎ *01932 228019.*
JGF Passenger Boats, *Walton Bridge, Walton on Thames, KT12 2NF* ☎ *01932 253374.*
Vjera Line Cruises, *Anglers Wharf, Manor Road, Walton on Thames, KT12 2PS* ☎ *01932 252520.*

Book Shop
WH Smith, *13 High Street, Walton on Thames, KT12 1DG* ☎ *01932 243262.*

Cinema
The Screen, *85 High Street, Walton on Thames, KT12 1DN* ☎ *01932 252825.*

Golf Course
Burhill Golf Club, *Walton on Thames, KT12 4BL* ☎ *01932 227345.*

Hotel
Ashley Park Hotel, *Ashley Park Road, Walton on Thames, KT12 1JP* ☎ *01932 220196.*

Library
SCC Lending Library, *High Street, Walton on Thames, KT12 1HZ* ☎ *01932 224818.*

Pubs
Anglers, *Manor Road, Walton on Thames, KT12 2PF* ☎ *01932 223996.*
Bear, *30 Bridge Street, Walton on Thames, KT12 1AH* ☎ *01932 253420.*
Dukes Head, *Hepworth Way, Walton on Thames, KT12 1BQ* ☎ *01932 220588.*
George Inn, *124 Bridge Street, Walton on Thames, KT12 1AH* ☎ *01932 223622.*
Halfway House, *40 Hersham Road, Walton on Thames, KT12 1RZ* ☎ *01932 244839.*
Old Manor House, *113 Manor Road, Walton on Thames, KT12 2PL* ☎ *01932 221359.*
Swan, *50 Manor Road, Walton on Thames, KT12 2PF* ☎ *01932 225964.*
◆Valentines, *66 Terrace Road, Walton on Thames, KT12 2SD* ☎ *01932 227145.*

Walton, *42 Terrace Road, Walton on Thames, KT12 2SD* ☎ *01932 227339.*
Weir, *Towpath, Sunbury Lane, Walton on Thames, KT12 2JB* ☎ *01932 784530.*
Wellington, *60 High Street, Walton on Thames, KT12 1BY* ☎ *01932 221862.*

Restaurants

Angelos, *68 Terrace Road, Walton on Thames, KT12 2SF* ☎ *01932 241964.*
Hoya, *35 Bridge Street, Walton on Thames, KT12 1AF* ☎ *01932 228579.*
Khyber Pass, *54 Terrace Road, Walton on Thames, KT12 2SD* ☎ *01932 231328.*
Mr Chongs, *111 Hersham Road, Walton on Thames, KT12 1RN* ☎ *01932 246986.*
Old Colonial, *40 Hersham Road, Walton on Thames, KT12 1RZ* ☎ *01932 244839.*
Oriental Curry Centre, *13 Church Street, Walton on Thames, KT12 2QP* ☎ *01932 244427.*
Passage to India, *33 Bridge Street, Walton on Thames, KT12 1AF* ☎ *01932 241923.*
Pecheur, *Thameside, Walton on Thames, KT12 2PG* ☎ *01932 227423.*
Pizza Hut, *35 The Centre, Walton on Thames, KT12 1QJ* ☎ *01932 243522.*
Pizza Piazza, *14 Bridge Street, Walton on Thames, KT12 1AA* ☎ *01932 220153.*
Swan Pool, *36 Church Street, Walton on Thames, KT12 2QS* ☎ *01932 225251.*
Water Margin, *12 The Centre, Walton on Thames, KT12 1QG* ☎ *01932 247380.*
Zio'Toto, *61 High Street, Walton on Thames, KT12 1DJ* ☎ *01932 222974.*

Sports & Leisure Centre

Elmbridge Leisure Centre, *Waterside Drive, Walton on Thames, KT12 2JG* ☎ *01932 245679.*

Swimming Pool

Walton Swimming Pool, *Kings Close, Kings Road, Walton on Thames, KT12 2RF*
☎ *01932 222984.*

Take-Aways

D Parr, *101 Terrace Road, Walton on Thames, KT12 2SG* ☎ *01932 243128.*
Kentucky Fried Chicken, *39 High Street, Walton on Thames, KT12 1DG* ☎ *01932 246419.*
McDonald's, *5 High Street, Walton on Thames, KT12 1DG* ☎ *01932 240325.*
Merryweathers, *Hersham Road, Walton on Thames* ☎ *01932 229772.*
River Bank Refreshments, *Walton Lane, Walton Bridge, Walton on Thames* ☎ *01932 221663.*
Solleys, *25 Church Street, Walton on Thames, KT12 2QP* ☎ *01932 225131.*
Sun, *45 High Street, Walton on Thames, KT12 1DH* ☎ *01932 229280.*
Wimpy, *63 High Street, Walton on Thames, KT12 1DJ* ☎ *01932 220121.*

Theatre

Riverhouse Barn, *Manor Road, Walton on Thames, KT12 2NZ* ☎ *01932 253354.*

Wine Bars & Cafe Bars

Blase Cafe Bar, *29 Bridge Street, Walton on Thames, KT12 1AE* ☎ *01932 232624.*
Sixties, *New Zealand Avenue, Walton on Thames, KT12 1QB* ☎ *01932 221685.*

See also Ashford, Chertsey, Cobham, Esher, Hersham, Hinchley Wood, Laleham, Molesey, New Haw, Shepperton, Sunbury, Weybridge, Whiteley Village. 2 miles from the Greater London boundary.

Walton on the Hill

A mainly Victorian village on the North Downs which has strong connections with the horse racing activities at nearby Epsom. It is well known also for its excellent golf course.

CHURCH OF ST PETER THE APOSTLE. The church possesses a beautiful Norman lead font, which is possibly the oldest in England. Around the bowl is an arcade of round-headed arches, beneath each of which is a seated figure, either reading or with a hand raised in blessing.

Antique Dealer

James Roberts, *43 Walton Street, Walton on the Hill, KT20 7RR* ☎ *01737 813147.*

Golf Course

Walton Heath Golf Club, *Walton Heath, Walton on the Hill, KT20 7TP* ☎ *01737 812380.*

Pubs

★Bell, *Withybed Corner, off Walton Street, Walton on the Hill, KT20 7UJ* ☎ *01737 812132.*
◆Blue Ball, *Deans Lane, Walton on the Hill, KT20 7UE* ☎ *01737 812168.*
★◆Chequers, *Chequers Lane, Walton on the Hill, KT20 7SF* ☎ *01737 812364.*

◆Fox & Hounds, *Walton Street, Walton on the Hill, KT20 7RU* ☎ *01737 812090.*

Restaurant
  Walton Heath Tandoori, *22 Walton St, Walton on the Hill, KT20 7RT* ☎ *01737 814206.*

Take-Away
  Walton Fish & Chips, *39 Walton Street, Walton on the Hill, KT20 7RR* ☎ *01737 813345.*

Tea Room
  First Tee, *15b Walton Street, Walton on the Hill, KT20 7RW* ☎ *01737 814050.*

See also Ashtead, Banstead, Betchworth, Box Hill, Buckland, Burgh Heath, Headley, Kingswood, Mickleham, Reigate, Tadworth.

Wanborough

Untouched by development and surrounded by farmland, Wanborough boasts the best tithe barn in Surrey.

MANOR HOUSE. The present house was built in the 17th century. Gladstone's Parliamentary Private Secretary, Sir Algernon West, lived here and later Herbert Asquith. During the second World War, the Manor House served as the headquarters of the Special Operations Executive.

ROMAN TEMPLE. Foundations of a Roman temple were excavated in 1985 and many artifacts were discovered, including 5,000 Iron Age gold coins.

ST BARTHOLOMEW'S CHURCH. A tiny church built just before the Norman conquest, and reconstructed by the monks of Waverley Abbey in the 13th century. It fell into disuse in the mid 1600s and was restored and re-opened in 1862, after some 200 years.

See also Ash, Compton, Eashing, Farncombe, Godalming, Guildford, Hurtmore, Loseley, Normandy, Peper Harow, Puttenham, Runfold, The Sands, Seale, Shackleford, Tongham, Wood Street, Worplesdon.

Warlingham

On a plateau 600ft up on the North Downs, the village grew around the green, which was formerly part of the extensive common land in the area, and which is now a public garden. There is farmland to the south and east of the village and new housing to the north.

CHURCH OF ALL SAINTS. Built in 1250 and restored by Sir George Gilbert Scott(1811-1878) and P M Johnston in the late 19th century, this is believed to be the place where the Prayer Book authorised by Edward VI was first used, at a service attended by Archbishop Cranmer.

CHURCH OF ST MARY THE VIRGIN, FARLEIGH. A Norman church which preserves many of its original features.

ST LEONARD'S CHURCH, CHELSHAM. Once centrally placed within the community it served, this medieval flint church is now isolated from the present village. Originally 12th century but largely rebuilt in the 13th century, it has a 15th century tower, and was restored in the 1870s. The church has a 13th century marble font and a 16th century screen which is intricately carved and probably Flemish. There is also a 13th century piscina, two angle shafts in the south east and north east corners.

WHITE LION INN. A 15th century pub with a passageway from the inglenook to a butcher's shop opposite.

Antique Dealer
  Village Antiques, *416 Limpsfield Road, Warlingham, CR6 9LA* ☎ *01883 623466.*

Garden Centre
  Knights Garden Centre, *Chelsham Place, Limpsfield Road, Chelsham, Warlingham, CR6 9DZ* ☎ *01883 622340.*

Hotel
  Villa Sonia, *432 Limpsfield Road, Warlingham, CR6 9LA* ☎ *01883 626910.*
Library
  SCC Lending Library, *Shelton Avenue, Warlingham, CR6 9NE* ☎ *01883 622479.*
Pubs
  Botley Hill Farmhouse, *Limpsfield Road, Warlingham, CR6 9QH* ☎ *01959 577154.*
  Bull Inn, *Chelsham Common, Warlingham, CR6 9PB* ☎ *01883 622970.*
  Hare & Hounds, *Limpsfield Road, Warlingham, CR6 9DZ* ☎ *01883 623952.*
★Harrow Inn, *Farleigh Road, Warlingham, CR6 9EL* ☎ *01883 622824.*
  Leather Bottle, *2 The Green, Warlingham, CR6 9NA* ☎ *01883 624201.*
★White Bear, *Fairchildes Road, Ficklesbole, Warlingham, CR6 9PH* ☎ *01959 573166.*
★White Lion, *3 Farleigh Road, Warlingham, CR6 9EG* ☎ *01883 624106.*
Restaurant
  Good Companions(Beefeater), *Tithe Pit Shaw Lane, Warlingham, CR6 9AW*
  ☎ *0181-657 6655.*
  Horseshoe(Chef & Brewer), *Farleigh Road, Warlingham, CR6 9EG* ☎ *01883 622009.*
Sports & Leisure Centre
  Warlingham School, *Tithe Pit Shaw Lane, Warlingham, CR3 9YB* ☎ *01883 722000 x454.*
Swimming Pool
  Warlingham School, *Tithe Pit Shaw Lane, Warlingham, CR3 9YB* ☎ *01883 722000 x454.*
Take-Away
  Mann's, *86 Limpsfield Road, Warlingham, CR6 9RA* ☎ *01883 623237.*
Tea Room
  Pantry, *Knights Garden Centre* ☎ *01883 622340.*

See also Caterham, Tatsfield, Whyteleafe, Woldingham. 2 miles from the Greater London
boundary.

West End

THE GORDON BOY'S SCHOOL. Founded in 1885 and housed in Victorian red-brick buildings
designed by William Butterfield(1814-1900), the school is named after General Gordon of
Khartoum(1833-1885). There is a museum devoted to objects associated with General Gordon.

Golf Course & Driving Range
  Windlemere Golf Centre, *Windlesham Road, West End, GU24 9QL* ☎ *01276 858727.*
Pubs
  Hare & Hounds, *Brentmoor Road, West End, GU24 9QG* ☎ *01276 858161.*
  Wheatsheaf, *42 Guildford Road, West End, GU24 9PW* ☎ *01276 858652.*

See also Bagshot, Bisley, Brookwood, Chobham, Horsell, Knaphill, Lightwater, Pirbright,
Windlesham. 3 miles from the Berkshire boundary.

Westcott

A Victorian village with a classic triangular green. Thomas Malthus(1766-1834) the
economist was born here at The Rookery, now demolished.

HOLY TRINITY CHURCH. Designed by Sir George Gilbert Scott(1811-1878) and built in 1852.

Antique Dealer
  Westcott Antiques, *The Studio, Parsonage Lane, Westcott, RH4 3NL* ☎ *01306 881900.*

Art Gallery
  Westcott Gallery, *4 Guildford Road, Westcott, RH4 3NR* ☎ *01306 876261.*
Inn
  Crown Inn, *Guildford Road, Westcott, RH4 3QG* ☎ *01306 885414.*
Pubs
  Cricketers, *Guildford Road, Westcott, RH4 3NW* ☎ *01306 883520.*
  Prince of Wales, *Guildford Road, Westcott, RH4 3QE* ☎ *01306 889699.*

See also Abinger Common, Bookham, Box Hill, Brockham, Dorking, Holmbury St Mary, Holmwood, Mickleham, Polesden Lacey, Ranmore Common, Westhumble, Wotton.

Westhumble

The village is set in the Mole Valley in the shadow of both Box Hill and Ranmore Common. In a field on what was once part of the Pilgrims Way opposite Chapel Farm are the ruins of a 12th century chapel, which is now owned by the National Trust. Fanny Burney(1752-1840) the novelist and diarist lived here from 1797 to 1801, with her French husband General d'Arblay, in a cottage they named Camilla after the novel she had written the year before.

CHAPEL FARM. A working farm set in 200 acres of magnificent countryside, with extensive farm buildings some of which are over 400 years old. A numbered animal trail guides children to the many friendly animals which are mostly accessible for hands on experience. Trailer rides are usually available and there are walks through the surrounding fields and woodlands.
BOXHILL AND WESTHUMBLE STATION. Now a listed building, the station was intended to be the most elaborate station on the Epsom to Horsham line, and was built in 1867 for guests travelling to Polesden Lacey and for day-trippers to Box Hill. The locomotive 'Box Hill' is in the York Railway Museum.

Farm Attraction
  Chapel Farm, *Chapel Lane, Westhumble, RH5 6AY* ☎ *01306 882865.*
Mountain Biking
  Action Packs, *The Booking Hall, Boxhill Station, Westhumble, RH5 6BT* ☎ *01306 886944.*
Pub
  Stepping Stones, *Westhumble Street, Westhumble, RH5 6BS* ☎ *01306 889932.*

See also Betchworth, Bookham, Box Hill, Brockham, Buckland, Dorking, Effingham, Fetcham, Headley, Holmwood, Leatherhead, Mickleham, Polesden Lacey, Ranmore Common, Westcott.

Weybridge

At Weybridge the River Wey flows into the River Thames and it was from this point that in 1653 the River Wey Navigation to Guildford was constructed, starting by the Wey bridge which was first built as a foot bridge in the 12th century. Weybridge was a quiet rural village dominated by Oatlands until the railway arrived in 1838, soon after which the Oatlands estate was broken up. More recently Weybridge became important for its motoring and aviation history. E M Forster(1879-1970) was living in Weybridge when he wrote 'A Passage to India'.

BROOKLANDS. In 1907 Hugh Locke-King built the first motor racing track in Britain, and it was soon being used by the early aeroplanes. In 1909 Brooklands became one of the country's first permanent aerodromes. Between the wars records were made and broken by famous men, such as Sir Donald Campbell, on the banked track and the test hill, which were designed to test the old racing cars to breaking point. During the second World War the Vickers factory here built Spitfires, Hurricanes, Wellingtons and Lancasters.

BROOKLANDS MUSEUM. Opened in 1991 on 30 acres of the original 1907 motor racing circuit, the museum features the most historic and steepest section of the old banked track, and the 1-in-4 Test Hill. Many of the original buildings have been restored and the Edwardian Clubhouse, the Brooklands racing car collection, Malcolm Campbell's workshop and a motoring village help to recreate the atmosphere of Brooklands in its heyday and tell the story of motor racing here from 1907 until it stopped in 1939. Also on show is a unique aircraft collection, including the Wellington bomber rescued from

The Club House - Brooklands

Loch Ness, which tells the story of 85 years of aircraft production at Brooklands.

ELMBRIDGE MUSEUM. Changing exhibitions throughout the year cover the social and natural history and archaeology of north western Surrey. There are displays of costume, trade and craft implements, and bygones.

OATLANDS PALACE. An established residence in Oatlands Park was transformed into a sumptuous Tudor palace by Henry VIII in 1538 for his new queen, Anne of Cleves. She never lived here, but it became the home of Elizabeth I, James I and Charles I who is said to have planted the fine cedar tree beside the driveway of the Oatlands Park Hotel. The palace was pulled down in 1650.

OATLANDS PARK. The Oatlands Park Estate was inherited in 1716 by the 7th Earl of Lincoln who built a new mansion, but his second son destroyed the elaborate formal garden and created a long lake known as the Broadwater out of the canal and other adjoining ponds. In 1846 Oatlands Park was sold for residential development and new large houses were built overlooking the Broadwater, although these have since been demolished in favour of more modern developments. The mansion became a hotel in 1856.

RIVER WEY & GODALMING NAVIGATIONS. See under Guildford.

ST JAMES'S CHURCH. Built in 1848 to replace the original 12th century church, and later enlarged. The stained glass east window portrays the Redemption, the reredos represents New Testament scenes, and the walls and floor of the chancel are richly decorated.

Antique Dealers
Brocante Antiques, *120 Oatlands Drive, Weybridge, KT13 9HL* ☎ *01932 857807.*
Church House Antiques, *42 Church Street, Weybridge, KT13 8DP* ☎ *01932 842190.*
Not Just Silver, *16 York Road, Weybridge, KT13 9DT* ☎ *01932 842468.*
Oatlands House Antiques, *124 Oatlands Drive, Weybridge, KT13 9HL* ☎ *01932 858284.*
R Saunders, *71 Queens Road, Weybridge, KT13 9UQ* ☎ *01932 842601.*
Village Antiques, *39 St Marys Road, Weybridge, KT13 9PT* ☎ *01932 846554.*
Weybridge Antiques, *43 Church Street, Weybridge, KT13 8DG* ☎ *01932 852503.*
Art Galleries
Cave's Picture Shop, *44 Church Street, Weybridge, KT13 8DP* ☎ *01932 844133.*
Edward Cross Gallery, *128 Oatlands Drive, Weybridge, KT13 9HL* ☎ *01932 851093.*
Art & Craft Equipment
Cave's Picture Shop, *44 Church Street, Weybridge, KT13 8DP* ☎ *01932 844133.*
Sunflower Graphics, *135 Oatlands Drive, Weybridge, KT13 9LB* ☎ *01932 846620.*
Book Shops
WH Smith, *13 High Street, Weybridge, KT13 8AX* ☎ *01932 852043.*
Weybridge Books, *28 Church Street, Weybridge, KT13 8DX* ☎ *01932 842498.*
Garden Centre
Barbeque Shop, *Station Approach, Weybridge, KT13 8UD* ☎ *01932 855521.*
Golf Course
St George's Hill Golf Club, *St George's Hill, Weybridge, KT13 0NL* ☎ *01932 842406.*

Guest Houses

Kingston Guest House, *15 Heath Road, Weybridge, KT13 8TE* ☎ *01932 856191.*

Hotels & Inns

Hand & Spear, *The Heath, Heath Road, Weybridge, KT13 8TX* ☎ *01932 845035.*

Kings Manor Hotel(Toby), *25 Oatlands Chase, Weybridge, KT13 9RW* ☎ *01932 253277.*

★Oatlands Park Hotel, *146 Oatlands Drive, Weybridge, KT13 9HB* ☎ *01932 847242.*

★Ship Hotel(Thistle), *70 High Street, Weybridge, KT13 8BQ* ☎ *01932 848364.*

Warbeck House Hotel, *46 Queens Road, Weybridge, KT13 0AR* ☎ *01932 848764.*

York House Hotel, *14 Hanger Hill, Weybridge, KT13 9XR* ☎ *01932 828705.*

Information Centre

Weybridge Information Centre, *Weybridge Library* ☎ *01932 856058.*

Library

SCC Lending Library, *Church Street, Weybridge, KT13 8DE* ☎ *01932 843812.*

Museums

Brooklands Museum, *Brooklands Road, Weybridge, KT13 0QN* ☎ *01932 857381.*

Elmbridge Museum, *Church Street, Weybridge, KT13 8DE* ☎ *01932 843573.*

Park

Oatlands Recreation Ground, *Oatlands Drive, Weybridge.*

Pubs

British Volunteer, *Waverley Road, Weybridge, KT13 8UT* ☎ *Ex Dir.*

Duke of York, *85 Queens Road, Weybridge, KT13 9UQ* ☎ *01932 843190.*

Farnell Arms, *33 Thames Street, Weybridge, KT13 8JG* ☎ *01932 855234.*

Flintgate, *139 Oatlands Drive, Weybridge, KT13 9LA* ☎ *01932 842721.*

Grotto, *Monument Hill, Weybridge, KT13 8RJ* ☎ *01932 842480.*

Jolly Farmer, *41 Princes Road, Weybridge, KT13 9BN* ☎ *01932 856873.*

Lincoln Arms, *104 Thames Street, Weybridge, KT13 8NG* ☎ *01932 842109.*

Mitre, *53 Heath Road, Weybridge, KT13 8TJ* ☎ *01932 847075.*

Old Crown, *83 Thames Street, Weybridge, KT13 8LP* ☎ *01932 842844.*

◆Prince of Wales, *Cross Road, Weybridge, KT13 9NX* ☎ *01932 852082.*

◆Queens Head, *1 Bridge Road, Weybridge, KT13 8XS* ☎ *01932 847828.*

Restaurants

Broadwater, *Oatlands Park Hotel* ☎ *01932 847242.*

★Casa Romana, *2 Temple Hall, Monument Hill, Weybridge, KT13 8RH* ☎ *01932 843470.*

Colony, *3 Balfour Road, Weybridge, KT13 8HE* ☎ *01932 842766.*

Far Pavilion, *125 Oatlands Drive, Weybridge, KT13 9LB* ☎ *01932 847158.*

Gaylord, *73 Queens Road, Weybridge, KT13 9UQ* ☎ *01932 842895.*

Go Sing House, *117 Queens Road, Weybridge, KT13 9UN* ☎ *01932 840246.*

Golden Curry, *132 Oatlands Drive, Weybridge, KT13 9HJ* ☎ *01932 846931.*

Hussain Tandoori, *47 Church Street, Weybridge, KT13 8DQ* ☎ *01932 847443.*

La Trattoria, *7 Temple Market, Queens Road, Weybridge, KT13 9DL* ☎ *01932 851178.*

L'Escales, *Ship Hotel* ☎ *01932 848364.*

Osteria Franco, *29 Baker Street, Weybridge, KT13 8AE* ☎ *01932 846362.*

Pizzeria Galleria, *8 Hanger Hill, Weybridge, KT13 9XR* ☎ *01932 849302.*

Sosio's, *108 Oatlands Drive, Weybridge, KT13 9HL* ☎ *01932 843131.*

Stumps Bistro, *8 Hanger Hill, Weybridge, KT13 9XR* ☎ *01932 828705.*

Sullivans, *41 Church Street, Weybridge, KT13 8DG* ☎ *01932 850545.*

Thai Garden, *47a High Street, Weybridge, KT13 8BB* ☎ *01932 846824.*

Well Spring, *43 High Street, Weybridge, KT13 8BB* ☎ *01932 846563.*

Special Pursuits

Go Karting, *Weybridge Trading Estate, Weybridge Road, Weybridge, KT15 2RW* ☎ *01932 820543.*

Take-Aways

Peking Garden, *3 Monument Hill, Weybridge, KT13 8RX* ☎ *01932 847891.*

Riverside, *16 Church Street, Weybridge, KT13 8DX* ☎ *01932 854273.*

Wimpy, *11 Church Street, Weybridge, KT13 8DE* ☎ *01932 852291.*

Tea Room

Sunbeam Tea Room, *Brooklands Museum* ☎ *01932 857381.*

Wine Bars & Cafe Bars
  Berkleys, *18 Baker Street, Weybridge, KT13 8AP* ☎ *01932 851333.*
  Bogart's, *2 Hanger Hill, Weybridge, KT13 9XR* ☎ *01932 828808.*
  Buffers, *Heath Road, Weybridge, KT13 8UE* ☎ *01932 855332.*
  Sullivans, *39 Church Street, Weybridge, KT13 8DG* ☎ *01932 847961.*

See also Addlestone, Byfleet, Chertsey, Cobham, Hersham, Hinchley Wood, Laleham, Lyne, New Haw, Ottershaw, Pyrford, Shepperton, Walton on Thames, Whiteley Village, Wisley, Woodham.

Whiteley Village

Completed in 1921, this retirement village is the legacy of William Whiteley who owned a store in Bayswater and died a millionaire in 1907. It was designed by R F Atkinson and opened by King George V and Queen Mary.

ST MARK'S CHURCH. Built at the same time as the village, but in medieval style.

See also Byfleet, Cobham, Downside, Hersham, New Haw, Ottershaw, Shepperton, Stoke D'Abernon, Walton on Thames, Weybridge, Wisley, Woodham.

Whyteleafe

Cinema
  Rank Organisation, *439 Godstone Road, Whyteleafe, CR3 0YG* ☎ *01883 623355.*
Pub
  Whyteleafe Tavern, *208 Godstone Road, Whyteleafe, CR3 0EE* ☎ *01883 624133.*
Restaurant
  Casa Pepe, *215 Godstone Road, Whyteleafe, CR3 0EL* ☎ *01883 622443.*
  Curry Garden, *242 Godstone Road, Whyteleafe, CR3 0EF* ☎ *01883 627237.*
  Royal Tandoori, *209 Godstone Road, Whyteleafe, CR3 0EL* ☎ *01883 626200.*
  Wise's Chinese, *226 Godstone Road, Whyteleafe, CR3 0EF* ☎ *01883 622708.*
Take-Away
  Whyteleafe Fish Bar, *2 Station Road, Whyteleafe, CR3 0EP* ☎ *01883 622510.*

See also Caterham, Chipstead, Warlingham, Woldingham. On the Greater London boundary.

Windlesham

CHURCH OF ST JOHN THE BAPTIST. The original church was built in the 15th century and was substantially rebuilt in 1874. The M3 motorway has since rather isolated it from the village.

Antique Dealer
  Country Antiques, *Country Gardens Garden Centre* ☎ *01344 873404.*
Garden Centre
  Country Gardens Garden Centre, *London Road, Windlesham, GU20 6LL* ☎ *01344 21411.*
Pubs
  Bee, *School Road, Windlesham, GU20 6PD* ☎ *01276 473359.*
  ★Half Moon, *Church Road, Windlesham, GU20 6BN* ☎ *01276 473329.*

Sun Inn, *1 Chertsey Road, Windlesham, GU20 6EN* ☎ *01276 472234.*
Surrey Cricketers, *Chertsey Road, Windlesham, GU20 6HE* ☎ *01276 472192.*
Windmill Inn, *London Road, Windlesham, GU20 6PJ* ☎ *01276 472281.*

Restaurants
Brickmakers Arms, *Chertsey Road, Windlesham, GU20 6HT* ☎ *01276 472267.*
FRESH HOME COOKED FOOD, ESPECIALLY FISH. BOULES TERRAIN IN PUB GARDEN.
Rashoi, *58 Updown Hill, Windlesham, GU20 6DX* ☎ *01276 452197.*

See also Bagshot, Bisley, Chobham, Knaphill, Lightwater, West End. 2 miles from the Berkshire boundary.

Wisley

The village comprises little more than Church Farm, a few cottages inhabited mainly by RHS employees and a tiny Norman church.

ROYAL HORTICULTURAL SOCIETY'S GARDEN. Wisley is a beautiful and world famous garden and a leading centre of horticultural practice, with pre-eminent trial grounds. Established in 1904, there are 240 acres of ornamental plants, fruit and vegetables growing in their appropriate settings. There is also an orchid house and a wide range of trees and shrubs.
WISLEY CHURCH. Built around 1250, there are traces of early wall paintings, and three crosses marked in the stonework at the church's consecration. The church's dedication has been lost.

Park & Gardens
Royal Horticultural Society, *Wisley Gardens, Wisley, GU23 6QB* ☎ *01483 224234.*
Plant Centre & Nursery
Royal Horticultural Society, *Wisley Gardens, Wisley, GU23 6QB* ☎ *01483 211113.*

The Royal Horticultural Society's Wisley Garden

Situated in some 240 acres, near Junction 10 of the M25 and the A3 Trunk Road, 7 miles from Guildford and 20 miles from London.

*From the springtime alpine meadows and the early summer displays of rhododendrons and daffodils, to the splendid traditional English herbaceous borders at the height of summer and the spectacular colours of autumn, this is a **Garden for all Seasons**.*

Admission
Open to the public Mon-Sat throughout the year (except Christmas Day), from 10am to Sunset (or 7pm in summer). Only members of the RHS are admitted on Sundays, from 9am.

Information Centre & Shop
The most extensive range of horticultural and botanical books in the U.K. available for sale, together with a wide range of quality gifts.

The Plant Centre offers over 8,500 varieties of plants. Inside the garden, Wisley's licensed **Terrace Restaurant** and the **Conservatory Cafe** are open all through the year.

Restaurant
  Terrace Restaurant, *Royal Horticultural Society* ☎ *01483 224234.*
Tea Room
  Conservatory Cafe, *Royal Horticultural Society* ☎ *01483 224234.*

See also Byfleet, Chertsey, Cobham, Downside, New Haw, Pyrford, Woking, Ripley, Send, Sheerwater, Weybridge, Whiteley Village, Woodham.

Witley

The history of Witley can be traced from Saxon times. During medieval times iron was smelted and cloth and glass were manufactured. The Victorian novelist Mary Ann Evans(1819-1880), alias George Eliot, was living here when she wrote 'Daniel Deronda'.

CHURCH OF ALL SAINTS. Originally Saxon, but dating mainly from the 12th century with many additions and renovations since then. The church has a 12th century wall painting on the south side of the original Saxon nave.

TIGBOURNE COURT. Built by Sir Edwin Lutyens(1869-1944) and thought by many to be his finest work.

WHITE HART. The 600 year old, tile hung, steep roofed White Hart is one of the oldest pubs in England and was originally built on to one of Richard II's hunting lodges.

Tigbourne Court

WITLEY COMMON. Witley Common was used as a camp for soldiers during both world wars. It is a haven for wildlife, and enjoyed by walkers along its three nature trails. The information centre run by the National Trust, is set in pine woods on the edge of the common, and offers an audio visual programme and exhibition explaining the history, natural history and management of Witley Common.

WITLEY PARK. A large house built here at the turn of the century was the home of Victorian financier Whitaker Wright who is said to have designed a billiard room or a ballroom under the lake. The house was demolished in the 1950s, but the lake and the colonnaded stone boathouse by Lutyens remain.

Nature Reserve
  Witley Common *(Enquiries* ☎ *01428 683207).*
Pubs
  Star Inn, *Petworth Road, Witley, GU8 5LU* ☎ *01428 684656.*
  White Hart, *Petworth Road, Witley, GU8 5PH* ☎ *01428 683695.*

See also Brook, Chiddingfold, Eashing, Elstead, Farncombe, Godalming, Hambledon, Hascombe, Hydestile, Milford, Peper Harow, Shackleford, Thursley.

Woking
(including Old Woking)

Little more than a group of rural villages until 1850, when the London Necroplis Company purchased 2,268 acres of common land for the new Brookwood cemetery. In the event only 400 acres were required, the remaining land was sold off in small lots, and the modern town of Woking developed. Old Woking dates back at least to the 8th century, and was the largest and most important of the local villages before the development of the new town. There was a forge, a brewery and a paper mill, but most of the population were employed in agriculture and nursery

The Peacocks

gardening. It is situated by the River Wey and possesses a character of its own.

CHRIST CHURCH. Built in 1889, and now modernised in a light and airy style.

PEACOCKS ARTS CENTRE. Surrey's newest theatre, the New Victoria theatre, is the flagship of the Centre and offers a wide range of top quality productions from drama to ballet, musicals to comedies, opera to pre and post West End shows.

ST JOHN'S CREMATORIUM. This is the first British crematorium, built in 1879, six years before cremation was legalised. It was first used on 26th March, 1985.

ST PETER'S CHURCH. The church has a Norman door, a 14th century east window, a Jacobean pulpit and a 17th century gallery.

SHAH JEHAN MOSQUE. The first mosque in Britain and probably Europe, founded in 1889 to cater for the spiritual needs of students attending the nearby Oriental Institute at Maybury. Now the mosque is the spiritual focus of Woking's Muslim community.

WOKING MINIATURE RAILWAY. A ground level miniature steam railway in a scenic location at Mizen's Farm on the banks of the River Bourne.

WOKING PALACE. Near the river in Old Woking are the remains of this moated royal residence, which dated from at least the 13th century and was pulled down in the 1620s after falling into disrepair. It was the home of Margaret Beaufort, mother of Henry VII and grandmother of Henry VIII, the home of Edward IV and Henry VIII, and birthplace of Mary Tudor in 1514. The remains are not open to the public.

WOKING PARK. This is Woking's premier leisure area and is home to the Leisure Centre and the Pool in the Park. It has extensive formal gardens, a scented garden and outdoor sporting facilities.

Antique Dealers
  Manor Antiques, *2 New Shops, High Street, Old Woking, GU22 9JW* ☎ *01483 724666.*
  Venture, *12b High Street, Old Woking, GU22 9ER* ☎ *01483 772103.*
  Wych House Antiques, *Wych Hill, Woking, GU22 0EX* ☎ *01483 764636.*
Art Gallery
  Barbers Picture Framing, *18 Chertsey Road, Woking, GU21 5AB* ☎ *01483 769926.*
Art & Craft Equipment
  Barbers, *18 Chertsey Road, Woking, GU21 5AB* ☎ *01483 769926.*
Arts & Entertainment Centre
  Peacocks Arts & Entertainment Centre, *Woking, GU21 1GQ* ☎ *01483 761144.*
Book Shops
  Berean Book Shop, *26 High Street, Woking, GU21 1BW* ☎ *01483 715358.*

Hammicks, *18 Wolsey Walk, Woking, GU21 1XU* ☎ *01483 726938.*

Cinema

Peacocks Cinema, *Peacocks Arts Centre* ☎ *01483 761144.*

Golf Course

Woking Golf Club, *Pond Road, Hook Heath, Woking, GU22 0JZ* ☎ *01483 760053.*

Worplesdon Golf Club, *Heath House Road, Woking, GU22 0RA* ☎ *01438 489876.*

Golf Course & Driving Range - Public

Hoebridge Golf Course, *Old Woking Road, Old Woking, GU22 8JH* ☎ *01483 722611.*

Guest House

Glencourt, *St Johns Hill Road, Woking, GU21 1RQ* ☎ *01483 764154.*

Hotels & Inns

Cotteridge Hotel, *Constitution Hill, Woking, GU22 7RT* ☎ *01483 762400.*

Maybury Lodge Hotel, *83 Maybury Road, Woking, GU21 5JH* ☎ *01483 720000.*

Northfleet Hotel, *6 Claremont Avenue, Woking, GU22 7SG* ☎ *01483 722971.*

◆Star Hotel, *Wych Hill, Hook Heath, Woking, GU22 0EU* ☎ *01483 772705.*

★The Dutch, *Woodham Road, Woking, GU21 4EQ* ☎ *01483 724255.*

Information Centre

County Information Centre, *Woking Library* ☎ *01483 771011.*

Library

SCC Lending Library, *Gloucester Walk, Woking, GU21 1HL* ☎ *01483 770591.*

Park

Woking Park, *Kingfield Road, Woking.*

Pubs

Albion, *Church Path, Woking* ☎ *Ex Dir.*

Bleak House, *Chertsey Road, Woking, GU21 5NL* ☎ *01483 760717.*

College Arms, *College Road, Woking, GU22 8BT* ☎ *01483 761730.*

Cricketers, *Westfield Road, Woking, GU22 9NQ* ☎ *01483 761409.*

Crown & Anchor, *100 High Street, Old Woking, GU22 9LN* ☎ *01483 766274.*

Fox & Flowerpot, *Goldsworth Park Centre, Woking, GU21 3LG* ☎ *01483 729288.*

Goldsworth Arms, *Goldsworth Road, Woking, GU21 1LQ* ☎ *01483 771744.*

Kingfield Arms, *Kingfield Road, Woking, GU22 9EQ* ☎ *01483 772179.*

Maybury Inn, *Maybury Hill, Woking, GU22 8AB* ☎ *01483 760613.*

Old Stillage, *12 Chertsey Road, Woking, GU21 5AB* ☎ *01483 725625.*

Princess, *24 Princess Road, Woking, GU22 8EQ* ☎ *Ex Dir.*

Queens Head, *40 High Street, Old Woking, GU22 9ER* ☎ *01483 728833.*

Red House, *Crown Square, Chobham Road, Woking, GU21 1HR* ☎ *01483 714162.*

Rowbarge, *St Johns Road, Woking, GU21 1SA* ☎ *01483 761618.*

Sovereign, *Guildford Road, Woking, GU22 7QQ* ☎ *01483 768868.*

White Hart, *150 High Street, Old Woking, GU22 9JH* ☎ *01483 763202.*

Putting Green & Crazy Golf

Woking Park, *Kingfield Road, Woking.*

Railway

Woking Miniature Railway, *Mizens Farm, Guildford Road, Woking* ☎ *01483 720801.*

Restaurants

Dragon Pearl, *58 Chertsey Road, Woking, GU21 5BG* ☎ *01483 764044.*

Fuente, *Glencourt Guest House* ☎ *01483 726264.*

Khyber Pass, *18 Broadway, Woking, GU21 5AP* ☎ *01483 722950.*

La Reggia, *44 Commercial Way, Woking, GU21 1HW* ☎ *01483 773097.*

Overtures, *Peacocks Arts Centre* ☎ *01483 776636.*

Piazz'Amore, *24 Chertsey Road, Woking, GU21 5AB* ☎ *01483 760784.*

Pizza Express, *65 Goldsworth Road, Woking, GU21 1LJ* ☎ *01483 750310.*

Pizza Hut, *19 Chertsey Road, Woking, GU24 8ND* ☎ *01483 755845.*

Sbarro, *41 Wolsey Centre, Woking, GU21 1XX* ☎ *01483 724114.*

Sinuessa, *16 High Street, Woking, GU21 1BW* ☎ *01483 770742.*

Soons Peking, *1 St Johns Road, Woking, GU21 1SE* ☎ *01483 726290.*

Spaghetti Western, *3 Guildford Road, Woking, GU22 7PX* ☎ *01483 721040.*

Thonburi Thai, *18 High Street, Woking, GU21 1BW* ☎ *01483 766649.*

Vojon Tandoori, *2 St Johns Road, Woking, GU21 1SE* ☎ *01483 725354.*
Woking Tandoori, *45 Goldsworth Road, Woking, GU21 1JY* ☎ *01483 725251.*

Sports & Leisure Centres
Chris Lane Indoor Tennis Centre, *Westfield Avenue, Woking, GU22 9PF* ☎ *01483 722113.*
Woking Leisure Centre, *Woking Park, Kingfield Road, Woking, GU22 9BA* ☎ *01483 771055.*

Swimming Pool
Pool in the Park, *Kingfield Road, Woking, GU22 1LB* ☎ *01483 771055.*
Woking Leisure Centre, *Woking Park, Kingfield Road, Woking, GU22 9BA* ☎ *01483 771055.*

Take-Aways
Best Fish Bar, *4 The Terrace, High Street, Old Woking, GU22 9ES* ☎ *01483 762365.*
Bonoful, *127 Princess Road, Woking, GU22 8ER* ☎ *01483 724202.*
Curry Centre, *3 The Shops, Kingfield Road, Old Woking, GU22 9EH* ☎ *01483 768902.*
Domino's Pizza, *9 Goldsworth Road, Woking, GU21 1JY* ☎ *01483 760761.*
Golden House, *181 High Street, Old Woking, GU22 9JH* ☎ *01483 720886.*
Haylees Lunch Box, *Victoria Gate, Chobham Road, Woking, GU21 1JD* ☎ *01483 740584.*
Jade Garden, *87 Walton Road, Woking, GU21 5DW* ☎ *01483 768132.*
Ketch, *17 St Johns Road, Woking, GU21 1SA* ☎ *01483 772163.*
Lais Fish & Chip Shop, *101 Goldsworth Road, Woking, GU21 1LJ* ☎ *01483 773241.*
McDonald's, *11 Chertsey Road, Woking, GU24 8ND* ☎ *01483 729755.*
Mr Cod, *6 High Street, Woking, GU21 1BG* ☎ *01483 715493.*
New Maxim, *8 Kingfield Road, Woking, GU22 9EH* ☎ *01483 765411.*
Sandwich Box, *49a Chertsey Road, Woking, GU21 5AJ* ☎ *01483 727020.*
Woking Kebab House, *5 Broadway, Woking, GU21 5AP* ☎ *01483 771072.*

Tea Rooms & Cafes
Garden Cafe, *Pool in the Park* ☎ *01483 751707.*
Martino's, *3 Goldsworth Road, Woking, GU21 1JY* ☎ *01483 720998.*
Peacocks Arts Centre ☎ *01483 761144.*
Sandies Cafe, *49 Goldsworth Road, Woking, GU21 1JY* ☎ *01483 772166.*

Theatres
New Victoria Theatre, *Peacocks Arts Centre* ☎ *01483 747422.*
Rhoda McGaw Theatre, *Peacocks Arts Centre* ☎ *01483 747422.*

Wine Bars & Cafe Bars
Beavers, *Kiln Bridge, 10 Hermitage Road, Woking, GU21 1TB* ☎ *01483 723440.*
Broadway, *14 Broadway, Woking, GU21 5AP* ☎ *01483 720452.*
Duval's, *30 Goldsworth Road, Woking, GU21 1JT* ☎ *01483 756180.*
Miss Demeanours, *99 Goldsworth Road, Woking, GU21 1LJ* ☎ *01483 772159.*
Oscars, *Peacocks Arts Centre* ☎ *01483 728259.*

See also Bisley, Byfleet, Chobham, Horsell, Knaphill, Mayford, Ottershaw, Pyrford, Ripley, Send, Sheerwater, Sutton Green, Wisley, Woodham, Worplesdon.

Woldingham

Until 1880 Woldingham consisted of a few farmhouses, some cottages beside the green and a very small church. The village is notable for the splendid views from South Hawke, owned by the National Trust.

St Agatha's Church. The highest church in South East England at 796ft above sea level and probably the smallest in Surrey.
St Paul's Church. Built in 1933 to replace St Agatha's, it is built in flint.

Art & Craft Equipment
Rembrandts, *9 The Crescent, Station Road, Woldingham, CR3 7DB* ☎ *01883 652508.*

Garden Centre
Knights Garden Centre, *Rosedene Nursery, Woldingham Road, Woldingham, CR3 7LA*
☎ *01883 653142.*
Golf Course
North Downs Golf Club, *Northdown Road, Woldingham, CR3 7AA* ☎ *01883 653298.*
Tea Room
Conservatory Coffee Shop, *Knights Garden Centre* ☎ *01883 652712.*

See also Caterham, Godstone, Limpsfield, Oxted, Tandridge, Tatsfield, Warlingham, Whyteleafe.
2 miles from the Greater London boundary.

Wonersh

A lovely mix of tile-hung and half timbered buildings, some of which date from a time when the village was a thriving centre of the clothing industry.

BRITISH RED CROSS MUSEUM. The museum traces the history of the Red Cross movement from its foundation in 1863. With its collection of uniforms from both world wars, photographs, drawings, embroideries and other memorabilia, it provides a comprehensive look at the humanitarian work of the Red Cross in aiding the victims of war and natural disasters, and its continuing health and welfare programme. The reference library and archives are available to researchers.
CHINTHURST HILL. A conical hill with a folly on the top, built during the Second World War.
GRANTLEY ARMS. This 14th century coaching inn is one of several architectural masterpieces in the Street.
PARISH CHURCH. The oldest parts of the church are the Saxon nave wall and the Norman tower base. It was partly destroyed by fire in 1793 but was restored and retains many interesting features. There are also some 15th century brasses.

Art Gallery
Jonleigh Gallery, *The Street, Wonersh, GU5 0PF* ☎ *01483 893177.*
Museum
British Red Cross Museum, *Barnett Hill, Wonersh, GU5 0RY* ☎ *01483 898595.*
Restaurant
★Grantley Arms, *The Street, Wonersh, GU5 0PE* ☎ *01483 893351.*

See also Albury, Blackheath, Bramley, Chilworth, Farncombe, Godalming, Hascombe, Loseley, Merrow, Newlands Corner, Shalford, Shamley Green, Shere.

Wood Street

The village has a well tended village green where a maypole has stood for over 150 years.

Garden Centres & Nurseries
Pinks Hill Nurseries, *Pinks Hill, Wood Street Village, GU3 3BP* ☎ *01483 571620.*
Woodlands Farm Nursery, *The Green, Wood Street Village, GU3 3DU* ☎ *01483 235536.*
Pubs
Royal Oak, *89 Oakhill, Wood Street Village, GU3 3DA* ☎ *01483 235137.*
◆White Hart, *White Hart Lane, Wood Street Village, GU3 3DZ* ☎ *01483 235939.*

See also Burpham, Compton, Guildford, Hurtmore, Loseley, Normandy, Pirbright, Puttenham, Wanborough, Worplesdon.

141

Woodham

Art & Craft Equipment
Lilytone Glass & Craft, *Bourne Valley Nurseries* ☎ *01932 352525.*
Golf Course
New Zealand Golf Club, *Woodham Lane, Woodham, KT15 3QD* ☎ *01932 345049.*
Nursery
Bourne Valley Nurseries, *Woodham Park Road, Woodham, KT15 3TH* ☎ *01932 342013.*
Pub
Victoria Inn, *427 Woodham Lane, Woodham, KT15 3QE* ☎ *01932 345365.*

See also Addlestone, Byfleet, Chertsey, Horsell, New Haw, Ockham, Ottershaw, Pyrford, Ripley, Shepperton, Weybridge, Whiteley Village, Wisley, Woking.

Worcester Park

Worcester Park is mainly in Greater London, but the southern edges are in Surrey.

Garden Centre
Garden Care, *Central Nursery, Old Kingston Road, Worcester Park, KT4 7QH*
☎ *0181-337 9922.*
Pub
Gamecock, *Vale Road, Worcester Park, KT4 7ED* ☎ *0181-337 9442.*
Restaurant
Hogsmill Tavern(Beefeater), *Worcester Park Road, Worcester Park, KT4 7QE*
☎ *0181-337 5221.*

See also Chessington, Epsom, Ewell, Thames Ditton. On the Greater London boundary.

Wormley

LOCKWOOD DONKEY SANCTUARY. Established in 1966 to care for sick elderly donkeys, but now offering a home to numerous other animals.

Animal Sanctuary
Lockwood Donkey Sanctuary, *Hatch Lane, Sandhills, Wormley, GU8 5UX*
☎ *01428 682409.*
Pub
Pig & Whistle, *Combe Lane, Wormley, GU8 5TB* ☎ *01428 682362.*

See also Brook, Chiddingfold, Eashing, Godalming, Grayswood, Hambledon, Hascombe, Hydestile, Milford, Peper Harow, Thursley.

NOTES

Worplesdon

MERRIST WOOD COLLEGE. One of the largest colleges of agriculture and horticulture in the UK, the 40 acre College estate includes a working farm, small animal care unit, nature trails, extensive ornamental gardens, glasshouse nursery and plant centre.

MERRIST WOOD HOUSE. A listed building by Norman Shaw, built in 1877 and now an agricultural college.

ST MARY'S CHURCH. The church dates from the 13th century, was recorded in the Domesday Book and was restored in 1866. The churchyard was formerly the site of a semaphore tower.

Antique Dealer
  Perry Hill Antiques, *Perry Hill, Worplesdon, GU3 3RD* ☎ *01483 236081.*
Art & Craft Equipment
  Two Hoots Crafts, *Holly Lane, Worplesdon, GU3 3PA* ☎ *01483 236634.*
Garden Centres & Nurseries
  Bonsai Centre, *St Mary's Garden, Worplesdon, GU3 3RS* ☎ *01483 232893.*
  Gunner John, *Sunnyside, Clasford Bridge, Aldershot Road, Worplesdon, GU3 3RE*
  ☎ *01483 233543.*
  J Ellis & Sons, *Lantana Nurseries, Fox Corner, Bagshot Road, Worplesdon, GU3 3PT*
  ☎ *01483 232118.*
  Tangley Garden Nursery, *Pitch Place, Worplesdon Road, Worplesdon, GU3 3LQ*
  ☎ *01483 232243.*
Guest House
  Hillside, *Perry Hill, Worplesdon, GU3 3RF* ☎ *01483 232051.*
Hotel
  Worplesdon Place Hotel(Beefeater), *Perry Hill, Worplesdon, GU3 3RY* ☎ *01483 232407.*
Pubs
  Fox, *Guildford Road, Fox Corner, Worplesdon, GU3 3PP* ☎ *01483 232520.*
◆Jolly Farmer, *Burdenshott Road, Worplesdon, GU3 3RN* ☎ *01483 234658.*
  Ship Inn, *Pitch Place, Worplesdon Road, Worplesdon, GU3 3LB* ☎ *01483 232343.*
  White Lyon, *Perry Hill, Worplesdon, GU3 3RE* ☎ *01483 232417.*

See also Brookwood, Burpham, Guildford, Knaphill, Mayford, Normandy, Pirbright, Send, Wanborough, Woking, Wood Street.

Wotton

ST JOHN'S CHURCH. Originally Saxon, the church is mainly 13th century but has an 11th century tower. It was restored during the 19th century and contains many monuments. St John's belonged for centuries to the Evelyn family, and John Evelyn(1620-1706) the diarist and author is buried here in the family burial place in the north chapel.

WOTTON HOUSE. Wotton House also belonged for centuries to the Evelyn family and John Evelyn was born here. From the age of five he lived away from here but returned to live in Wotton for the last 12 years of his life. The house is now largely 19th century, but the landscaped gardens were laid out from 1643 onwards.

Restaurant
★Wotton Hatch, *Guildford Road, Wotton, RH5 6QR* ☎ *01306 885665.*

See also Abinger Common, Dorking, Gomshall, Holmbury St Mary, Holmwood, Peaslake, Polesden Lacey, Ranmore Common, Shere, Westcott.

Wrecclesham

Situated on the Hampshire border, Wrecclesham was renowned until early this
century for green pottery made to designs which had been popular in London since
Elizabethan times. Originally manufactured in Farnham, the pottery was moved to
Wrecclesham in 1872 by Absolom Harris, a distant cousin of William Cobbett.
Pottery is still manufactured by A Harris and Sons although they now specialise in
horticultural ware.

Hotel
  Trevena House Hotel, *Alton Road, Farnham, GU10 5ER* ☎ *01252 716908.*
Pottery
  Farnham Pottery, *Pottery Lane, Wrecclesham, GU10 4QJ* ☎ *01252 715318.*
Pubs
★◆Bat & Ball Inn, *Bat & Ball Lane, Wrecclesham, GU10 4RA* ☎ *01252 794564.*
  Bear & Ragged Staff, *48 The Street, Wrecclesham, GU10 4QR* ☎ *01252 716389.*
  Cricketers, *1 The Street, Wrecclesham, GU10 4PP* ☎ *01252 714937.*
  Royal Oak, *59 The Street, Wrecclesham, GU10 4QS* ☎ *01252 716845.*
  Sandrock, *Sandrock Hill Road, Wrecclesham, GU10 4NS* ☎ *01252 715865.*
Take-Away
  Top Table Fish Shop, *13 The Street, Wrecclesham, GU10 4PP* ☎ *01252 726537.*

See also Badshot Lea, The Bourne, Farnham, Frensham, Hale, Heath End, Rowledge, Runfold,
The Sands, Tilford. 1 mile from the Hampshire boundary.

NOTES

Index of Personalities

146

King George V - Whiteley Village.
King George VI - Polesden Lacey.
King James I - Byfleet, Loseley Park, Weybridge.
King John - Egham, Reigate, Shere.
King Henry II - Farnham, Guildford.
King Henry VIII - Bletchingley, Chertsey, Ewell,
  Gatton, Loseley Park, Molesey, Reigate,
  Weybridge, Woking.
King Richard II - Godstone, Witley.
King Richard III - Shepperton.
King William I (the conqueror) - Stoke
  D'Abernon.
King William III - Molesey.
Knight, Captain C R - Camberley.
Knyvett, Sir Thomas - Stanwell.
Lamb, Edward - Englefield Green.
Lambert, William - Burstow.
Langtry, Lily - Compton.
Langton, Stephen - Abinger Common.
Leadbetter, Stiff - Clandon.
Leoni, Giacomo - Clandon.
Lloyd George, David - Churt.
Locke-King, Hugh - Weybridge.
Lovelace, Earl of - Horsley.
Lovelace, Lord - Ockham.
Lucan, Earl of - Laleham.
Ludlam, Mother - Farnham, Frensham.
Lutyens, Sir Edwin - Abinger Common,
  Godalming, Shere, Thursley, Witley.
Malthus, Thomas - Westcott.
Manningham, General Coote - Bookham.
Marlborough, Sarah, Duchess of - Chilworth.
Martin, Elias - Sunbury.
Matthews, Olive - Chertsey.
Maufe, Sir Edward - Guildford.
Melbourne, Lord - Bletchingley.
Menuhin, Sir Yehudi - Stoke D'Abernon.
Meredith, George - Abinger Common.
Middleton of Cork, Lord - Peper Harow
Monsel, John - Englefield Green.
Monson, Lord - Gatton.
Moore, Arthur - Fetcham
More, Sir William - Loseley Park.
Nelson, Lord & Lady - Dorking, Ripley.
Nightingale, Florence - Compton.
Onslow, Arthur - Guildford, Thames Ditton.
Paine, James - Chertsey.
Palmerston, Lord - Bletchingley.
Parker, Eric - Hambledon.
Pearson, J L - Redhill.
Pepys, Samuel - Ewell.
Pirbright, Lord - Pirbright
Prince Leopold - Esher.
Princess Charlotte - Esher.
Pugin, Augustus W - Albury, Peper Harow.
Queen Anne of Denmark - Byfleet
Queen Elizabeth I - Chiddingfold, Ewell, Loseley
  Park, Weybridge.
Queen Elizabeth, Queen Mother - Polesden
  Lacey.
Queen Mary I (tudor) - Woking.

Queen Mary II - Molesey.
Queen Victoria - Bagshot, Chobham, Esher,
Farnham, Godstone.
Raleigh, Carew - Horsley.
Raleigh, Sir Walter - Horsley.
Redgrave, Sir Michael - Farnham.
Rennie, George - Staines.
Rennie, John - Staines.
Repton, Humphrey - Clandon.
Roberts-Austen, Sir William - Blackheath.
Rose, Joseph - Reigate.
Roubiliac, Louis - Walton on Thames.
Rutherwyke, John - Bookham.
Rysbrack, Michael - Guildford, Ockham.
Sandby, Paul - Virginia Water.
Sandby, Thomas - Virginia Water.
Scott, George Gilbert - Ottershaw, Ranmore
  Common, Tandridge, Warlingham, Westcott.
Scott, Lady Gilbert - Tandridge.
Scott, Sir Giles Gilbert - Godalming, Godstone.
Shannon, Field Marshal Viscount - Walton on
  Thames.
Shaw, George Bernard - Hindhead.
Shaw, R Norman - Chipstead, Worplesdon.
Soane, Sir John - Albury, Brockham.
Spring, Major R - Camberley.
Stael, Madam de - Mickleham.
Stanley, Sir Henry - Pirbright.
Stone, Nicholas - Stanwell.
Street, G E - Banstead, Headley, Holmbury St
  Mary.
Swift, Jonathan - Farnham.
Sutton, Thomas - Godalming.
Talleyrand - Mickleham.
Temple, Sir William - Farnham.
Tennyson, Alfred, Lord - Haslemere.
Thorndike, Dame Sybil - Leatherhead.
Thorpe, Rose Hartwick - Chertsey.
Tonebridge, Richard de - Bletchingley.
Townsend, C H - Blackheath.
Tupper, Martin - Albury.
Vanburgh, Sir John - Esher.
Vaughan Williams, Ralph - Coldharbour,
  Dorking.
Villiers, Barbara - Ewell.
Warrenne, William de - Reigate.
Watts, George Frederick - Compton.
Watts, Mary - Compton.
Wayneflete, Bishop William of - Esher.
Wells, H G - Horsell
Wesley, John - Leatherhead.
West, Dame Rebecca - Brookwood.
West, Sir Algernon - Wanborough.
Weston, Sir Richard - Sutton Green.
Wheatley, Dennis - Brookwood.
Whiteley, William - Whiteley Village.
Winchester, Bishop of - Farnham, Frensham
Woodyer, Henry - Buckland, Dorking.
Wright, Whitaker - Witley.
Wyatt, Richard - Farncombe.

Index of Locations
(which do not include place names in their title)